I0889749

Ritual, Myth, and Mysticism in the Work of Mary Butts

ROSLYN RESO FOY

Ritual, Myth, and Mysticism in the Work of Mary Butts

Between Feminism and Modernism

THE UNIVERSITY OF ARKANSAS PRESS

Fayetteville 2000

Manufactured in the United States of America

04 03 02 01 00 5 4 3 2 1

Frontispiece: Mary Butts in 1929. *Photo courtesy Camilla Bagg.*

Designer: Sheila Hart

♾ The paper used in this publication meets the minimum requirements of the American National Standard for Permanence of Paper for Printed Library Materials Z39.48–1984.

Library of Congress Cataloging-in-Publication-Data

Foy, Roslyn Reso, 1945–
Ritual, myth, and mysticism in the work of Mary Butts: between feminism and modernism / Roslyn Reso Foy.
p. cm.
Includes bibliographical references and index.
ISBN 1-55728-581-0 (alk. paper)
1. Butts, Mary, 1890–1937—Criticism and interpretation. 2. Feminism and literature—England—History—20th century. 3. Women and literature—England—History—20th century. 4. Modernism (Literature)—England. 5. Mysticism in literature. 6. Ritual in literature. 7. Myth in literature. I. Title.

PR6003.U7 Z66 2000
823'.912—dc21 99-053090

For Ed and Edna

Acknowledgments

I am grateful to friends at the University of Connecticut, who were generous with their time and advice in the development of this project. My very dear friend, David A. Leeming, was invaluable in offering support and encouragement for several years during the writing process. He was extremely generous with his time, read the manuscript several times, helped me find the right direction when necessary, and offered important advice and moral support at various stages along the way. Glen MacLeod and Margaret Higonnet offered very helpful advice and fine insights. The publisher of Mary Butts's books, Bruce McPherson, was an invaluable source of information and contacts. I relied on his advice and friendship at numerous crossroads. I also extend sincere thanks to Camilla Bagg, Mary Butts's only child, whose friendship I have come to treasure and whose generosity and support for this study helped me over difficult hurdles. Nathalie Blondel, who wrote the biography of Mary Butts, was kind enough to read early versions of this manuscript and offer encouragement for its development. This is an opportunity, also, to thank my remarkable friends (far too many to name), the memory of my loving father, and my extraordinary family for their unconditional love and encouragement throughout my life, especially my mother, Edna C. Reso, who made everything possible. Above all, my husband, Edmond J. Foy, has shown forbearance and enthusiasm, along with love, intelligence, and generosity, throughout the entire process. To all of them I extend my sincere and deep gratitude.

Contents

Preface

In June of 1996, after several years of reading and studying the work of Mary Butts, I traveled to England to meet with Butts's only child, Camilla Bagg. Camilla agreed to take my husband and me through Butts territory, both physical and spiritual, for several days.

Leaving Camilla's home near Reading, England, we drove south through Dorset to Poole Harbour where Butts's vision came clearly into focus. The places she had described intimately in her autobiography of childhood, *The Crystal Cabinet,* rang out with the beauty and wonder of nature (although greatly changed by the progress Butts so dreaded in her own lifetime). The land surrounding Poole Harbour extends like palms of a hand caressing and protecting a rare part of the natural world. Far south and surrounded by water, the land is lush and green.

Camilla had made arrangements for us to visit the family home of Salterns, which also figures vividly in Butts's *The Crystal Cabinet.* Although time has brought change and modernization to the great eighteenth-century home, much of what Butts describes in her autobiography remains preserved and treasured by the family that now owns it. A presence lingered in the house and the area: its gardens were perfect, the view to the harbor beautiful and inspiring.

We took a ferry across the harbor to the Isle of Purbeck to visit Corfe Castle (the namesake of one of Butts's most striking poems), walked through the ancient village, and discovered the power of the ruined castle whose history Butts likened to that of Delphi. From there we went to Badbury Rings, a series of prehistoric mounded circles several miles northwest of

Poole, well preserved by the National Trust. This site, of particular importance to Mary Butts, offers a vision of both the wildness of nature and the ordering of spiritual chaos in one magnificent spot. Here, truly, the mystery of Butts's writing came alive.

The next day in Camilla's home she allowed me to look at the journals that Butts kept for twenty-one years. Many entries offer insights into the emotions of a young woman who experienced great extremes during her lifetime. Camilla showed me numerous family photos not available elsewhere and was a gracious host and keeper of her mother's heritage. We discussed her own life, which was virtually devoid of the opportunity to be with or to know her mother. She perhaps has learned most about her mother from the journals, and some of the entries are painful to her, even now.

Camilla was also kind enough to arrange a meeting with Nathalie Blondel. Blondel had sole rights to the journals and had spent over seven years working on a biography of Mary Butts. We found that we agreed significantly on interpretations and attitudes. Nathalie invited us to her home, where she permitted me to view her manuscript, showed me several more pictures I had not seen, offered copies of articles I had not been able to unearth in the United States, and talked for several hours about Butts's work. Her comments and discussions helped validate my own work.

On the last day of our visit, Camilla drove into Reading from her home in nearby Bradfield to spend the afternoon with us and to have our last dinner together. Once more we discussed events in her own life as well as her relationship with her mother and her father, John Rodker. I left England gratified to have had firsthand experience of Mary Butts's life and of the land that was so sacred to her.

In April 1998, just after the publication of Blondel's biography, Camilla Bagg visited my home in Metairie, Louisiana, and generously gave me an ivory bracelet that had belonged to her mother during the wild days of the 1920s. This gift is particularly special and treasured because Camilla has so little of her mother's life in her possession. During several conversations, Camilla explained more of the details of why she had maintained possession of the Butts papers for such a long time. When Mary Butts died in 1937, she left her friend (and literary executor) Angus Davidson instructions that Camilla was to receive all her papers, journals, and belongings when she reached age twenty-five. Shortly after that time (1945), Camilla was contacted by Norman Holmes Pearson of Yale University (through the intermediaries of Angus Davidson and Harcourt Wesson Bull), who asked Camilla to arrange for the twenty-one years of journals and the Butts letters and papers to go to the Beinecke Library. Pearson was in the process of collecting the papers belonging to some of the most interesting figures of the 1920s, including H. D., Ezra Pound, T. S. Eliot, Gertrude Stein, and others. Camilla had a letter from Pearson explaining to her how significant it would be to have the Butts papers at the Beinecke along with, as Camilla remembers it, "so many well-known people" and claiming "that it would be the right place for my mother because so many of her friends were there."[1] By the time that initial contact occurred and some discussion back and forth between Pearson and Harcourt Wesson Bull took place, it was 1950, and Camilla expected the papers would go to Yale. Then everything stopped for nearly eleven years. During that time, Camilla had a chance to reconsider her decision. When Pearson finally wrote to Angus Davidson in 1961 with instructions to ship the journals and papers, Camilla had grown up a bit and decided not to let these "great men" push her about.

After the deaths of Mary Colville-Hyde (Mary Butts's mother) in 1947 and two of Colville-Hyde's sisters, in 1951 and 1952, Camilla had inherited an enormous number of letters to add to the collection. To the dismay of Davidson and Bull, she wrote to Pearson and told him that she would not send the Butts papers to the Beinecke because she wanted more time with them herself to discover things about her mother that she was denied as a child; these journals and possessions were nearly all that was left of her mother and her life. During those years Camilla had married, was raising her own children, and felt she needed to hold on to her mother's belongings a while longer. Bull and Davidson were anguished and wrote to her asking if she really knew what she was doing, but Camilla remained adamant in her decision.

Then in 1963 two American academics wrote to her and requested access to the journals. By this time Camilla realized she needed to make some decisions about the papers and agreed to allow them the opportunity to work with the Butts papers. After nearly twenty years of "messing about" with the academics, Camilla was back where she started. The association had been a disappointing one.[2] Eventually, she heard from a young scholar in California, Elena Storer-Nitzberg, whom she visited and who then became involved with a conference on Mary Butts organized by Christopher and Barbara Wagstaff in 1984, which included the poet Robert Duncan, Robin Blaser, and numerous scholars.[3] After her association with academia, Camilla claims she was exhausted; she attended the conference in California and returned home. Then in the early 1990s, Nathalie Blondel contacted Camilla. They met, and Camilla was reticent about beginning another round of academic wrangling. But Blondel was persistent, and Camilla liked and respected her. Eventually, she gave sole rights to the Butts papers to Nathalie Blondel. Blondel's biography, *Mary Butts: Scenes from the Life,* appeared in March of 1998.

Also in 1998 Camilla arranged for the Mary Butts papers to go to the Beinecke Library at Yale University after all; she ended where she had begun nearly fifty years earlier. Among the papers, in addition to a revealing essay "Bloomsbury," published in *Modernism/Modernity* in 1998 and a short story published in the *New Yorker* in the same year, there is an extraordinary novel, *Unborn Gods*. Camilla explained that "it seems to be merely an exercise in expressing what she [Butts] thought about men and sex. . . . I think already she was beginning to feel that she had some sort of magic power with men, but what was she to do about it?"[4] There is also poetry, some published in little magazines of the day but never collected, an unfinished historical novel, *Julian the Apostate,* and other unfinished work. One can only speculate about what the reputation of Mary Butts would have been today had Camilla agreed to release the papers to Norman Holmes Pearson in the 1960s. Now that they will be available to scholars, interest in Mary Butts's work should continue to grow.

Corfe

MARY BUTTS

I

Corfe, the hub of a wheel
Where the green down-spokes turning
Embrace an earth-cup of smoke and ghosts and stone.
The sea orchestrates
The still dance in the cup
Danced forever, the same intricate sobriety
Equivocal, adored.

But when I remember you Corfe, I remember Delphi
Because your history also is a mystery of God.

"And God is no blind man and God is our father's"
But like lovers
Your cup is full of the courts of other princes
Disrupting you.

Very sweet is the sacred wood
In the gold clearing, in the mustard patch;
But at night comes a change
Like a gold ball thrown out
And a black ball thrown in
(Not a sunset behind Tyneham Cap
On a night without a moon.)
But a shift of potencies
Like a black ball thrown in
And a gold ball thrown out
And the players are princes
Of the turf and the weed
And the wind-moulded trees
And the hazel thicket
And the red blackberry thorn.

Never trust a hemlock
An inch above your mouth.
An ice-green hemlock
Is a lover
In the wood.
Now every way the wind blows this sweetie goes
In the south
Where goes the leaf if the rose
And the evergreen tree.

II

Inside the house, above the wood
Look out of the tall windows squared
With wood-strips painted white.
The wild grass runs up the wild hill
The wild sky runs over itself
And goes nowhere.

A man crosses the rough grass
Up the wild hill;
Strong graceless kharki [*sic*] legs in silhouette
Tired and tough, treading the hill down.

He will not wear it down
Let him try!
He is here only because this place is
A button on the bodies of the green hills.

III

God keep the Hollow Land from all wrong!
God keep the Hollow Land going strong!
A song a boy made in a girl
Brother and sister in a car
Over the flints, upon the turf
Beside the crookbacked angry thorn
Under the gulls, above the dead
To where the light made the grass glass.

Until they came to the world's end
The sea below and under them
The gulls above and over them
And through the thunder and the wailing
Sun full of wings was over them
In a glass world made out of grass.
"God keep the Hollow Land from all wrong!
God keep the Hollow Land going strong!"

Curl horns and fleeces, straighten trees,
Multiply lobsters, assemble bees.

Give it to us for ever, take our hints
Knot up its roads for us, sharpen its flints,
Pour the wind into it, the thick sea rain,
Blot out the landscape and destroy the train.
Turn back our folk from it, we hate the lot
Turn the American and turn the Scot;
Take upropitious [*sic*] the turf, the dust
If the sea doesn't get 'em then the cattle must.

Make many slugs where the stranger goes
Better than barbed wire the briar rose;
Swarm on the down-tops the flint men's hosts
Taboo the barrows, encourage ghosts.

Arm the rabbits with tigers' teeth
Serpents shoot from the soil beneath
By pain in belly and foot and mouth
Keep them out of our sacred south.

Quoted by permission of Camilla Bagg. In Glen E. Morgan, "Mary Butts," *Antaeus* 12 (Winter 1973): 144–46. The "Hollow Land" metaphor comes from a song at the end of William Morris's "The Hollow Land: A Tale." There is a bell in "The Hollow Land" called Mary and "When Mary Rings the Earth Shakes." *See The Collected Works of William Morris* (Routledge/Thoemmes, 1992).

Introduction

When Mary Butts died on March 5, 1937, at the age of forty-six, she was, as Douglas Goldring tells us, "in a fair way towards becoming one of the most respected of our 'high brow' woman writers."[1] Author of three novels, three volumes of short stories, an autobiography of childhood, two historical narratives, a novella, uncollected poetry, two pamphlet-length essays, and numerous reviews, Mary Butts was published in most of the literary periodicals of the day, including Ford Madox Ford's *Transatlantic Review,* the *Dial,* and the *Little Review,* and she moved in the circles of the now "established" modernist writers. Bryher (Annie Winifred Ellerman) recognized that "[Butts] was from the start one of the few who matter, a builder of English, and I have never doubted since I read her first story that she belonged to the immortals."[2] After her death her reputation suffered a mysterious decline (perhaps because her only child, Camilla Bagg, held on to her papers and journals for over fifty years), and it is only now experiencing a revival.

In 1984 several poets and scholars gathered at the University of California, Davis, to celebrate Butts's work. From that gathering grew an eclectic collection of essays, letters, interviews with people who knew her, memoirs, and an extensive bibliography called *A Sacred Quest: The Life and Writings of Mary Butts* (1995), edited by Christopher Wagstaff, one of the organizers of the conference.[3] Barbara Wagstaff, John Ashbery, Robin Blaser, and Paul West have written forewords and afterwords to recent reissuings of her work. Ruth Hoberman and Mary Hamer have included chapters on

Butts in recent publications, a biography *(Mary Butts: Scenes from the Life)* by Nathalie Blondel appeared in 1998, and some previously unpublished work is beginning to appear since Butts's daughter released the papers and journals to the Beinecke Library at Yale University in 1998. Yet, until now, no sustained critical study has been done on her work.

As Bonnie Kime Scott, Alicia Ostriker, and others have suggested, for critics at mid-century, modernism "was unconsciously gendered masculine"; women's writing was "rarely collected for academic circulation."[4] Ostriker rightly contends that professors and critics of the 1950s and early 1960s formed opinions on poetry primarily by reading male poets. As a result, what was believed to be universal was only partial.[5] But contemporary feminist criticism has made significant advances toward changing that situation. Rita Felski, Marianne DeKovan, Kathleen Wheeler, Bonnie Kime Scott, and others have made recent contributions to reassessing and renegotiating definitions of modernism in relation to gender.[6] Sandra M. Gilbert and Susan Gubar suggest that women's "increasingly successful production of literary texts throughout the nineteenth and twentieth centuries" has given us an "entirely different modernism."[7] An exploration of Mary Butts's work will enhance and contribute to this richer and more diverse definition of modernism.

Born in 1890, a great-granddaughter of Thomas Butts, who was a patron and friend of William Blake, Mary Butts grew up in her family home at Salterns in Poole Harbour, Dorset, England, surrounded by forty-two of Blake's original pictures. Growing up with a background of security and affluence, Mary Butts apparently exaggerated the social status of her family throughout her life, characterizing it as aristocratic with a pedigree dating back to the twelfth century.[8] The accuracy of this lineage is questionable, and Butts's daughter seems to feel that the best that could be said of the Butts family is that they had a wealthy background something like country gentry, yet certainly not aristocratic. Mary Butts, however, played on the notion of her social status and class, yet had no qualms about begging friends for money after she had used up her own on parties and drugs.

Whatever the truth concerning her social class, Salterns became the center of Butts's life and, with the surrounding harbor and countryside, her primary inspiration. *The Crystal Cabinet,* her autobiography of childhood, records the formative years of a child raised by a father, Capt. Frederick Butts, who had already lost two sons to tragedy and had married a woman thirty years his junior (Mary Jane Briggs) in an attempt to rebuild a family. According to Mary Butts, her mother was of a different class, bringing with her a Victorian sense of womanhood and women's education that even Butts as a child found offensive. Moreover, in *The Crystal Cabinet,* Butts says that after her father's death, her mother took his "French" books (which Mrs. Butts considered pornographic) and burned them in the woods, an event that made a very strong impression on the mind of the child. Many of these issues are explored in Butts's *The Crystal Cabinet,* yet it should be noted that this is an autobiography written from the perspective of over forty years. Still, Butts felt a closer connection to her father and continued to disparage her mother and her mother's way of thinking for the rest of her life.

When Captain Butts died in 1905, Mary Butts was only fourteen years old, but her father had already encouraged in her a love of learning, provided an education in the classics, and instilled a passion for the land and a sense of her place within the class of country gentry. Fifteen months after her father's death, Butts's mother remarried. He was an old friend of the captain's called Francis Frederick Musgrove Colville-Hyde, and they adopted the name Colville-Hyde from then on. Mary Butts was fond of her stepfather (she called him Tiger-Tiger). According to Butts's account in *The Crystal Cabinet,* her mother felt she was a bit too fond of her stepfather and accused her of impropriety with him—a situation, whatever the truth of it may have been, that created a deeper breach between mother and daughter.[9] Mary was soon sent to boarding school at St. Leonard's School for Girls in St. Andrew's, Scotland, where she experienced emotional hardship. She had lost her beloved father, was ripped from the home and land she loved, and felt extremely lonely and disconnected. Used to her own solitude, she had difficulty relating to the interests and concerns of the other girls. Yet, in spite of these hardships, she received one of the best educations a girl could hope for at the time.

Mary Butts later became estranged from her mother and her beloved younger brother, Tony, mainly over issues of money.[10] She studied briefly at Westfield College in London from 1909 to 1912, attended the London School of Economics from 1912 to 1914 (she graduated in 1914 with a social science certificate), worked with the London County Council, the Children's Care Committee (with the Australian painter Stella Bowen), and the National Council Against Conscription during the early years of World War I. She also had an affair with Eleanor Rogers, during which time Butts started her twenty-one years of journals, beginning July 21, 1916. She also met John Rodker, the son of Jewish immigrants. She eventually broke things off with Eleanor, married the poet and publisher Rodker in 1918, and worked with him at his Ovid Press, whose publications included Ezra Pound's *Hugh Selwyn Mauberley* and T. S. Eliot's second book of poetry, *Ara Vos Prec.* She experienced a failed pregnancy, whether from miscarriage or abortion is unclear. Nathalie Blondel records the fact that Butts wanted a child but feared the repercussions of a child on her work.[11]

Although she disliked the feeling of being pregnant, she recognized the restirrings of the mystical while in the pregnant state. By the end of 1918, Butts had met Wyndham Lewis, Ezra Pound, and Roger Fry, with whom she began to fall in love, but she struggled against the idea of becoming sexually unfaithful to Rodker. Her libido was to create conflict throughout her life and relationships. Then in 1920 she met the physically and psychically wounded Cecil Maitland, a Scottish artist and Joyce critic, and began an emotional—if a not yet physical—affair with Maitland because of "the delicious states he evokes in me."[12]

Cecil Maitland's knowledge of and interest in magic touched the core of Mary Butts, yet the relationship remained unconsummated sexually because, by the end of February 1920, Mary Butts was once again pregnant. The marriage to Rodker was failing, and her fascination with Maitland and magic continued to grow. Her only child, Camilla, was born on November 7, 1920. Butts did not find motherhood easy, once again feared its influence upon her work, and was preoccupied with Maitland, his drugs, his despondency, and his suicide attempt. By December Cecil and Mary had become lovers. In January 1921, while in Spain, John Rodker discovered their affair after reading an entry from her 1920 diary. Shortly afterwards he moved out of their apartment. Butts waited three days, left Camilla with a friend whom she paid to look after her (Camilla was shuffled around for a good bit of her life but was finally raised primarily by her great-aunt Ada), and went away to Paris with Maitland.[13] Maitland deepened her involvement with drugs (cocaine, opium, hashish, heroin), introduced her to the black magic of Aleister Crowley ("The Great Beast" with whom she soon became disenchanted) and his occult group in Cefalu, Italy, and left her damaged and hurt. With her pale skin and red hair (which Butts called "scarlet"), she then pursued a wildly bohemian life in London, Paris, and Villefranche, accounts of which appear in numerous memoirs of the time. Her lifestyle afforded her the freedom she sought as a woman; she moved easily among artists, writers, lesbians, and homosexuals in the avant-garde world of the 1920s. Butts was a free spirit who lived her life exactly as she chose. She also read widely, worked diligently, and explored avenues to ritual and the sacredness of nature, all the while testing the limits of her experience with drugs and alcohol.

Letters between H. D. (Hilda Doolittle) and Bryher, both of whom knew Butts and admired her work, indicate that excesses in her behavior stunned even the other bohemians: "Mary has apparently shocked everyone in Paris, but I don't think it matters. Because she is so wild I think people would hardly believe anything she says."[14] Yet, Butts's daughter and her biographer, Nathalie Blondel, agree that her lifestyle did not affect the intensity of her devotion to her work. It did, however, affect subsequent response to her work. Blondel correctly asserts that Butts was so outrageous that the memoirs of the period expend great energy recording her behavior. As a result, a greater emphasis and interest were later placed on this behavior than on her work, which was, in fact, better known during her lifetime than now.[15] Perhaps, as Bryher notes in her memorial after Butts's death, "She was exploring thc new type of emotion for which we have not yet words."[16] Edward Sackville-West best explains the disparity between Butts's lifestyle and her writing in his assessment of Butts in the year of her death:

> Yet few writers can ever have been more different from her books than she. In her life she was diffuse, uneasy, awkward in friendship, impulsive in all the wrong as well as all the right ways, hopelessly generous. Clever discrimination, balanced judgement, sufficient scholarship, were not qualities which one associated with her living presence. Yet these were the very qualities which, together with a real and original talent, combined to make her so remarkable a writer.[17]

We are only now attempting to separate the lifestyle from the remarkable abilities of the artist.

During the 1920s, Butts developed a close relationship with the composer Virgil Thomson. Jean Cocteau, another close friend, illustrated her book *Imaginary Letters*. She moved among the most famous artists and writers of the time, including Gertrude Stein, Virginia Woolf, T. S. Eliot, W. B. Yeats, Ezra Pound, and Ford Madox Ford, yet she remained on the edges of any one "group." She was snubbed by Woolf and the Bloomsbury Circle, for example, who believed her to be a "member of the underground" (although she apparently had a relationship with Roger Fry).[18] By 1930 her struggle with drugs and poverty led to a breakdown from which her mother rescued her. Shortly after, in the same year, Butts married Gabriel Aitken, a handsome but alcoholic young English artist. She and Aitken moved to Sennen Cove, near Land's End in Cornwall. By 1934 Aitken, a homosexual, left her, and Butts spent the remainder of her life in the natural world she had loved as a child and where she now became an Anglo-Catholic. She never relinquished her addiction to opium but did manage to write her autobiography of childhood, two historical novels, two pamphlets, and numerous reviews. She died in 1937 at West Cornwall Hospital in Penzance, where she was taken after she collapsed. Blondel quotes Butts's brother, Tony, writing to John Rodker that she died "after an operation for gastric ulcer—which should—one imagines have been diagnosed long before—but which was not."[19] The love of her life had been Cecil Maitland, whose departure and death had left her, as she wrote to her friend Angus Davidson, "alone in a way difficult to define."[20]

Butts had much in common with early modernists. Like many of them, she imbued her work with myth, ritual, and mysticism, as well as with psychoanalysis and anthropology. Like W. B. Yeats and H. D., she was also interested in the occult and in magic.[21] She resembled T. S. Eliot, in that she was an intellectual who sought a way to give meaning and shape to a world which she believed had lost its soul. She can also be associated with D. H. Lawrence, with whom she shared an interest in primitive religions, nature mysticism, and the primitive subconscious.[22] She blends all these interests in her fiction by turning, as did her contemporaries, to the gods of the pagan world. As Jascha Kessler suggests, she "longs to believe in their reality above and beyond the reality of human psychology."[23]

Myth, ritual, mysticism, and occultism all grow out of the human sense of a connection to nature and to the numinous world. *Myth* for Butts was tied up with the notion of a *sacred* past that would help explain and define her present.[24] The mysterious, repetitious aspect of *ritual* serves to link Butts's central characters to a racial memory, one that facilitates a connection between what she observes as the *seen* and the *unseen* worlds. Butts perhaps best defines her brand of *mysticism* in a 1933 review she wrote on *The Later Life of Wordsworth*. Here, in her attempt to define Wordsworth's mysticism, she gives us insight into her own sense of union with the Absolute: ". . . in his mysticism Paganism and Christianity met and were fused at that white heat which alone puts an antithetic good into men's possession."[25] Problematically, the revelation of this "Absolute" defies expression in words; it is rather, as William James suggests, a "state of feeling" which must be directly experienced.[26] In a letter to her friend Hugh Ross Williamson, Butts tells him that the mystical experience meant everything to her, "the one way of finding out what things are."[27] In her quest to discover meaning, Butts also examined mysticism as related to *occultism* with its emphasis on magic, secrecy, and ancient wisdom.[28]

Butts incorporates *myth, ritual, mysticism,* and *occultism* into her work in an attempt to reconnect humanity with its primal center. When T. S. Eliot defined "the mythological method" in his 1923 essay "*Ulysses,* Order and Myth," for example, he described artists using myth to establish a structural as well as a spiritual context in literature. Myth offered that "order and form" so necessary for the modern world through its focus on the eternally recurrent in experience. Butts, with a particular kind of religious sensibility in which she blends pagan and Christian topoi, integrates Eliot's "method" with her own mystical "seeings." These personal mystical experiences appear in *The Crystal Cabinet,* particularly in connection with her early immersion in the poetry of Blake, Wordsworth, and Shelley, which clearly affected Butts's evolution into a creative artist. For Butts, the authenticity of the initiate is established by a ritual initiation or joining with the land (represented in her own life by her family's land at Salterns) and its mythical and primitive origins, a theme which dominates her fiction (especially in *Ashe of Rings* [1925], *Armed with Madness* [1928], and *Death of Felicity Taverner* [1932], as well as numerous short stories).

Lillian Feder tells us that "the conquest of helplessness and fear through understanding and control . . . is inherent in all ritual."[29] Butts's work suggests that she hoped a mythic and ritual connection to the sacredness of nature could lead toward a conquering of the helplessness and fear prevalent in the early twentieth century. So, like W. B. Yeats, Butts explored the occult and magic in the face of the void brought on by the indifference toward belief that was in fashion in the Western World.[30] She sought a way to make the center hold in a world marked by the dislocation and loss that were the result of World War I and the chaos which followed in the 1920s in London and Paris. In a 1927 entry in her journal, Butts elucidates her concerns:

> What apart from the specific work of writing is what interests me? Nothing but spiritual development, the soul living at its fullest capacity. That is the lever, the new synthesis, or vision or faith. . . . And many of the things we do are not wrong, it is our way of doing them. . . . What do I love, outside writing and clothes and opium and the weather and my friends? I have always had since I can remember an incomparable pleasure in finding someone psychically sick, and learning about it, and seeing if there is a way out."[31]

This interest in "spiritual development" and healing the "psychically sick" is important in Butts's work. Her pleasure in "finding someone psychically sick" and trying to find a way out was part of the struggle she felt as woman and artist, a struggle to find answers for her own psychic clarity. In a diary entry from 1930 recording the early stages of her relationship with Gabriel Aitken, she claims parenthetically, "(He never *has* understood that psychically and nervously I'm almost as ill as he is—in some ways worse having an artist's sensibility and a woman's)."[32] If she could find the origins of others' psychic illnesses, then perhaps she would be closer to discovering her own difficulties. Drugs, investigation of the occult, her love of the sacredness of nature, the exploration of the role of myth and ritual in both history and the present, her sincere interest in truth and the human soul, and her writing were her ways of moving toward that discovery. Her art fused with her life as a means of survival, or at least as a way to deal with the reality of her own existence. By joining her reality to a larger, mythic one, she managed to survive and at the same time found the basis of her art.

These investigations also contributed to the establishment of her own voice, a voice Jascha Kessler describes as "so individual that one can believe one hears her speaking."[33] In this voice the mystical excitement at the center of her work reverberates. As Virgil Thomson explains, all her stories deal with moments when her characters are "caught up by something, inner or outer," and the "resulting action therefore is definitive, an ultimate clarification arrived at through ecstasy."[34] Like Yeats, Butts located evil not in the experimental searchings of a misguided society but in the inevitable changes brought on by war, technology, science, and progress. Butts saw these changes fragmenting her culture and invading the natural world, the sanctuary which nonetheless offered answers for the authentic initiates of its magic. What mattered was the purity of the quest to redefine and recapture the "center."

In Butts's fiction the authentic initiate is most often (but not always) a female figure who represents the sacredness of nature and its curative supernatural mysteries. She acts as an instrument of healing for the wounded society in which most of Butts's characters are caught up. This female, like the ancient mysteries and myths to which she is joined, embodies both good and evil, light and dark—the seemingly contradictory elements which Butts, like Wordsworth, was aware of in the mystical realm of nature. The Butts heroine is at once healer, sacred priestess, earth goddess, lover, and daimon/demon. Furthermore, she mediates between the past and the future—leading back to the primal source. Butts is certain that the true or authentic initiate, represented by this female figure, is the key to preserving what is real and sacred.

Mary Butts's interest in spiritual development and healing corresponds to Alicia Ostriker's notion that women mythmakers sought the figure of the "female creatrix" rather than the "abstract father god who creates the universe *ab nihilo*."[35] Although Butts's mythmaking is not so revisionist as, say, H. D.'s concept of myth, like H. D., she explores female initiates and female origins (which Butts connects to nature) and the "life force which infuses all organic and spiritual things with the power of growth, synthesis, and resurrection."[36] Yet it is important to note that Butts is not presenting her female characters in opposition to maleness but merely as human beings playing out their role; these characters hearken back to an authentic past that helps define their present. As Mary Hamer states about one of Butts's female characters, "She may be born of woman but all the rest of her has been formed by men."[37] This statement reinforces Butt's own strength of intellect, an intellect that incorporates and does not reject the masculine past in its endeavor. A consideration of the work of Mary Butts will add to our understanding of what female modernists do with myth by recalling the origins and powers of the female divine for both men and women and by translating those powers into healing forces for contemporary concerns.

Sir James Frazer's *The Golden Bough* first appeared in 1890 and laid the groundwork for studies connecting magic and religion and for interpreting humanity's cultural past. It had a significant influence on modernist thought, as did Jessie Weston's *From Ritual to Romance,* which explored the nature of the Holy Grail quest. The themes of death and rebirth so prevalent in Frazer and the link between Christianity and the Pagan Mysteries in Weston assisted Butts in creating and developing her own vision of how the past and its rituals relate to humans' present spiritual condition and thinking.

Butts's view of ritual and primal sources was particularly influenced by the work of the Cambridge Ritualists (Jane Ellen Harrison, Gilbert Murray, Francis M. Cornford, and, to a lesser degree, Arthur Bernard Cook), a group of classical scholars working primarily during the period from 1900 to 1915. Harrison and Murray are both mentioned by Butts in *The Crystal Cabinet* and in her 1932 essay *Traps for Unbelievers.* For Harrison and Murray, ritual was an acting out to assure fertility or to prevent disaster, and both stressed the primacy of ritual over mythology; myth can change over time while the ritual itself tends to remain the same.[38] Both Harrison and Murray were leading Hellenists of their day, and Butts apparently drew from their work as sources for her own. Specifically, Harrison's *Themis* on primal origins shapes Butts's notion of *mana* (an elemental force that individuals try to acquire from a totem animal or god). The idea of *mana* permeates *The Crystal Cabinet,* the novel *Armed with Madness,* the essay *Traps for Unbelievers,* and numerous short stories. Like Harrison, Butts sought the source of the religious impulse (Blake's "inmost form") and agreed with Harrison's assertion that the "function of ritual was to ensure the continued existence of the group."[39] Ruth Hoberman defines Butts's "mythical method" as involving "ritual not story, and is associated with fluidity, nurturing, and jouissance. It evokes a totemistic world whose passing she, like Harrison, mourns."[40] Hoberman's connection of Butts's method with Harrison's views and with *jouissance* links Butts to Julia Kristeva's cyclical and monumental time and the various myths of resurrection which "perpetuate the vestige of an anterior or concomitant maternal cult,"[41] and this connection unites Butts with Harrison's interests more so than with Frazer's focus on male death and resurrection. For Butts, the interest lies in being able to move outside of linear time within the rhythm of the natural world. For Harrison and for Butts, this points to the primal female principle that revels in its identification with the natural world and with the cosmic order outside subjective time and space. In a sense Butts is prophetic in anticipating female characters who, as Kristeva contends, "rejoin, on the one hand, the archaic (mythical) memory and, on the other, the cyclical or monu-mental temporality of marginal movements."[42]

Harrison, in addition, perceived the gods of Greek religion as a projection of the collective unconscious of the group,[43] an idea that connects her with Jungian theory. Although Butts was skeptical of the influence Freud and Jung might have on her, she recognized their potency in her world and utilized their ideas throughout her work.[44] Harrison and the Cambridge Ritualists served Butts by connecting myth to ritual and by showing the significance of ancient rites to the modern psychoanalytical and archetypal work of Jung and Freud.[45]

• • • • • •

Mary Butts did not fit into any particular literary circle. Positioned between feminists, on the one hand, and male modernism, on the other, Butts did not write anything like the "Feminist Manifesto" of Mina Loy or reflect the strongly feminist views of other female modernists, yet her work and her lifestyle (that of a woman who attempted to define herself on her own terms) distinctly promote the independence of female intellect and spirit. In fact, Butts writes principal females (and characters in general) who are not concerned with gender identity and who are instead interested in their own way, in what Toril Moi describes as the "goal of the feminist struggle," of deconstructing or breaking down binary oppositions of masculinity and femininity.[46] Although Moi's comments are directed at Virginia Woolf's Lily Briscoe of *To the Lighthouse,* I argue that many of Butts's female protagonists do, in fact, situate themselves in a gender role that satisfies their individual needs. Unlike the solitary and isolated Lily Briscoe, Butts's females instead retain the qualities of a Mrs. Ramsey (e.g., those elements of a primal past and an immediate past) and join them to their newly defined independence to create a broader definition of the modern woman—a definition simply of what it means to be a human being. As women emerging from a patriarchal order toward a completeness, they are able to balance and juggle both positions—earth-mother/life-giving force with modern woman defining herself and her place in the changing world. Butts's female protagonists are both independent and womanly, self-defining and nurturing.

In this way Butts is prophetic in recognizing, as did Woolf and others, that the time had come to redefine the nature of womanhood. Yet, unlike many other female modernists, Butts celebrates those female qualities that nurture, defend, protect, and unite, and as a result her female characters take on a sort of stability within chaos, understanding within confusion. By fusing the qualities of the past with the present, Butts's fiction argues that women do not have to eradicate essentials within their nature in order to be whole. In a review of Mark Perugini's *Victorian Days and Ways* published in *The Bookman* in May of 1932, Mary Butts reflects on the struggle of women like herself growing up in Edwardian England, an "agonised, ridiculous, exhausting, confusing, nerve-wrecking, complex-forming struggle" for the right to grow into whatever they might choose to be: "And it is a paradox of that extraordinary age, of which the girls' war was one of the death-throes, that it produced the greatest intellectual statements of women's rights to be human beings that the world has ever known."[47] By joining feminine qualities of the past with those of the present, she manages to reject the rigid structures of a Victorian past professed by her own mother, while paradoxically valorizing the healing power of the female. Her females are devoted to wounded men, yet draw their strength from a primal goddess source, the uniting of a Judeo-Christian spirituality with a matrilineally pagan one. This potential contradiction does not seem to compromise Butts's vision; instead, it promotes the position in the quotation above: it is an intellectual statement of a woman's right to be a human being and to interpret that humanity in terms of her own past and her own qualities, all the while dealing with the world's past and present. Marianne DeKovan's words in one of her discussions of reassessing modernism may be applied to what Mary Butts achieved, a modernist form which "maintains difference while denying hierarchy."[48] Butts's modern reinterpretation of ritual and myth underscores a particularly female modernist vision.

Although at present Mary Butts is not part of the "canon" of modernism, her work moves closely along the lines of modernism. At this point it is difficult to clarify Mary Butts's place in literary modernism, and it is yet to be determined how much Butts was influenced by other modernists or how much she influenced them. In 1932 the poet and essayist J. C. Squire compared a collection of her short stories with the work of Katherine Mansfield and Henry James, but also commented that "[r]ough comparisons of one author with another are usually invalid as criticism."[49] Butts's complexity and her enigmatic concerns with timelessness, the classics, her race and its heritage, the reality of the mystical experience and of magic, the relation of art to magic, and numerous other interests make her work and her vision difficult to categorize, particularly in relation to her fellow modernists. As a literary term, "modernism" is still a nebulous and even controversial term, especially when describing literature written by women between 1900 and 1935. Numerous studies addressing the definition of modernism attest to this fact. Malcolm Bradbury and James McFarlane state in the preface and introductory chapter to their classic work, *Modernism: 1890–1930,* that "[t]he Modern tradition was, and knew it was, a paradox" and that this era of literary and aesthetic achievement was the "art that makes life, the drama of the artist's consciousness, the structure that lies beyond time, history, character or visible reality, the moral imperative of technique."[50]

Butts's technique is one that assumes a substantial amount of knowledge and attention on the part of the reader, is elliptical, difficult, and confusing.

In modernist terms she does, in fact, disrupt conventional syntax; she separates subjects from verbs, confounds referents and their sources, forcing readers to reread and reconnect on their own; pronouns and antecedents resist easy association. The rereading to discover this association forces readers to rethink what is being said, a difficult disruption with a purpose. Mary Hamer suggests that Butts's writing

> makes Mary Butts a woman who cannot be dismissed. At the first encounter with one of her sentences, a reader wonders if she has ever heard the English language treated with such authority before. . . . [S]he used writing as a way of feeling forward, feeling beyond and through the old ways of putting things together. The arbitrary and unfamiliar syntax, the odd juxtapositions, grow out of this. If the reader feels challenged, this is perhaps not a mistake.[51]

Although Butts's technique is unique, the narrative flow is fairly standard. Her stories have a beginning, middle, and ending; it is what takes place in between that suggests a modernist notion that fits Ezra Pound's dictum to "make it new." Butts was an intellectual, and in spite of the wild lifestyle that she so eagerly pursued, her writing challenges and forces readers to think in new ways, to reorganize the way they think about the world. Like D. H. Lawrence, Butts explored relationships that ignored gender boundaries; like T. S. Eliot, she intertwined her knowledge of classical mythology with contemporary concerns; like James Joyce, she sought imaginative expression of consciousness; and, like many other modernists, Butts struggled to find what Bradbury and McFarlane identify as "the structure that lies beyond history, character, or visible reality," the discontinuity that takes us "behind familiar reality."[52] In this sense her work certainly belongs among the work of other modernists who challenged existing patterns of language and communication. Butts saw herself as something of a seer, a mystic who had much to reveal to a world that she saw crumbling around her. In her diary in 1921, two of Butts's seven aims of her writing included the following:

> V. I want to make this world into material for the art of writing.
> VI. I want to observe the pairs of opposites, remembering that which is below is as that which is above. From this I wish to formulate clearly, the hitherto incommunicable idea of a third perception. This is a perception of the nature of the universe as yet unknown to man, except by intuitions which cannot be retained, and by symbols whose meaning cannot be retained also. I want to fix it in man's mind.[53]

Rather than through an emphasis on technique, Butts's modernist thrust is such that it confronts and reinterprets reality in extraordinary ways. To do so, she must challenge readers to think outside their ordinary patterns of thought, to suspend disbelief temporarily, yet finally to accept the extraordinary as true. Hers is a perplexing style that forces her readers to reevaluate incomprehension, something like the paradigm shift that was taking place in physics at the time—a way of looking at the new by reinterpreting the old, shaped by self and consciousness. Her fiction does this through the use of myth, the magic of ritual, and the spirituality of mysticism. And for Butts the process of writing rests on a specific acceptance and acknowledgment of life, both seen and unseen. But the reasons for reconsidering Butts's work are not simply to enlarge the canon of modernism; rather, as Jascha Kessler notes, "it is precisely our potential reciprocation of her passion today that should lead to her being unearthed and exhibited, as one would say of a buried hoard in archaeology."[54]

The difficulty in attempting a study of Mary Butts's work is due to the fact that she is extremely hard to categorize; in fact, Bruce McPherson, the publisher who reissued Butts's books in the United States, calls her a "sort of literary Rorschach test,"[55] and I wholeheartedly agree. From any given perspective, one can only attempt a reading of influential intellectual factors. I chose to introduce her work by finding a focus central to most of her fiction—myth and ritual with an underlying sense of the mystical. Her work is so rich in allusion and intellect that each subsequent reading sparks new analyses. Any first study will, as a result, seem incomplete. However, if this book acts as a springboard for future evaluation of Mary Butts, it will have fulfilled its purpose—one that establishes a foundation for critical inquiry rather than pretending to be an exhaustive study. My hope is that this book stimulates critical responses that veer from those presented here and offers a position against which to write other and varied criticism. For these reasons, I have not emphasized a feminist reading of Butts's work, although there is certainly room to do so, nor have I delved into the area of gay studies or queer theory in regard to Butts's relations with homosexual men. Her work and her vision are rich in opportunities for exploration for those who are specialists in these areas. There is fertile ground for another and somewhat different study of Butts's work. Instead, in addition to establishing a critical base from which to draw, I have tried to place her within a literary context in relation to her intellectual milieu and to explore her vision from a particular intellectual framework—specifically, how myth, ritual, and mysticism permeate her work and help create her own unique vision within the period of literary modernism. In writing for both a general audience as well as an academic one, I have combined scholarship with straightforward discussion and analysis.

For the reasons listed above concerning the specific literary focus of this study, I have chosen to address Mary Butts's two historical novels, *The Macedonian* (1933) and *Scenes from the Life of Cleopatra* (1935), in an appendix rather than within the main text. I concur with the reviewer Helen Moran, who said in her contemporary review of *The Macedonian* that "[t]his is very different from her other books. What will she do next?"[56] Both *The Macedonian* and *Scenes from the Life of Cleopatra* mark a point or shift in Butts's thinking, a revelation of sorts of her place in tradition and history. Since I view her historical novels as something of a departure from my own focus in the book, the appendix is a way to explore these novels independently, instead of trying to make their vision coincide with her earlier work. In regard to her poetry, most appeared in little magazines in the 1920s and 1930s, and it has never been collected. I have used her poem "Corfe" as an overview for this study because it elucidates the major themes crucial to Butts's fiction. There is a need for the poetry to be collected and a separate study done. The poet Kenneth Irby at the University of Kansas has been working on such a collection for several years.

Mary Butts is a writer who speaks to us now and whose sibylline prose looks into the future. She loved England, the land, its power, and those who understood this beauty. She lived between two centuries with the sensibilities of each; she loved freedom and truth and found these in her connection to the past and to racial memory. Perhaps like Blake, whose presence permeated her home and her life, she knew that only a very few would understand her passion. For Bryher, "[h]er mixture of clarity and metaphysics, of charity and intolerance, made easy fame impossible."[57] But the writings of a "soul living at its fullest capacity" deserve serious consideration.

CHAPTER ONE

"I Strove to Seize the Inmost Form": The Crystal Cabinet *(1937)*

"In a glass world"

As the great-granddaughter of Thomas Butts, patron and friend of William Blake, Mary Butts took the name for her autobiography of childhood from Blake's enigmatic poem of the same name, "The Crystal Cabinet." Choosing that title, Butts acknowledges the mystical influence of Blake on her life and her writing. Her desire to live in and out of time, to make the invisible visible originates within the natural world surrounding Salterns, her beloved family home. *The Crystal Cabinet* also identifies the personal influences on Butts's intellectual development that would later weave through her fiction. But it is the mystical quality of Blake's art and poetry, combined with the sanctity of the natural world that she treasured and adored, that is at the nucleus of her memoir, and the words "I strove to seize the inmost form" suggest the mystical focus of all her life and work.

To begin a study of an artist with one of her last completed works, published posthumously in 1937, the year of her death, may seem somewhat out of order. Her autobiography, however, permits us to search for the roots of the sacred and the mystical in her childhood. Robin Blaser has suggested that "Mary Butts's reputation, like that of H. D., suffered because of the complexity of the sacred in her twentieth-century mind, heart, and work."[1] This was a time of scientific and technological advancement, yet instead of looking to science, Butts, like many other modernists, turned to the past and its primal offerings to help define and explain the confusion of her world. The mystical impulse, which she discovered in her natural world at Salterns and in the pictures and writings of William Blake and the Romantics, takes on a special significance in this very personal record of those influences and memories.

Mary Butts was an intellectual child of nature, in the tradition of Wordsworth and the nature mystics. Although Blake was her earliest Romantic influence, what she also discerned in William Wordsworth and Percy Bysshe Shelley helped create the artist she would eventually become. With a father who took responsibility for her education until his death when she was only fourteen, Butts discovered the world of literature, classical myth, and primitive ritual that were as much a part of her life as the sacred, natural world of the countryside.[2] In a letter to her friend Hugh Ross Williamson (1934), Butts explains her passionate interest in and feeling for the "mystical experience": "It means everything to me—I mean as a thing separate from any practice, from love or the arts or work of any kind, the pure quiet sudden thing, like a fire—no, a light . . . it is the thing, the only thing, men live by . . . the one way of finding out what things are."[3] Salterns offered her what we might call the primal experience of autochthony, "the feeling of *belonging to a place.*"[4] In what she labeled her "Sacred Wood," Butts began her discovery of the origins not only of her literary inspirations but also of her spiritual and mystical "seeings" (what she termed her "*Amor Intellectualis Dei*"), a "way of finding out what things are."

This immersion in the magic of literature and nature alienated her from the Victorian notions of womanhood and women's education and finally from her own mother. Butts, even as a child, was a free spirit, a woman who demanded her own place and her own right to an education that any exceptional child necessarily requires. In *The Crystal Cabinet* we learn that this was a natural development of her existence as long as her father lived; once he was gone, however, Butts had to find a way to fit the very complex intellectual development of a young girl into her mother's and society's norms. She never managed to completely understand her mother's way of thinking, and, as a result, the remainder of her childhood and her young womanhood were filled with painful and difficult experiences.

What did sustain her through emotional difficulties was her knowledge that there was something in nature which offered insight into a world beyond. Although feminist critics of Romanticism, such as Anne K. Mellor, Margaret Homans, and Marlon Ross rightly point out numerous difficulties with female representations in Blake, Wordsworth, and Shelley,[5] the early influence of the Romantics marks Butts's emotional and intellectual development. As Mellor and Ross observe, the Romantic ego was "potently male"; it was also capable of "incorporating into itself whatever attributes of the female it desired to possess."[6] The Romantic poet could "deify" the male ego even as it "cannibalized the attributes of the female,"[7] most specifically by appropriating the reproductive process, i.e., the poet/savior giving birth to art. Marlon Ross explains that the "romantic poets write from a perspective that it would be impossible for a woman living during the time to take" and that, as a result, these women were categorized as "extremely minor romantics."[8] Butts suffers some of the same fate as her female romantic predecessors, yet she draws from the male-dominated world what she needs as a female artist with her own voice and her own interpretations. The influence of Blake, Wordsworth, and Shelley perhaps accounts for her unique modernist vision, one which embraces and supports men as creatures who need protection and nurturing. This is a way of thinking which prevails in her life as well as in her art. She never doubted at any time that her intellectual abilities were equal to those of her peers, male or female. Perhaps her exploration of Blake, Wordsworth, and Shelley initiated a strength of intellect with which she could face the challenges of her own times.

The thesis in Blake most clearly reflected in Butts's vision is his insistence that change can take place through each person's individual power to imagine, and the corollary that dreams and visions are not for escape but for change and renewal.[9] Like Blake's persona in his poem "The Crystal Cabinet," Butts "strove to seize the inmost form." In her book, Butts discusses her mystical "seeings" and compares her own mind to a "crystal cabinet like the one Blake wanted to live inside and outside of at once."[10] From Blake's mythmaking, Butts culled his search for "simultaneous possession of eternal life" (237). Although Butts writes that "[c]onsciously the Blakes had very little influence on me" (34), Blake's mystical impulse and his aim of attaining spiritual truth apparently awakened and helped define her own mystical yearnings.

Brooding on several of Blake's works, Butts explains what it meant to move through her home as a young child among the "mystical" drawings: "Until slowly, not the execution but the conception, the kind of seeing that there was in William Blake, in the end affected me both unconsciously and profoundly" (34). This is the "wonder" of Blake's mystic impulse that Helen White noted in her 1927 study, *The Mysticism of Blake,* "the wonder of very little, and usually very commonplace, things that we pass by every day without any appreciation of how extraordinary they are,"[11] and, like Blake's innocent child, Butts enjoys her moments of insight in her personal Eden at Salterns. Whatever effects the Blakes "unconsciously" had on Butts, she expresses a desire similar to Blake's to return to a time before the human race had been corrupted or oppressed by physical life. Butts's longing for spiritual development, "The soul living at its fullest capacity,"[12] clearly resembles Blake's affinity for a prelapsarian state, while a childlike innocence permeates whatever "mystic" experiences they share.

The Crystal Cabinet ends at what Butts terms "the edge of my maturity"

(262) and falls very much into the tradition of Wordsworth's *The Prelude.* As the author, like Wordsworth, explores her childhood through her connection to nature, this immersion in nature creates a fascination with both its "loveliness and power," which, as Butts explains, "Though the loveliness comes direct, power, as Wordsworth was at such pains to make immortal words explain, is not so easily learned by a child" (22). In Wordsworth's words, "Fair seed-time had my soul, and I grew up / Fostered alike by beauty and fear."[13] Butts's "child," like Wordsworth's, recognizes that

> when Nature ceases to be the Mother, the all-nourisher, you are left without her, or with those aspects of her which are hostile to men who have not made their submission. It is only by obedience and conquest, or by blinding ourselves, that we cease to see how strange she is, the potential terror lying dormant, that the shifting of a stone will evoke. (15)

Or the surging of a storm across Poole Harbour could conjure the idea of nature as a living being: "I could not think of it as anything else but a live thing, as visible as it seemed to Wordsworth that it might be . . . a true daimon, as the young of each race first see power" (10–11). Her personal experiences with this mix of beauty and power, related in detail and variety in her memoir, incite her interest and her desire to "live in two worlds at once, or in time and out of it" (13).

Butts then, even in her early youth, longs to understand the "mystic" inclinations of Wordsworth and to define and incorporate her own mystical leanings into her life's desire and into her work. Her childhood "seeings" bring together the fascination of Wordsworth's nature with that of Blake's innocent who nearly loses human identity in the mystical experience. For Butts, writing her childhood memoir from the perspective of her forties, a combination of both notions identifies experience that is at once reflective and immediate, intuitive and profound. Nature is both an object of sacred reverence, as it is for Wordsworth, and a vision of angels, which Blake describes as youthful divinations.

But the most influential Romantic for Butts and the one who pervades her memoir is Percy Bysshe Shelley. Butts devotes an entire chapter to Shelley, draws from his youthful vigor and excitement, and reminds us throughout *The Crystal Cabinet* that

> Only there is a world where things are different, the world Shelley knew. The heavenly world, only not the parson's heaven, more like the 'many mansions' Our Lord said heaven meant.
>
> Only to know about it is truly a great adventure, and you have to dare things. As Shelley did. (113)

Butts apparently read widely in Shelley, and she recognized in him a companion for what she considered her own daring adventures. In experiences such as those described in "Hymn to Intellectual Beauty," Shelley perceived an eternal reality beyond the mortal world, a Platonic "unseen Power" which is part of the "invisible" world Butts had intuited from early childhood. "Arethusa" and *Prometheus Unbound* introduced Butts to Shelley's own mythmaking. In his independence of mind, intense admiration for ancient Greece, struggle against evil in the world, and youthful longing for a return to primal innocence, she found what would become primary concerns of her own fiction. Shelley could help transform the painful experiences of her youth and her isolation into insights "beyond the moon": "Beyond the moon you could fly on Shelley's wings, wings he lends so generously to girl and boy" (114). Here, "beyond the moon" Butts finds parallel moments of visionary ascent toward the eternal where poetry and art are created.

From Shelley's "Hellas," Butts learned a way to incorporate contemporary events into art. Writing about the Greek struggle for independence from the Turks during his time, Shelley was able to express his hatred of contemporary oppression as well as his admiration for the culture of ancient Greece. Shelley converts life into art and assists Butts to understand what to do "if one were to meet heavy weather" (116), while she learns to metamorphose her own times through mythical interpretations of the past with "Hellas the beginning and the end and the significance of all" (114).

Perhaps, however, Shelley's *Prometheus Unbound* offered Butts most of what she needed to define her art and her life. *The Crystal Cabinet* reveals Butts's youthful struggle to understand her uniqueness and difference as a young woman thinking thoughts beyond those of her mother's generation. In a discussion of Prometheus and Asia, Butts grapples to explain what it all meant to her "nearly thirty years ago" (114). Quoting the final passage from *Prometheus Unbound,* Butts searches "[u]ntil it seemed that in the hero Prometheus the meaning of human life was to be found—Prometheus, the rebel, the fire-bearer; who told people they might do things they had not been allowed to do—that was why he was called Saviour" (115). Like Prometheus, Shelley and Butts longed for a way to combat the forces which struck out against them. The final passage of *Prometheus Unbound* offered solutions:

> To suffer woes which Hope thinks infinite;
> To forgive wrongs darker than death or night;
>   To defy Power, which seems omnipotent;
> To love, and bear; to hope till Hope creates
> From its own wreck the thing it contemplates;
>   Neither to change, nor falter, nor repent;
> This, like thy glory, Titan, is to be
> Good, great and joyous, beautiful and free.
> This is alone Life, Joy, Empire, and Victory.[14]

The influence of the three romantics, Blake, Wordsworth, and Shelley, then, played an important role in the fashioning of the artist who is Mary Butts—at once child, visionary, lover of the natural world, and fighter for emancipation from oppression in whatever form it takes.

For Butts, one form of oppression was not having the freedom to explore and examine the intellectual and mystical incidents she experienced in her youth. In a chapter entitled "Regiment of Women," she recounts her very difficult stay at a boarding school at St. Leonard's in St. Andrews, Scotland. Although she feels grateful for the "lifting of the taboo laid on women against the free use of their faculties" (180) at St. Leonard's—"from the beginning, to be given a real education was the one desire of which [she] was sure" (180)—she had been torn from her family and her beloved Salterns after her father's death. At St. Leonard's she found herself alone and frightened by a rigidity and coldness in the personalities of the teachers and the other girls that duplicated the Scottish climate. The severity of this "regiment of women" threw her into a nervous state and, except for the brief friendship of one teacher, the entire experience was negative, painful, and severe. Bryher calls Mary Butts a "specially gifted child" and explains that

> It was an additional tragedy for Mary that she was not a rebel, she would not then have been so isolated, she wanted to co-operate with authority; her revolt was only against the system that crushed her overwhelming desire for scholarship and insistence that she conformed to a pattern they never even troubled to explain to her.[15]

The excessive discipline, the lack of any individuality or freedom, and the extreme loneliness and sense of loss induce her to recognize that she "was leading a life entirely in two worlds—the school world with its deadly pressure, and a world within, where every song that Shelley ever wrote sang in a kind of super-chorus together" (189).

This lonely austerity of boarding school in Scotland offered her a "'seeing' which comforted me" (221), says Butts, and it lifted her out of despair. Praying on a little rosary of "nutmegs and tiny macrocarpa cones, carved beads from the east and pierced tonquin beans. . . . All strung together, with a queer Russian cross attached, four equal arms engraved with stiff, hieratic figures. . . . A mixed lot, pagan and Christian and one or two I had made up" (221), Mary Butts related her primitive, mythical world to the unseen, the invisible. She emphasized how a sense of place defined and rooted her mysticism:

> Just as it was quite dark, out of the chill and the stones and the grimness, out of Scots magic which is quite different from English magic, out of the hardness and grimness, out of all that is Scotland and not England or France or Spain, out of a world that seemed the very opposite of a fairy-tale—or was perhaps its own unique fairy-tale—it came.

> On the long grass court, between my walk and the outer Abbey wall, turf used in winter for lacrosse and in summer for nets, from somewhere out in the middle of it I heard a voice say: "Round the stem of the fairy tree". That, I remember, came from a song old Andrew Lang, who sometimes you saw out walking on the Links, had made up. About the Garden of the Hesperides. Then I looked, and out on the grass where the voice came from there was a tree. Not the Hesperidean, but a young slight one, a birch I think, with something gold as oranges glimmering in its branches, only more golden. A Tree with a delicate air. Sprung up there just by itself, for comfort. What the Bible called a remembrancer. A magic thing to remind me that all the inside things were true.
>
> Not to be looked for again. Or asked for. Only to be remembered. I stood still, adoring it. I never saw it again. (221)

The "remembrancer," like the *mana* of nature, remains an essential element of her vision. This episode has at its center the "concrete," similar to what Helen White identifies in Blake's handling of his "mystical experiences."[16] In one's perception of the experience is a kind of divination that Butts carries with her into her dealings with the external world. Like the world of Blake's crystal cabinet, the "inside" things are true. Butts's "earthly 'unearthly'" (133) takes form in the ballad she recalls in this "seeing." In "The Wife of Usher's Well" Butts recognizes the birch tree as the tree from which a woman's sons come home to her, "wearing hats made of the bark of a birch that grew 'at the gates o' Paradise,'"[17] a sign that the sons are no longer of this world; they return from the world of the dead, an "earthly 'unearthly.'" Butts's "world within" defines her mystical quest. To live "in two worlds at once," for Butts, means to exist with an inwardness always present in the real world. Butts's sincere searching and mystical thinking go hand-in-hand with the aesthetic creation of art and the magic of discovering the divine within. If we take Mary Butts at her word, the spiritual manifests itself not only in her sacred, natural world but also emerges from the artist in the creative process, and this spirituality or mystical comprehension, she believes, are as real as the concrete elements of the natural world. Art is another manifestation of what she, and others who claim mystical seeings, experiences in nature.

The concrete image of the tree, then, transforms into a reflection of the eternal, the macrocosmic and microcosmic world that Hazard Adams, in his discussion of Blake's poetry, associates with Blake's crystal cabinet.[18] This macrocosmic image serves Butts as a reminder that the microcosmic (inside) world is true and safe. At this stage of her life, feeling abandoned and alone, Butts had to look within to understand the contrast of her happy, early life with the isolated, lonely existence she now found herself encountering. She was a child who treasured learning and who possessed an exceptional intense mind, a mind seeking both independence and solace. Bryher explains that "[w]hatever strange and reckless actions happened in her later life, were the direct result of these unhappy, neglected years."[19] Mysticism, its offer of internal clarification and of a connection between the natural world and the spiritual world, became something of a quest from this very early age.

Mary Butts defines her brand of mysticism as the awareness of "a much smaller, nearer, form of supernatural life, an immediate earthly, 'unearthly'" (133) linked to the world of the dead and the power of her ancestors. From the beginning, we see that her mysticism is clearly rooted in her sense of place, nationality, and ancestry. She tells us that until the war, she had worked out for herself the "same religion as Plutarch. As Glover says: 'Radiant with amiability —and everything a symbol of everything else, and all is beautiful and holy'" (133). Seeing the mirror of the divine in her external world, "in and out of doors; in patches, and often, as in the case of the great pine-tree, especially attached to things" (133), Butts recognizes that this nearer form of supernatural life is "infinitely less than God. The thought of God could send 'it' scattering in an instant—if you remembered in time. Only there were bits of it, come upon suddenly round corners, so terrifying that they caught you before you could remember Him" (133–34). This "terror" leads her to participate in the mystical quest and to discover her spiritual inwardness as "primitive man did" (134), youthful and alone, with exhilarating fear and awe.

In the sense that her visions represent a true inwardness of life in this world, perceived through a kind of magical-aesthetic thinking, Butts's mysticism moves clearly between the inner and outer worlds rather than sensing the divine through prayer or the customary stages of the Mystic Way described, for example, by Evelyn Underhill as

> (1) The awakening of the Self to consciousness of Divine Reality . . .
> (2) Purgation . . .
> (3) Illumination . . .
> (4) Dark Night of the Soul . . .
> (5) Union: the true goal of the mystic quest.[20]

Butts's mysticism makes a crucial distinction between two mystical realms in that her mystical "seeings" focus on how the external world and her spiritual ancestors mirror the divine within her own life. She lives in this world but longs for and recognizes a fusion with divinity perhaps more in line with William James's description of mysticism as that which "defies expression," offers "states of insight into depths of truth unplumbed by the discursive intellect," is "transient" and after an hour or two "begins to fade into the light of common day," and puts one's own will "in abeyance" as if "grasped and held by a superior power."[21] Whether or not Butts read James's more liberal explanations of the mystic state, her mysticism implies a broader definition than that of mystical pantheism or traditional religious disciplines. Butts's approach and experience combine with a more primitive sense of belonging, which she derives from the ghosts of her ancestors and the spirit of the land. Her mysticism germinates in her inner world so intimately connected to her past and the land she held sacred.

By taking her title from the Blake poem, Butts links herself with a longing for "the inmost Form," similar to the "mystic state" identified by William James as "windows through which the mind looks out upon a more extensive and inclusive world."[22] She senses a consanguinity with the natural world at Salterns, what she identifies as a "secret common to our blood. A secret concerned with time and very little with death, with what perhaps medieval philosophers called *aevum,* the link between time and eternity. With which goes an ability to live in two worlds at once, or in time and out of it" (12). This secret belongs to Butts and her ancestors, and in her mind their kinship to the land of Salterns affords the opportunity to be both in and out of time.

Sensing consciousness in the elements of nature, Butts found a way to identify and unite with them on a mystical level. As a young child, she writes that she was awakened one night and was told to "get up and look." She knelt on the window-sill and looked out beyond and above the trees to view the stars:

> I knew what they were called, I knew that they were there, but for the first time I saw them as the host of heaven . . . I adored. And have managed to keep the same eyes that saw them that night—the eyes of the same child. Understanding, without the least difficulty, that this was the answer to my worry about God, establishing in my mind where God was to be looked for, and how things could be called 'like' God. (10)

Like those of Blake, who influenced her so "profoundly," Butts's visions were immediate, an instant affinity with spiritual life. Like Wordsworth, she sought a communion with nature but was able to maintain the "eyes of the same child." Richard Coe, in his study of the autobiography of childhood, points out that Wordsworth, who certainly recognized the importance of the child's vision and who sought communion with the "One Great Mind," was never able to complete his "submission to this pantheistic, mystic spirit of the world"; instead, he retained "his own strong sense of individual identity, as a force separate from, and in some ways in opposition to, the greater force outside him."[23] For Butts, the childhood communion with her natural world informs the entirety of her existence and sustains her through the madness of the 1920s. By writing about her childhood near the end of her life while immersed in the countryside and nature of Cornwall, her life comes full circle as she returns to the nature, although now altered by progress, which had offered her early inspiration.

Caught between two worlds, the Victorian Protestant orthodoxy of her mother and her father's skepticism (as well as that of "the new physics"), and fusing what she discovered in the Romantics and in mythology, Butts sought to define her world in her own terms in her search for what is true. The mysterious, magic force of living nature, combined with the power celebrated in myth and poetry, transformed her experiences into mystical associations with the world of her youth. Jane E. Harrison, whose work Mary Butts knew well, clarifies mystical elements of nature that conform with Butts's vision: "from the multitude of things that have *mana,* there arises the notion of a sort of *continuum of mana,* a world of unseen power lying behind the visible universe, a world which is the sphere . . . of magical activity and the medium of mysticism."[24] The extraordinary magic associated with Badbury Rings (prehistoric mounded circles northwest of Poole), the salt marshes and woods surrounding her home, the poetry of Shelley, Blake, Wordsworth, and others, a sense of ritual, and Norse and Greek mythology merge to form the *mana,* the elemental force of nature embedded in an object or person, which sums up Butts's desire to unite the temporal and the timeless.

In her classic work on mysticism, Evelyn Underhill observes that "the end which the true mystic sets before him is conscious union with a living Absolute."[25] In the sense that Butts's work and her life at Salterns attempt to define this union, the discovery of the seen and unseen, Butts's experiences and language qualify as mystical, and *The Crystal Cabinet* relates several experiences which help her to lift this veil of the unseen temporarily. She tells us that in her youth after reading Shelley, the five words, "Love and man's unconquerable mind," become "one short passionate key to everything" (115). Later, in London near the end of the war she feels a sense of panic during air-raids "screaming out of the high winter sky" (117). Frightened and alone, she hides herself in a little outbuilding and encounters those words once more:

> I can only try and tell what happened as I tried not to crouch there. Which was a clear, thrilling, quiet voice repeating: "Love and man's unconquerable mind. Love and man's unconquerable mind"; and I was suddenly charged with knowledge that, somehow, it mattered that I should command myself; that, in some unrealizable way, I had it in me to give or take away the life from those words.
>
> Repeating them, I went back; and inside the studio and the racket overhead there was a quiet into which I entered where both fear and death were swallowed up. (117)

Mistakenly, Butts associates the line "love and man's unconquerable mind" with Shelley when it actually appears in a Wordsworth poem, "To Toussaint l'Overture."[26] In remembering this line, which appears again later in her work, Butts perhaps makes this error because she associates it with Shelley's independence of mind and spirit. Love and the unquenchable power of the mind are, for Butts, driving forces carried by the elements. In reflecting on these forces in her memoir, she recognizes the essential role they play in defining her existence. In fact, in *The Prelude,* Wordsworth relates an experience similar to that of Butts in which he tells of taking shelter from an approaching storm under the brow of a rock:

> Thence did I drink the visionary power;
> And deem not profitless those fleeting moods
> Of shadowy exultation: not for this
> That they are kindred to our purer mind
> And intellectual life; but that the soul,
> Remembering how she felt, but what she felt
> Remembering not, retains an obscure sense
> Of possible sublimity, whereto
> With growing faculties she doth aspire,
> With faculties still growing, feeling still
> That whatsoever point they gain, they yet
> Have something to pursue.[27]

As *The Crystal Cabinet* makes clear, Butts's "divine property of first seeing," her *"Amor Intellectualis Dei,"* what she defined as "perception of a hierarchized universe, awakened by every order in the external world" (258), combined with the force of her creative abilities and a sense of Wordsworth's "visionary power," serves to sustain her throughout her full, if brief, life. "Love and man's unconquerable mind" support her through her father's death when she was fourteen; her mother's burning of her father's "dreadful books" after his death, an act in which she declared her mother had "murdered beauty" (108); her mother's accusations of impropriety with her stepfather; her estrangement from her beloved brother, Tony; the loss of Cecil Maitland, the love of her life; her battle with poverty and drugs, which led to an eventual breakdown; and the entire sense of loss associated with World War I. "Love and man's unconquerable mind" join her to the eternal world for which she longs.

Near the end of her memoir, Butts returns to Blake's poem in an attempt to give definition to her experiences. The conclusion of Blake's "Crystal Cabinet" is a kind of breaking through, while Butts's memoir serves as an interpretation of experience:

> I strove to seize the inmost Form,
> With ardor fierce & hands of flame,
> But burst the Crystal Cabinet,
> And like a Weeping Babe became—
>
> A weeping Babe upon the wild,
> And Weeping Woman pale reclind;
> And in the outward air again
> I fild with woes the passing Wind.[28]

Just as for Butts the sacred world of nature is the opening to an inner world, a seeing, the crystal cabinet itself is, according to Hazard Adams, "an area just short of vision, holding within itself all the possibilities of vision."[29] For Harold Bloom, in Blake's cabinet "Everything in the outer Wild has its counterpart in this inner world,"[30] and "The inmost form is reserved for art."[31] For Butts, this transformation translates as the art of writing, which helps preserve her through her difficulties. Writing is Butts's glimpse into the "inmost form," a way to interpret the opportunities the cabinet offers and to translate her experiences into Platonic reflections of what she constantly refers to as "another world." Her belief that this world is a reflection of some other, more meaningful world, a world where "between two dream states there is an instant of change, as of a barrier passed, as between two levels of consciousness" (137), is essential to her art. These transitional states of consciousness, a very real part of her life from early childhood, were her opportunity to glimpse that "other" world: "They have 'something to do'—that is, sometimes, they are not wholly, I think, unrelated to one's state of perception when moved by art or by natural beauty" (138). These two worlds, then, become central to Butts's quest. She says, "In 'another world'? What world? In one sense the rest of my life was to be a search for the answer to that" (136). Her mystical impulse, she knew, could not be induced "by any drug, stimulant, suggestion, or desire" (137), even though she had tried that and sought opportunities to "lift the veil" throughout her life. Her art, then, became a medium, a way to create and explore what she knew existed in a realm she only touched upon in moments of perception; Blake's poem is the perfect metaphor for such a search.

In Blake's world, Adams explains, "proper vision lies in an inward expansion in which one's own spiritual body surrounds that 'other England' within the grain of sand. Any violent reaching out destroys the vision."[32] Blake's speaker bursts the Crystal Cabinet in his fierce attempt to "seize the inmost Form." For Mary Butts, much like Blake, the mystical reaching would help define her place in the universe. In 1921 she listed as one of her seven aims of writing: "I want by various mystical practices and studies to produce my true nature, and enlarge my perceptions."[33] In *The Crystal Cabinet* Butts explores the secrets of Blake's cabinet through the secrets of her mind:

> I was seeing my mind as though it were a cabinet, furnished with all sorts of shelves and cupboards and drawers. . . . Yet still on the whole an empty cabinet, a crystal cabinet like the one Blake wanted to live inside and outside of at once. Perhaps that was what learning to live meant, really learning. Not the half-learning, which seemed as much as most people learned. Anyone can live outside it, and a very few, like the duller saints, altogether inside. But to do what Blake said—and be inside and outside the cabinet at once? Wasn't that what someone called the 'same thing and simultaneous possession of eternal life'? Wasn't that what Delphi had tried to show the ancient world? (237)

And isn't that what Butts's language in *The Crystal Cabinet* indicates? It is an attempt to live inside and outside at once, to experience the seen and the unseen, to lift the veil to reveal the invisible, to see the "shining out of a God," whatever that god may be, to unite momentarily with the salt marshes, the land, the sea, Pan, Hermes, Apollo, Shelley. This is the language and the struggle of the mystic and of Mary Butts. Her literary and ancient ancestors become the same as the landscape in which she lives, even though they live in her mind, while the externals of nature remain outside but offer insights or openings into the realm of truth she struggles to see and to define. In the language of the mystic, Butts yearns for the opportunity to fill the secret cupboards and drawers where memory holds the moments of connection with the unseen. The elements of nature were her *mana,* the elemental forces and essential components of her sacred game.

The concluding chapter of *The Crystal Cabinet* tells of her mystical initiation at Badbury Rings. The sacredness of Badbury Rings is essential to her connection with what is sanctified in nature and the world she inhabited. Although she refuses to "tell the secrets of Badbury Rings" (265), Butts emphasizes the importance of what they came to represent in her life by examining the clarifying quality of ritual, a theme prevalent throughout her novels and stories. Like primitive man, Butts is initiated into the ancient purification of the Rings:

> That afternoon, I was received. Like any candidate for ancient initiations, accepted. Then in essence, but a process that time after time would be perfected in me. Rituals whose objects were knitting up and setting out, and the makings of correspondence, a translation which should be ever valid, between the seen and the unseen. . . . Like any purified, I was put through certain paces; through certain objects, united to do their work, made from the roots of my nature to such refinements of sense-perceptions as I did not know that I possessed, made aware of those correspondences. (266)

Without the ancient magic ensconced in the Rings (recalling the "bliss" of past ritual), Butts states that she would have been swept up in the choices of her age, "on the merry-go-round of the complex and the wish-fulfillment and the conditioned reflex, with Jung and Pavlov, Julian Huxley and Bertrand Russell, in all the consciousness of my group" (265). Instead, the Rings offer "that business which included in itself end and beginning and all sequences that run between" (264), what she terms the "contact between the visible and invisible, the natural order and the supernatural" (265). The "seeings" join her work to her vision. Myth, magic, and a kind of visionary madness lead her toward "a theophany, a shining-out of a God" (186), but not the orthodox Christian God nor the mythic pagan gods; instead, it is a blend, a co-joining of primitivism with what is sacred in the natural world.

On her mystical journey, Butts is difficult, elliptical, and confusing, yet those very elements enhance the poetry of her work. Butts perhaps suggests a transformation through contact with the sacred in nature which may alter our vision of God as we recognize in "terror" a vision of the invisible which is not necessarily human. In *Traps for Unbelievers,* a pamphlet written in 1932, Butts examines the substitutes for God which act as traps for skeptics and unbelievers, "For the potency of the human god wanes, and his end is horror; rebirth, but for their human nature, terror."[34] In this rebirth, Butts offers a vision of her "visible Pan" in the sacredness of nature which so inspired and nourished her and which offered solace from the terrors, large or small, of existence:

> The meaning of everything was there, and would make itself plain in due course. When I was old, or perhaps not till after I was dead, but the pattern was being shown me there, the patterns and the meaning of the pattern. The visible and the invisible world, and the veil between drawn exactly as much as I could bear. Not only such knowledge as Wordsworth drew from lake and hill, but knowledge of house and breed and good and evil men; what spiritual income I had; how to invest it. . . . (262)

Similarly, her art helped sustain resistance to the underlying terror of existence behind the veil so carefully drawn to reveal "the meaning of the pattern." The artist, in her perception of the invisible, modifies this world through language. In a 1927 entry in her journal, Butts elucidates the link between art and life: "What apart from the specific work of writing is what interests me? Nothing but spiritual development, the soul living at its fullest capacity. That is the lever, the new synthesis, or vision or faith."[35] By joining with the potency of the Rings, Butts solidified her connection with the ability "to live in two worlds at once, or in time and out of it" (13), and she confirms this idea in a second selection from her journal. Enjoying the countryside of France in October 1929, she looks out of the train window and says, "I blessed the Power which has filled my life with poetry."[36] Like her initiation at Rings, art is her other true joining with the unseen world she sought so diligently.

Moving from romanticism to classicism to modernism, Butts weds together her childlike examination of nature and its magic, her blend of pagan and Christian myth, and her "seeings" as a child and as an adult. These joinings, in turn, place her within the confines of the mystic experience and, in a sense, extend the definition itself. Many of Butts's characters possess a childlike innocence, awed by the magic of nature and myth even in the midst of madness, yet within the madness of drugs, decadence, and the occult, Butts longed for the visions she knew briefly throughout her life, and their importance to her appears throughout her writings. While visiting Aleister Crowley in Cefalu, she writes, "The idea is to find an authentic means of inducing the mystic state."[37] It is the authenticity of vision which she seeks and which she convincingly evinces in *The Crystal Cabinet.*

Butts cannot be pigeonholed into neat, academic views. Like the sacred nature she so loved and feared, her work and ideas are rich and open. She is not a "type" and therefore has been marginalized for her personal vision. However, Butts needs closer study because the bulk of her small body of work transcends the personal and explores universal beliefs and terrors. Unique in her vision as well as in her mystical qualities, Butts sought to define her world in her own terms through the mysterious, magical force of her natural world. Writing in her journal in 1927, she asks herself about the source of her mystical leanings: "This mysticism of mine, enough for me because I 'get' and 'know' things which I cannot describe or explain, on what is it based? To make, under no matter what image or indirection, a living clarity of it, great art and power—life giving—would flow through me, enough at least to refresh my generation."[38] It was not until she wrote *The Crystal Cabinet* shortly before she died that she was able to explain her memory of Salterns, Badbury Rings, and the mystical qualities of the natural world of her childhood; she realized that without the magic of her Dorset childhood she would not have found the connection between her art and her spirituality, between the visible and the invisible worlds, the natural order and the supernatural that carried her through the times and set her apart as an artist. Robert Byington quotes one of many references in her journals that explain the intensity of her belief in the mystical connection: "There is more divine life in me than in any man I have known. I wish to formulate a theory—a perception of the universe as yet unknown to man."[39] The elements of nature served as her *mana* in an authentic quest for "spiritual development, the soul living at its fullest capacity."

CHAPTER TWO

A "War-fairy-tale": Ashe of Rings *(1925)*

"Better than barbed wire the briar rose"

Ashe of Rings, Mary Butts's first novel, was written between 1916 and 1919.[1] It was serialized in the *Little Review* in 1921, published by Robert McAlmon's Contact Editions in Paris in 1925 and shortly after in America, yet it did not appear in England until 1933. It was recently reissued by McPherson & Company in 1998. Examining this novel in the context of biographical evidence revealed in *The Crystal Cabinet,* published in 1937, one cannot ignore the parallels between the narrative of *Ashe of Rings* and Butts's vivid account of her own youth. In an afterword to the London edition, Butts calls *Ashe of Rings* "a fairy story, a War-fairy-tale, occasioned by the way life was presented to the imaginative children of my generation."[2]

The merger of war with the fairy tale form in *Ashe of Rings* creates the central metaphor of the novel, while, at the same time, establishing characters that will become significant in Butts's fiction in the future. Since the major portion of the book takes place in England in 1917, we find several typical Butts characters, whose way of life has been irretrievably altered, living on the edges of war, along with those who have been more directly damaged by the war or revolution raging not only in Europe but also within the hearts and souls of the characters themselves. These characters come from various backgrounds and embody a society struggling to maintain the status quo in an inevitably ever-changing present.

In this present Butts creates a heroine (one who will appear in various guises throughout her fiction) who hearkens in a very Wordsworthian way to an idealized past when humans and nature lived in close proximity and when people had a better understanding of that interrelationship. This heroine, Vanna, embodies what Butts will later identify in *Armed with Madness* as "the female principle of life," reaching back into the enchanted past of her ancestors who knew and worked within the realm of magic. As an ancient priestess, this modern female draws her strength from a primal past and recognizes the terror and beauty so inextricably mingled in the natural world, the core of her family's history and mystical magic.

Butts's heroine unites the disparate elements of nature and, as an authentic heir to ancestral mysteries, she strives to live in "two worlds at once" (232). In her Shelleyan pursuit of truth and spirituality, this female becomes the priestess offering her magic to help heal those whose contact with war and its effects has been more direct and personal. The female principle in each novel has her masculine challenge: in some instances she saves him; in others she senses a possession of evil too strong to overcome. But Butts makes it clear that the true priestess will carry on against the odds of the negativity surrounding her. The priestess believes in *magic*—the ability to make things happen—and she does make things happen in nearly every instance. Believing unequivocally in the certainty of these two worlds—that of the mind and spirit and that of the external, natural world—Butts's heroine takes her role as healer, priestess, and nurturer firmly to heart.

Anthropologist Sherry Ortner notes in "Is Female to Male as Nature Is to Culture?" that "both the subversive feminine symbols (witches, evil eye, menstrual pollution, castrating mothers) and the feminine symbols of transcendence (mother goddesses, merciful dispensers of salvation, female symbols of justice)" indicate that women "can appear from certain points of view to stand both under and over (but really simply outside of) the sphere of culture's hegemony."[3] Butts's heroines do exactly that: good or evil, they stand "outside" the realm of society in their transcendent role. Butts's goddess heroine attempts to use her ancient, secret knowledge in a society usually controlled by male hegemony and moves in a sphere all her own. War, then, is a focus for this first novel; it is, in fact, "one of the first modern novels to deal with persons 'on the run' from military service."[4] At the same time Butts adds other ingredients to the mix to emphasize the power of the primal past and of those whose authority is real and supernatural.

In *Ashe of Rings* this mix moves us into another realm of the two worlds Butts so curiously explores, the world of fantasy and fairy tale. What makes it a "fairy-story," Butts tells us in the afterword, is that it

> had to end happily. . . . Yet one sees now that this would not necessarily have been the true end; that is, as things are, there would have been far less chance of peace for the Ashe children; nor would the mother have so easily accepted the magical leading, or her dead husband's will. The essential triumph, with which the book ends, would very likely not have happened. (232)

Of course, this happy ending was never to be a part of Butts's own complicated childhood and life. In a September 18, 1917, entry in her journal Butts writes, "Notes for *Ashe.* Take for the central theme the hatred of age for youth, of the old for the new, of yesterday's 'rose' for today's, expressed in a cruelty, part intuitive, part consciousness. This for a larger stage, implied throughout, war and its consequent *repression* and destruction."[5] With the passage of fourteen years between the writing of the novel and the afterword, Butts may have discerned how much this book contained the wish-fulfilling fantasies of a young woman. A 1925 review of *Ashe of Rings* sums it up best: "*Ashe of Rings* is a lovely, but somewhat misty legend of the anguish of a sensitive spirit under the lash of the war."[6] This "sensitive spirit," in looking back on her novel, found it "impossible to alter," while recording "a tension of life and a sense of living in at least two worlds at once" (232).

The magic form of the fairy tale proposes a way to assist Butts's understanding of living in two worlds: perhaps most explicitly, by appropriating the fairy tale form, Butts can better understand the inner world of William Blake's crystal cabinet, the "inmost form," and the external world of loss, fear, and what she calls "dis-ease." One of the characters in *Ashe of Rings* comments that "I think we are living in an enchantment," and defines this dilemma by stating, "I mean that we are spectators of a situation which is the mask for another situation, that existed perhaps [in] some remote age, or in a world that is outside time" (44). In a sense the fantasy of the fairy tale form helps interpret the connection between events of Butts's youth and what she had become in the present. Throughout her life, Mary Butts sought some kind of magic to help her survive in "two worlds at once." The ideas behind fairy tales, the occult, legend, myth, and ritual, along with the associations and interactions among them, become the means of disentangling and interpreting mystical and psychological occurrences which permeated her life, her thought, and her work.

Bruno Bettelheim's discussion of the fairy tale's influence on the child's maturation process supports the notion that the childlike impulse in Butts's first novel serves to examine this inner life. He writes, "[M]ore can be learned from them [fairy tales] about the inner problems of human beings, and of the right solutions to their predicaments in any society, than from any other type of story within a child's comprehension."[7] Similarly, Lillian Feder notes that folktales or fairy tales "are stories expressing significant psychological experience in the form of stylized and patterned behavior."[8] By identifying her first novel as a "War-fairy-tale," Butts sets it in a particular time and place that gives it a both a personal and universal pattern of psychological significance.

The "fairy tale," a story for children with psychological effects and solutions to the child's inner turmoil and development, becomes for Butts an initial approach to what would later produce her very intricate and enigmatic art. This early novel is much more than a fantastic tale. It initiates a fictional form which is not merely linear narrative; rather, the association with myth, folklore, and daimons and witches enriches the form by intertwining unreality with reality.[9] Never simple, always introducing more and more complexity and associations, Butts develops a style that now seems familiar. When the book was reissued in 1933, the review in the *Glasgow Herald* claimed: "Today we may read the work with understanding and fascination which on its first publication was too innovative stylistically."[10] When asked to provide a preface to the 1933 London edition, Mary Butts noted in her diary: "The truth is that I was tight on Joyce at the time, as we all were; and that now having found how to reproduce half-conscious thinking, most of the fun has gone out of it. Yet it can't be taken out. Say that I could do it—now—just as deeply and more conventionally now."[11] Although this is perhaps her most stylistically innovative novel, precisely in the sense that she describes of reproducing "half-conscious thinking" (although she was to continue to experiment with such techniques in her short stories), the Joycean comparison works as a way of describing technique but does not reflect the reality of her own unique method. She described this method in 1919: "Grasp of the technique of free association of ideas, plus a structural unity."[12]

Butts met Joyce in 1920 in Paris, and her writing would be compared with his throughout her life. Yet, the mechanics of style were not the main influence of Joyce; rather, it was his sense of newness or originality in thinking about fiction that makes the comparison a legitimate one.[13] She wrote in her diary in late 1917 about the craft of writing: "Up to now we have had writers who have been marvelously close, with complete realism of detail. What we want is a new way of seeing—a complete new attitude of approach. In fact a new imagination. The analysis has been made, now for a new synthesis. Joyce, Eliot, Lewis—?"[14] The "new way of seeing" was what Butts desired and sought in her pursuit of the fairy tale form and the mythological world. She longed imaginatively to enter into these worlds through her art. Yet, in writing about her short stories in 1922, Douglas Goldring stressed that "she has real originality and if she can only succeed in forgetting *Ulysses,* she ought to make a name for herself as soon as she gets known."[15] Leaving behind the realism of the late nineteenth century and experimenting with "ways of seeing," through an imaginative approach, was what most appealed to Butts about James Joyce.

Numerous reviews of *Ashe of Rings* draw comparisons with Butts from Dostoievski to Dorothy Richardson and May Sinclair. Another contemporary influence most associated with Butts is D. H. Lawrence. Her insight into re-evaluating gender, relationships, and sexuality in bold, new ways makes her writing an easy comparison with Lawrence in more than one instance. In 1926, for example, the *Saturday Review of Literature* claimed that "*Ashe of Rings* sometimes suggests the Lawrence of *Women in Love*. There is the same lyrical writing and consciousness of beauty; there is the same stripped reality side by side with a turbid guesswork of motive and actions; there is something of the same perverted types of humanity."[16] And there is something humorous looking back on these reviews with a 1990s sensibility; much of what she was accused of (e.g., like Joyce, of "being clever beyond your audience") in the 1920s is all too familiar today.[17]

The originality of Butts's own style and voice, one roughly established in *Ashe of Rings,* includes her among her fellow modernists yet also sets her apart in her own unique approach to her subject and especially in her treatment of character. Her use of ancient narrative forms blended with modern techniques gives her fiction a very contemporary feel. Another review of the 1933 London edition of *Ashe of Rings* identifies her style as a "feverishness of vision which at once sees the surface of life with an intense clarity and, through it, to phantasmal 'Thrones, Principalities, and Powers,' angels and dœmons behind."[18] The otherworldly qualities of her characters, the mystical and magical setting, and her staccato dialogue full of ellipses give her writing a "cinematic sense" that John Ashbery finds in her short fiction as well.[19]

By intermingling the magical and the mystical, Butts shows us imaginatively in fiction, as T. S. Eliot does with poetry in "Tradition and the Individual Talent," that the inner life of the mind and its origins are continuous. There may be paradigm shifts, but our thinking about our place in the world continues along a similar path of searching for reassurance and understanding of the world we inhabit. In this search we long to comprehend the relationship between the external world and the inner world of the unconscious mind. For Butts, this quest initiates in the spiritual inner self, which stores primitive yearnings and understandings that intimately connect us to the magic of the natural world. An adult fairy tale is the perfect place to begin exploration into the adaptations of folktale and myth in art.

Lillian Feder observes that

> All of Yeats's adaptations of myth indicate a need to impose order and unity on an apparent anarchy in his own mind and in the universe; he does so by equating individual with universal experience, seeking some eternal element in the human soul. Ultimately his purpose is to use myth as a guide to reality, both unconscious or personal, and historical or general.[20]

In a similar manner, Butts will eventually adopt myth as a way to order and seek the eternal in her own personal vision and in the human soul in general.

Also like W. B. Yeats, Butts begins with the fairy tale form in search of answers and insight to both the conscious and the unconscious in humankind. In spring in Paris 1927, Butts gives us some insight into the fairy tale's magic. She questions whether she can ever "make a poem out of this a spring day"; the "sun [is] shifting in through the shutters," and Paris is in the background. This beauty brings "tears because there are fairy tales in which the pain stops, a miraculous right-about-turn of misery into accomplishment that never happens."[21] The fairy tale then offers a chance to stop the pain; it is what Yeats identifies as "the cry of the heart against necessity."[22]

Linda Dégh, in her investigations into the fairy tale, has noted that

> The tale symbolizes elementary reality with its dangers and struggles, and it demonstrates that cleverness, skill, courage, and perseverance lead to victory. The legend, on the other hand, is concerned with forces and figures which, in their often supernatural existence, cannot be defeated. The tale takes place in the "once upon a time" "never-never land," on a different level of existence, whereas the legend brings its fearsome mysteries down to earth. It happens here and now, in our home, perhaps even in the nursery. The tale gives relief from anxiety; the legend arouses it and leaves man alone with his anguish. The tale—the real one—is very useful. The legend—the real one—is very dangerous.[23]

In *Ashe of Rings* Butts adopts the traditional formula of the heroine who must venture out from the home; the family situation that has disintegrated and is no longer the center of stability and security impels her toward some fantastic situation. Once the home becomes intolerable, or the bad mother—originally the source of sustenance and security—neglects or abandons the child, flight offers the opportunity to strike out on one's own to seek one's fortune. In the magical/real world, the hero, claims Maria Tatar, "encounters villains with powers far more formidable than those of the villains he left behind. . . . The evil forces at home habitually reappear, with all their deformities magnified . . . the performance of feats in the magical world prepares the way for return to a new home."[24] In *Ashe of Rings,* Butts's heroine, Vanna, meets the parallel evil forces in the magical/real world, which then lead her back to her original home and her rightful position as heir to the magic and enchantment of Rings. Indeed, the fairy tale offered Butts a place to start her investigation into her writing life while at the same time suggesting an imaginative way of dealing with her personal human problems, putting them into a specific context, and extending them to relate to the confusion of World War I society.

The importance of family tradition and authentic relations with the natural world that surrounds and protects those who are its initiates and willing participants in its magic, the loss of a loving father, the conflict between an unenlightened mother and her daughter, the tension between the elder daughter and the brother she wishes would love and understand her, the intrusion of the madness of war and its aftermath on the very English country-gentry way of life, the displacement and "dis-ease" of the generation that has experienced the loss of that privileged lifestyle, and the role of myth, ritual, magic, folklore, and legend in the twentieth century world—all these ideas which abound throughout Butts's work are introduced in *Ashe of Rings*. These issues, of course, are the wish-fulfilling "fairy tale" of Mary Butts's own life. Her work may have autobiographical elements, but we soon learn that Butts utilizes narrative and ritualistic structures of the past as tools to examine larger, more complex issues, and these structures imitate Yeats's quest for "insight and knowledge."[25] In fact, in her list of seven aims of writing noted in her journal in 1921, Butts states, "I don't only want to find my true will. I want to do it. So I want to learn how to form a magical link between myself and the phenomena I am interested in. I want power." She adds that she wants to write a "book to show the relation of art to magic, and shew the artist as the true, because the oblique adept."[26] Writing *Ashe of Rings* gave Butts the power to learn about and define her beliefs and her vision and provided the "link" to the "two worlds" she struggled to comprehend, a struggle she would continue to pursue as an artist.

How to endure the madness and "dis-ease" of her contemporary society becomes an important issue for Mary Butts. In *Ashe of Rings,* Anthony Ashe, the aging patriarch of Rings (reminiscent of Butts's own Badbury Rings, a set of prehistoric mounded circles near her family home at Salterns), explains to his young bride, who is questioning the mysterious and pagan aspects of the priestly house, that "Christianity is a way, a set of symbols, in part to explain and to make men endure, the unutterable pain that is in the world. There are other sets, like chessmen. But only one game" (20). In this single game, as Butts sees it, whatever set of symbols one chooses to assist in withstanding the "unutterable pain" is totally acceptable, and the fairy tale offers at least one set of "chessmen" with which to play and unravel the past in order to make it bearable.

Butts's narrative in *Ashe of Rings* traces the fortunes and misfortunes of its heroine, Vanna Elizabeth Ashe, from conception to young womanhood. Butts structures the narrative in three parts: part 1 is set in 1892, and parts 2 and 3 in 1917. At the opening Anthony Ashe, in his old age, seeks a young wife to beget an heir (an echo of Mary Butts's own father and her young life described in *The Crystal Cabinet*). Anthony Ashe selects a woman from the village as his second spouse, gives her the name of Melitta, and tells her to find out what it means, and this suggestion invites us to do the same. *Melitta* comes from the Greek, suggesting bees and the sweetness of honey, and the implication is that Melitta is chosen because of her fertile childbearing abilities and not for any other reason.[27] She is not a blood member of the ancient Ashe family and is never absorbed by the inhabitants of the house. As the guardian of the Rings, Anthony observes "how the house, like a hive of quintessential bees, had enclosed her, not with honey, but with wax as though she were some insect trespassing" (27). She remains an outsider even after the birth of her red-haired daughter, Vanna Elizabeth, who is a true and natural heir to Rings, its magic and its mystery.

After more than seven years have passed, recognizing that she is not accepted by Vanna Elizabeth—"The baby did not like her" (28)—or by Rings itself, Melitta transforms into the fairy tale bad mother and seeks revenge upon the estate and the family by beginning an affair, on the very sanctified center of the third circle of Rings, with her neighbor Maurice Amburton. The mystical three rings and the ruined tower nearby stand at the core of the pagan rituals and activities of the past, such as a crucifixion of Florian Ashe, an ancestor who lived during the reign of Henry VI (by his wife's relatives) and various exploits of a great-great-grandmother named Ursula, who introduced the family to magic and witchcraft and who delivered her children on Rings Hill—"a place of evocation. Where the word is made flesh . . . where the shapes we make with our imagination find a body" (150).

Once Anthony Ashe discovers Melitta's adulterous indiscretion with Lord Amburton, he tells her, "Cheer up, I shan't last long. You'd better marry Amburton" (38). Anthony's concern is not that he has found her unfaithful but that he has discovered them together at the sacred center of the Rings. He orders them to leave, then brings clean leaves to "cover the place where they had lain" (39). Three weeks later Anthony dies, and we learn that Melitta is pregnant. The child is Valentine Evelyn Ashe.

Within three months Melitta becomes Lady Amburton, and the Amburtons and the children live alternately at Amburton and Rings. For a year Betty (Vanna Elizabeth) runs wild, celebrating her youth and her natural inheritance of the Rings' magic and mysticism, a "precinct like Eleusis" (104). In true fairy tale fashion, the natural world and its magic take the place of her father and extend his protection, yet Betty is still mystified and questing for her place in the world and as heir to Rings. After her father's death, Evans, the tutor who was chosen by her father and who will soon be dismissed, recognizes that "[a] fever runs in these people. If you nurse their imaginations, you raise insoluble terrors" (46). Betty explains to Evans that "Daddy said that there were things in the world, good and bad, and a thing called sophrosynê[28] that helped you through both of them. On the road to Delphi, you know?" (46). Evans understands and clarifies her fear:

> "Betty, you want the world to be good. Like everyone else, I'm not at all certain that it is good. An Ashe has to learn that there is life outside good things and bad. Most people don't get so far. Confound you, child! You must learn to take it easily. You'll drive us mad and yourself."
>
> "Can't take it easily. There is a beast tearing inside me."
>
> "Lots of stories end *and they lived happily ever after.* What about that?"
>
> "Only fairy stories." (46)

Later, Betty queries, "Would the beast stop tearing your heart if you were sorry for people?" (47). Now the stage is set for the adult Betty/Vanna's struggles to search for answers and to begin her attempt to heal and pity those who seem to need her magical solace, and for Butts to find a way to make things end "happily ever after."

As the true adept or priestess and guardian of the Ashe family's inheritance, Betty must grapple with her mother, who fails to comprehend the value of the past and its function. Thanks to Anthony, in addition to her innate connection to the land, Betty/Vanna has been tutored in Greek, Latin, and French and formally educated in the liberal arts. However, her mother soon puts an end to the liberal education her father had insisted upon by employing a governess to teach her "[t]hings a little lady must know. How do you know that you will not have to earn your living some day? And suppose you should marry, you do not understand what that means, but men don't like women who learn things" (49). This admonition echoes the words of Mary Butts's own mother in *The Crystal Cabinet* where Butts discloses her stepfather's "cheerful contempt for the arts" and her mother's "declaration that men did not like women who 'knew things.'"[29] In the novel, as in life, Butts reveals her battle to overcome such thinking, while in *Ashe of Rings* Betty scorns the new governess by telling her that if she stays at Rings something will eat her, "[b]ecause you are here not to teach me what I want to know" (50).

In the final section of part 1, we learn that Rings is finally shut up, Amburton has become unfaithful to Melitta, Betty has been sent away to school, Valentine Ashe has been accepted by Amburton, "but not Rings" (52), and Melitta has plotted her mission to make Valentine her "slave." These events allow them to withdraw, leaving the priest/butler Clavel in charge of the sanctity and magic of Rings until its true heirs return to resume their rightful place. Structurally, part 1 has set the stage for the events to follow in London and again later at Rings Hill once the characters return.

When part 2 opens, twelve years have passed, and Betty, now called Vanna or Van,[30] is living in London "the year before the end of the war, when there was very little to eat; and along with the strengthless food and the noises at night, friendship had lost its generosity and passion turned *à rebours*" (57). Cast out and disinherited by Melitta because she did not fit into the social life Melitta valued, Van, on a small allowance, shares a flat with Judy Marston. The main tension of the remainder of the novel concentrates on the struggle between Judy and Vanna over the soul of Serge, a white Russian émigré and artist who is the pivotal center of the novel—somewhere between desire and death. He has escaped two wars. He is fleeing the revolution of his own country and hiding from the world war that surrounds them all. In fact, he is "on the run" from military service. Serge, "little more than a thin ghost out of Russian fiction,"[31] marks the introduction of a character Butts will continue to explore and develop in her later work.

In Butts's afterword, she recognizes the "overwhelming influence of Dostoievsky" (232). Serge fits the Dostoievskian character who must seek redemption through suffering and who should somehow recognize the healing power of love. However, in spite of Vanna's attempts to heal and love Serge, he is trapped by the megalomaniacal Judy and her witchcraft, which mingles pleasure and pain, forbidden mystery and sensual bliss: "She would rehearse the turns of her screws on him at night. By day she would forget, because they acted exactly as she wished, but not as she had foreseen" (58).[32] In typical Dostoievskian fashion, Serge wrestles with the healing force of love yet finally must reject Vanna's magical efforts; love does not redeem him.

Eventually, Vanna and Serge travel to Rings to escape the city, where Vanna meets her brother Val and reclaims her rightful inheritance. Judy reappears, discloses her plan to marry Vanna's cousin, the shell-shocked Peter Amburton, for his money and, in a frenzy, demands that Serge choose between her and Van. Serge tries desperately to hold onto Van's power, but Judy's curse is far too strong. After numerous events, including an attempted rape of Vanna by her cousin Peter (orchestrated by Judy) and a sacrifice of Peter's dog on the sacred outer ring in an attempt to call up the infernal spirits and desecrate the sacred realm, the novel eventually ties up the loose ends of fairy tale, unites Vanna and her brother Val, and reconciles Vanna to her estranged mother, Melitta. Butts has her prescribed happy ending, coming full circle and mirroring the circles of Rings Hill.

The elements of fairy tale, witchcraft, and the occult mingle in this novel mainly through Butts's description of character rather than through narrative. Judy Marston, for example, acts as Vanna's foil. A dark, angry, evil, and troubled girl, Judy, once she has ensnared Serge, soon develops into the archetypal fatal woman, the *femme fatale*/witch who attempts to destroy Vanna and deprive her of her inheritance. Serge cannot separate from Judy because he has replaced the reality of war with the metaphor. Judy "loves" war and is, according to Vanna, a "microcosm of it" (67). As an artist, Serge's sensibilities reject war and what it represents, but his guilt and cowardice force him to become enamored of the very thing he fears. Judy embodies it all. She is both witch and goddess. Judy moves into this role with a swiftness and certainty that her *black witchcraft* guarantees; her actions function for evil purposes, against humanity and community and against the laws of God and nature. She is the antithesis of Vanna's *white magic* (change for good); she is a throwback to ancient aggressions and sorcery that Vanna must struggle to combat.

During a sexual escapade with Serge, for example, Judy, in ceremonial witchlike fashion, dances before a mirror with a small sickle knife when she thinks Serge is not looking. She is calling up her demons, and symbolically she castrates Serge; he is afraid to act, and the terror he feels with Judy only enhances the spell she holds over him. Ironically, the sickle is also an emblem of the harvest, pitting issues of impotence and fertility against each other, yet binding them together in this passage and foreshadowing the sickle's appearance later in the narrative. When Melitta encounters the same knife at the end of the novel, it is stuck through the basket which has always held the first-born of the house and, of course, which held Vanna as a child. Melitta does not understand the implications of the evil that Judy embraces, but Vanna does, and recognizing that the knife symbolizes Judy's "vile intentions" (230), Vanna must perform her own ritual to rid them of Judy's curse: "Take the knife, and stick it in the stone of his [Florian Ashe] tower, and leave it there. Hang a cocoanut on its handle for the birds, and if ever I find out the whole truth, I'll let you know" (230–31). Vanna at this moment becomes the goddess whose authenticity ensures fertility; the Ashe family will remain safe and their magic will abide.

Another example of Judy's role as witch occurs when she ends her affair with Serge. When he refuses to "[make] a decent defence" (80) against her railings that he is a "slacker" who can "come back in khaki or not at all" (79), she springs at him and bites his wrist. He leaves and looks back at her lying on the floor, sucking his blood from her sleeve as if "evoking an evil spirit" (80).[33] This drawing of blood prefigures Judy's intentions to call up the infernal spirits once she arrives at Rings with Vanna's cousin Peter Amburton, whom she refers to as a "shell-shocked lump of carrion" (116), as her fiancé. Her pursuit of Peter is undertaken to make certain that Vanna's brother inherits Rings and that she and Peter will have Amburton Hall.

An early review of the novel distinguishes the "dusky magic" of witchcraft from traditional fairy tale witchcraft. It suggests that in the earlier witch story, the witch was a clear vehicle for her evil and understood completely the dark forces with which she contended and which she controlled. The reader was not allowed a glimpse into the witch's head; rather, he/she viewed only the external maneuverings and results of the witchcraft. In *Ashe of Rings,* however, "[i]n this novel of psychologized witchcraft the witch knows little of the dark powers whose currents flow through her, but the reader sees all that goes on in her head and what little she herself knows of it is at his disposal."[34] In spite of the fact that we do get into Judy's "head" in this novel, we never completely unravel the secret of her mystery. Judy is a modern, war-mad fatal woman whose frustration we understand but who remains an enigma and plays into the magic of the tale itself. Judy, however, fails to comprehend the extent of Vanna's power. In her wickedness, Judy makes her quest clear to Vanna, and Vanna responds with the knowledge of a true adept of the ancient wisdom of Rings, the "last bee of her swarm" (137):

> You get out of it [Rings] what you put in. The same as with everything else, only more intensely. That is the first rule of magic, as you ought to know. . . . You've been mixing yourself up with some devil's hocus-pocus; going bad the way people do sometimes in the tropics. And the years we are living through have stirred the same thing up here. It's a state, a turn of the soul, people are making. But you keep bad company, if it's only in your own thoughts. (86)

Vanna's understanding of her inheritance establishes her place as heir to Rings. If Vanna is the embodiment of an ancient priestess who authentically practices the ritual and magic that her ancestors so clearly bequeath to her, she is also closely connected to the animism of the land. For her, divinity is inseparable from the land and is immanent in nature. Her reality, like that of her pagan ancestors, is polytheistic, multiple, and infinite. For Vanna, the sacred quality of Rings offers a way to reintegrate with a forgotten existence—to live in "two worlds" at once or finally to come home to participate in the unity of these two worlds. Judy, on the other hand, is a metaphor for war and the evil aspects of humanity that war represents, a diabolical ancient priestess. The magic of Rings Hill, which she longs to possess, offers her a fertile, mystical place to call up the infernal spirits, the demons in the service of Satan, to do her bidding and to assist in destroying Val and Vanna and the healing power that they embody. Rings is a center of mystical opportunity, be it good or evil, or as Serge describes it to Vanna, it is where "extreme life—that's you—and extreme anti-life—if that is Judy, meet" (150).

With the definitions of magic (black and white), the occult, pagan ritual, and witchcraft so closely intertwined, Butts utilizes these connections to enhance and advance the story. In 1921 Margaret Alice Murray, a distinguished Egyptologist, published *The Witch-Cult in Western Europe.*[35] Butts probably did not encounter Margaret Murray's work until after completing this novel, but she, like Murray, moves witchcraft out of the fairy tale status and places it in a modern setting with witches as ordinary people performing extraordinary tasks. Murray promoted the idea that the witch was no longer the hideous hag of fairy tales; she who chose to serve the older religion could be a member of a community. Murray restricted her study to Great Britain, with occasional recourse to French and Flemish sources, but her anthropological work opened the way for scholars to look at witchcraft as a survival of a primitive religion rather than simply as a historical report of witch trials in Europe and New England. In *Ashe of Rings* Butts connects fairy tale witches to ancient priestesses practicing their pre-Christian religion in the service of Satan and the infernal forces. Butts's novel and the combined work of all these scholars serve to recall the significance of the remnants of folk and primitive beliefs to later modern ideologies. *Ashe of Rings* mixes up a modern brew of ideas which all come together in the service of her art.

In her role as witch, Judy draws blood for the second time once they are all ensconced at Rings. She demands that Serge choose between her and Vanna, between Judy's infernal powers and Van's sacred authority. It marks a shift in the novel from fairy tale to the occult:

> There rose, over the back of his head, a distorted face, crimson, the mouth open and wet. It closed down on him, snatching at his eyelids. The teeth bit down between eyes and nose. Fingers raked his throat. He was sobbing as he tore her off, his tears meeting blood, blinding him. Then, a moment later, Van had followed her back into the room.
>
> "Get out, you filthy devil," she cried. The fear currents swerved. Judy was afraid. (119)

This ritual offers more insight into Judy's evil. Later, Vanna reminds Serge that Judy has "drawn your blood, and blood is the life. Mix it and you mix souls. A very old ritual: she's opened a vein in you, a leak in the body of the world's peace. The infernal powers are loose, in a place of evocation" (151). Judy is indeed practicing witchcraft and calling up infernal powers to assist in her mission. As an agent of evil incarnate, Judy initiates Serge into the blood ritual/sacrifice of her own private cult. Margaret Alice Murray discusses various accounts of witch covens who draw blood "at the admission of the neophyte."[36] The signing of a contract in the blood of the initiate, Murray explains, usually followed. Judy is obviously playing on this notion of blood sacrifice by creating an initiate in Serge. He is caught in her spell and allows himself to be drawn in as far as she desires; he is both attracted to and repulsed by her and her actions just as human beings are attracted to and repulsed by war.

The mix of desire and revulsion associated with war and people, like Judy, who revel in it explains not only the horror of war and its spiritual destruction but also examines the ancient history of humankind and its drive toward death and destruction. Vanna's words to Serge clarify Butts's point:

> Consider the war. Have you known anyone who loves the war as Judy loves it? *Stoop then and wash.* She dips her tall, white body in the blood and rolls it in her mouth, and squeezes it out of her hair. She is a delicate woman of good family; I know nothing in her history to account for it.
>
> Am I clear? There is the war. There is Judy and her kind. The individual state bred the general state, that bred the catastrophe. Oh, I know tribal instincts and heroism, and love of a row. . . . Other people conduct a war, and suffer in it; get a man's job out of it or physical death. People like Judy live on the fact of it, and get spirit-nourishing food out of the ruin of so much life. (149)

Quoting Robert Browning, "*Childe Roland to the dark tower came,*" and identifying Browning's tower as the "vortex of death, or of a life under a form absolutely inimical to man," Vanna claims that Judy is Serge's dark tower; "[s]he is a death-hound following us" (149), eager and driven to have his soul. For Butts, Judy symbolizes all that has been lost and destroyed by war. Judy is a parasite who draws her strength from the suffering of others. Witchcraft and occult practices, then, become vehicles to explain war and its history, just as Vanna's past connects her to spiritual growth and healing.

This shift to the *occult,* the secret understanding of ancient wisdom, and to *witchcraft,* the practice of pre-Christian religion, deepens Butts's notion of the power of *pagan* (non-Christian) ritual in her novel, an approach present in other modernist work. In *The Birth of Modernism,* Leon Surette has noted the influence and power that occult investigation and participation contributed to modernist writing in general and to the work of Pound, Eliot, and Yeats in particular. Surette tells us in his preface that "the ubiquity of myth in modernist literature must be attributed at least in part to the occult belief that myths represent a record of contact between mortals and the *au delà.*"[37] Surette contends that in the past, scholars skirted the issue of the occult in representative modernist works, such as *The Cantos* and *The Waste Land,* because the occult was considered such a "disreputable subject."[38] Butts, thoroughly educated in ancient wisdom and the Hermetic tradition so familiar to Yeats, Pound, H. D., and others, also drew on this knowledge and incorporated it into her writing blatantly and without fear of being tainted with labels such as black magic, demonology, sorcery, or the like, and Surette's study in a sense validates this exploration into the occult and witchcraft in Mary Butts's work. Although she was later to meet and fall in love with Cecil Maitland, who deepened her involvement in the occult and induced her to participate in the cult group associated with

Aleister Crowley, Butts apparently had already read widely and seriously in magical and occult lore. We can only speculate as to what prompted this interest, but Linda Dégh claims that the fairy tale is

> a need, especially for children between four and ten, but in many cases this need lives on beyond the tale-age, late into adulthood. Children who are deprived of the tale by force will sooner or later suffer from the consequences. It might be that the mystic cults and irrational sects, mushrooming in our days, take their victims from among those who substituted childhood vision with the rationalism of adult society much too early.[39]

Butts was not deprived of fairy tales as a child, but she certainly had to grow up quickly and deal with the "rationalism of adult society." In a sense she never completely relinquished the fantasy of her early childhood; interest and participation in the occult may very well have served to extend the fantasy and allowed her to pull it into her adult life.

And so it is that throughout the novel Butts moves back and forth between fairy tale and occult practices. One of the most striking scenes in the novel takes place on Rings Hill when Judy and Peter sacrifice Peter's dog in order to desecrate the place of enchantment and once more to call up the infernal spirits to assist them. These scenes of devil worship remind us that Butts is again fusing the ancient and the modern. Judy shouts at Van, "We've found out all about your filthy, mystery-mongering place. It drinks blood. Give it a drink, and it works. We've given it a drink" (186). The blood rite of witches, Margaret Murray tells us, was offered to please their god, the Devil. "The animals offered were generally a dog, a cat, or a fowl, and it is noteworthy that these were forms in which the Devil often appeared to his worshippers."[40] Butts's depiction of Judy assures us as readers that Butts is exploring a realm outside the external world, a demonic side of reality that Butts spent a great deal of her life pursuing in an attempt to sort out the good from the evil. Judy serves all purposes.

Peter, on the other hand, is a reluctant participant. He, like Serge, is caught up in the spell of Judy's madness. Peter unsuccessfully attempts to rape Vanna on the sanctified center of Rings Hill, where Vanna calls on the sanctuary of her race by wrapping herself in magic. She undresses, melds her body with the stone (a voluntary placing of her body on the sanctified altar), and prays to her ancestors "Florian and Ursula, my father and mother in Ashe" (188). Peter reveals his weakness when he whispers to Van, "I'm afraid of that girl, Judy. She wants something deep, too deep for me. . . . If you don't answer me, I'll have to do what she says. Must obey orders" (189). But Vanna fulfills her role as sacred priestess, and Peter knows her magic is powerful. Her magic is, in fact, stronger than Judy's dark power in this fairy tale version of occult practice. Peter acknowledges the power of the elemental forces alive on Rings Hill: "I won't touch that stone. It's alive—we woke it up earlier. I remember. The dog's blood turning into a white poison and moving the stone. Oh, God!" (189). The white magic of the true adept succeeds in its battle against the evil of Judy and Peter's attempt at black magic.

One additional scene must be examined to clarify Butts's uniting of pagan and Christian symbols in this tale so intricately mixed with various forms. An encounter between Judy and Vanna reveals the depths of Judy's madness and, although she desires the exacting of Vanna's blood, she remains satisfied with threats and spiritual darkness:

> Judy was running a thorned bramble sucker into her palms, she drew it out and whirled it at Van. It caught in her hair and tore her forehead. . . . She pulled out the thorns, but she did not think she could go away. She wanted to stay there and argue, till their conversation should reach an indescribable climax, and the question should be finally answered—for whom was Judy understudy? Answered, the role would cease. (192)

The obvious Christian symbolism of this scene sets Van apart from the others as a Christian parallel to the satanic magic or sorcery of Judy. Van is willing to suffer to save others. She endures torment with a clear understanding of her role as savior and priestess to Serge and to her and her brother Val's past. She is also Briar Rose, the fairy tale goddess about to awaken and renew the land. Butts merges Christian and pagan ideas of death and regeneration: as Judy's evil fades, Van's saving magic gains force.

Although Peter may be lost because he has to contend with his return from the war as well as his bizarre relationship with Judy, Serge takes on the role of the "psychically sick" that Butts was so fascinated with in her fiction as well as in life. Serge tries but cannot accept the healing force and goodness that Vanna embodies. He remains, enigmatically, drawn to Judy and her darkness. Serge's attempt to explain his feelings to Vanna only make understanding more difficult, yet it reveals an internal battle he has already reconciled. It is necessary to cite a large passage in order to have a sense of Butts's purpose and style:

> *Van:* "Isn't it possible, Serge, that this hating of me is an excuse you have to make to yourself for ceasing to care for me. Which might have happened anyhow?" Mother of God, what have I found out?
>
> *Serge:* "It is not that. I've been fighting it for years. Then I met Judy. It came through. I shan't live long. I mean, I shall change. I can feel the change moving. Another soul is changing with the one that was mine. . . .
>
> "I know, Van, you're a decent creature, but you're like a weak drawing."
>
> *Van:* "Why won't you live long?"
>
> *Serge:* "You won't recognize me. I shall be another person, and a nasty one."
>
> *Van:* "It's an hysteria."

Serge: "You can psycho-analyse it. Only I know. I didn't know exactly till you brought me up here to this abominable gallery in the dark. It's quite dark now, isn't it? There's a blaze over my eyes."
Van: "Quite dark, Serge. Will you join the army?"
Serge: "No, because I want to paint."
Van: "Are you going straight back to Judy?"
Serge: "I don't suppose so." And then: "I want her to be what you once were—
Van: "Oh, my son—"
Serge: "What?"
Van: "You can't have it both ways. If she has made you understand life from a new point of view, why do you break down and want her changed to me?"
Serge: "I don't know. I suppose I can't stand it. It's the inside knowledge that life is evil——" (224–25)

What we are to understand from this cryptic exchange is part of the magic of Butts's style and narrative. What she implies, however, is that Serge, who thoroughly enjoys his suffering, believes what he says—that life has turned evil.[41] Serge, however, retains a foot in both realms, good and evil, and the novel takes on another significance by commenting on the hazards of sexuality in the modern era. Just as in T. S. Eliot's wasteland, relationships are filled with danger. Butts again suggests that solutions can be found in a distinct connection to the past, its rituals, and its spiritual interactions between inner and outer reality. For Serge, Judy, then, is more real than the goodness that Van represents. Like a "weak drawing" in Serge's demented and distorted view, goodness seems merely illusion, while pain and suffering are real and true, reflecting the actuality of the war-torn society. Van, unlike her mother Melitta, understands the darkness behind the veil to which Serge refers. As a true priestess of her heritage, she recognizes the forces of good and evil always present in the world. One of Butts's journal entries from Paris, December 10, 1929, gives us a glimpse into her own waking dreams:

> The black curtain that hangs across the way I must go, receding with my step but *then,* is a little transparent this night.
>
> Think of a corridor, a passage white-wood panelled with a green carpet strip as at Salterns. My passage in life is down one of these, and I have passed many windows, some with pleasant views out onto several different lands. . . . And there have been some, cob-webbed at the corner of their panels, and in the cobwebs dead bees. . . . It is one of the fears that I shall have lived with that black curtains [*sic*] overcast my mind.
>
> The veil however is thinner tonight, as it recedes before me between the white walls.[42]

Vanna's power is love and authenticity. She is the true adept whose healing must come through the magic of Rings, which has crowned her its heir and which helps make the veil between the visible and invisible world occasionally transparent.

What is left is to examine Vanna's relationship to her newly found brother, Valentine Ashe. Nearly eighteen, Valentine comes under the protection of his older sister while he obtains his own authentic inheritance, even though Serge observes that only Van gets the blessing of Rings, "not even the boy" (286). Valentine, if he is not to be the chosen blessed of Rings, plays an essential role in supporting Van and her authenticity, similar to the minor role of Clavel, the butler, who reintegrates Vanna into her biological connectedness with her ancestors and with the land. His patient watchfulness and evident loyalty to the Ashe children give him the appearance of a "djinn to the word of power" (211), and in this role he extends and supports the supernatural magic of the Ashe family. Val serves a similar purpose of authenticating and supporting Vanna's role as true heir.

It is perhaps significant to note that the name *Valentine* has a connection to the Hermetic tradition. Basil Valentine was believed to be a "veiled master" of the fellowship of the Benedictine Brotherhood of St. Peter of Erfurt in the second half of the fifteenth century. His identity, however, remains something of an enigma. The name means "mighty king," and the writings attributed to him suggest those of a mystical alchemist, one who can transform reality through magic.[43] Whoever the true Basil Valentine was is not important; rather, what is important is that Butts's choice of Valentine as the name of Van's brother clearly marks an association with the secret mysteries of Hermetic brotherhood, an example of Butts's assumption of knowledge on the part of her readers and perhaps reason for her work being called difficult and too clever.[44] In the relationship between Vanna, her brother, and the powerful, supernatural forces supporting them, Butts sets up a power which cannot be combated by evil forces, even those which epitomize war.

At the beginning of this chapter, I noted that it was possible, with the knowledge of the narrative presented in *The Crystal Cabinet,* to draw parallels between events in *Ashe of Rings* and in Butts's own life. Indeed, much of what Butts writes conjures images of her childhood and her life, including Vanna's red hair, her jade earrings, the mother's accusation of impropriety with her stepfather, the physical description of the family home patched together for ages, "each bit in terms of its time" (141). For this reason, any careful examination of the novel must include scrutiny of the plot itself. The similarities are striking and obvious. However, as Butts tells us, this is a fairy tale, one that has an unbelievable happy ending in which all family members are reconciled and wounds are healed. This happiness, Butts recognized after fourteen years had passed, was never to be accomplished in her own life. Her life instead followed a more realistic pattern; yet, by finding it "impossible to alter" after "thinking it over for months," she suggests that she still believes in fairy tales and their magic, even if, as

Serge says to Vanna, "[i]t's the inside knowledge that life is evil" (225). Butts, like Vanna, never gives in to that evil. She quests continuously to find the magic that life and its past offer and, in doing so, creates heroines unlike the mother she portrays in *The Crystal Cabinet* and *Ashe of Rings.*

These heroines, whether or not we identify them with Butts herself, then become the center of most of Butts's writing. Vanna and Butts's heroines in general are never victims; they fight to maintain a tradition, a sense of place and of self that is so vital to their existence and their identities. There is, of course, a difficult struggle as they fight to assume their natural roles of reconciliation and healing, of priestess and initiate; in the movement of those roles, these women strive not only to live in the external world of "dis-ease" and disaster but also continue to search for a way to avoid living with the "black curtain" covering their minds. They are modern women refusing the status quo. Her heroines look into themselves, their pasts, and their authentic association with that other world of the unconscious, which, in turn, connects them to a spiritual past that continues into eternity.

Perhaps many modernists were searching for a spirituality through myth and an examination of the past; Butts attempted to make her spirituality a reality in her life as well as in her fiction. However decadent or confused her search became, it was a true seeking throughout her life, which she manipulated with a selfishness of single vision and a focused desire to succeed in her quest. In *Ashe of Rings* Butts sets the stage for her later fiction. The fairy tale with which she begins her work turns to the reality and danger of legend in her next novel, *Armed with Madness,* and legend succumbs to ritual and murder in *Death of Felicity Taverner.*

Most of Butts's fictional characters have a source in *Ashe of Rings,* and, with the fairy tale as the external form of this first novel, she establishes a paradigm for the narrative form of her later novels. Her external contouring of plot moves us from the realm of autobiography to that of fiction, a shaping that creates an aesthetic distance between the text and the reader and that is a constant reminder that we are experiencing art, not life. The structuring produces a *gestalt* peculiar to Mary Butts's style and a successful rendering of her developing aesthetic.

CHAPTER THREE

"Dis-ease": Armed with Madness *(1928)*

"Embrace an earth-cup"

In her journal in 1927 Mary Butts states that *Armed with Madness* "might well have been called 'The Wasteland.' Eliot always anticipates my titles. . . . Eliot and I are working on a parallel."[1] In late December she says, "T. S. Eliot . . . the only writer of my quality, dislikes me and my work, I think. But what is interesting is that he is working on the Sans Grail, on its negative side, the Waste Land."[2] In *Armed with Madness,* which is also about the wasteland of modern society, Butts takes a more positive approach to what Eliot sees as a world of decay and spiritual deprivation, emphasizing instead the hope of regeneration through a reestablishment of contact with the mysteries of the natural world. Drawing on the themes of death and rebirth so central to Jessie Weston's *From Ritual to Romance,* both Butts and Eliot turn to the Grail quest as a modern retelling of what Weston saw as Christianized versions of ancient fertility cults. By way of the "mystery" religions, Weston had established a link between the present and the ancient past: "I firmly believe that it is only in the recognition of this one-time claim of essential kinship between Christianity and the Pagan Mysteries that we shall find the key to the Secret of the Grail."[3] For both Weston and Butts, what that secret entails revolves around the need for humanity to seek what primitive peoples knew existed in the cycles of nature. With an innate understanding of the birth, death, rebirth process in the natural world, primitive cultures located something unchanging in a constantly changing world. This desire to return to a more primitive past associated with the rites of the natural world also connects Butts to her Romantic ancestors, as well as to the pagan mysteries elucidated by Weston, Sir James Frazer, and Jane Ellen Harrison and the Cambridge Ritualists.

Myth offered many modernists a way to create some order within the chaos of their world. When Eliot defined the "mythological method" in "*Ulysses,* Order, and Myth" (1923), he called for artists to create a continuity between the past and the present in order to give structure to the confusion they would inevitably confront:

> In using the myth, in manipulating a continuous parallel between contemporaneity and antiquity, Mr. Joyce is pursuing a method which others must pursue after him. . . . It is simply a way of controlling, of ordering, of giving a shape and a significance to the immense panorama of futility and anarchy which is contemporary history.[4]

By incorporating myth and ritual into her work, Mary Butts develops a modernist style that not only is an attempt at order but also looks to the past in a way distinct from other female modernists. In *Gendering Classicism: The Ancient World in Twentieth Century Women's Historical Fiction,* Ruth Hoberman argues, along with Judith Kegan Gardiner and Alicia Ostriker, that women writers did not feel the anxiety of "male modernist's fragmented self" because women writers "could not mourn the loss of the coherent individuated self they had never fully experienced."[5] Her position is that because women modernists embraced the ideas promoted by Jane E. Harrison, their sense of how mythic material was to be used was different from that of males, specifically in regard to Eliot's "mythological method," which offered a way of ordering the chaos of contemporary history. Hoberman suggests that because Butts was so heavily influenced by Harrison that she, like other female modernists, looked beyond myth to primitive ritual in Greek thought and to Harrison's interpretation of pre-Olympian religion, which led her to "think back the 'many' we have so sharply and strenuously divided, into the haze of the 'one,'" and thus "linking it to matriarchy, collective emotion, and totemism." Hoberman asserts that "[s]uch formulations don't provide a 'way of controlling or ordering,'" as Eliot contends.[6] Her point is that female modernists, in agreement with Jane E. Harrison, generally reject the analytical, the scrutiny of reason that separates and divides.

Although this may apply to other modernists, like H. D. and Mary Renault, or even, as Gardiner suggests, to Dorothy Richardson, Gertrude Stein, and Virginia Woolf, I see things differently for Butts. Mary Butts certainly disdained pure scientific reasoning as a solution to the world's problems and sought the "one" through her mystical "seeings." However, instead of turning strictly against the mythic past exemplified by male modernists, she incorporated all of it into her own vision and narrative method. She unquestionably does turn to myth as a way of ordering the world around her and as a means of helping to define her personal art. Ritual may precede myth and may even stand outside of myth, but the narrative of myth helps define. Butts uses both pre-Olympian and Olympian myth in modern and even fantastic ways to carve out her own place in modernism.

Mary Butts has been marginalized in part because she does not fit neatly into the categories of other female modernists and because of her spirituality in pursuit of her vision. This vision is all-encompassing, locating a source of strength from which women could draw and establishing a place for women as equals alongside that of males in modernism. Her voice is not one in opposition to that of men, nor does it oppose Harrison's suggestion to give up analysis. As a modernist she stresses the need for society to explore origins. She recognized, for example, that many men failed to acknowledge or understand their own origins as humans. In her 1936 essay "Bloomsbury," Mary Butts critiques the Bloomsbury group as having lost what Eliot found in "Ash Wednesday." She identifies "[t]he thing that always gets lost when men set themselves to live as they have lived as Olympians playing, yet uncertain of the validity or the origin of their power. The quality we call among other things Simplicity of mind, by which alone values are preserved. . . ."[7] This "Simplicity of mind" she finds not only in primitive female origins (Harrison's "non-differentiation") but also in what Butts calls *"Amor Intellectualis Dei,"* a perception of eternal love common to origins of both male and female. The emphasis on Harrison's notion of pre-Olympian ritual is for Mary Butts a natural hearkening to women's (and humanity's) past. It may be a source of power for Butts, but the fact that she looks to these origins, to the power of pre-Olympian religion, does not mean that she negates or rejects what followed.[8] In a sense, through her art Butts anticipates what Toril Moi would later suggest: the "goal of the feminist struggle must be precisely to deconstruct the death-dealing binary oppositions of masculinity and femininity."[9]

Butts's quest for humanity to strive for origins and perceptions of the ultimate source of those origins is the focus of her work and can be found in *Armed with Madness* in Scylla's relationship to the men in her life, her forgiveness, and her participation in the quest for the cup the group has designated the "Sanc Grail." Her modern retelling of the Grail quest combines all the qualities and concerns mentioned above—a search for origins, spirituality, ritual, and subsequently the narrative of myth and legend, forgiveness for those who do not comprehend, recognition of both male and female roles in the game they create, acceptance of gender roles that do not necessarily conform to a prevailing sociocultural order, and an understanding that ritual is a vital connection to the source they seek.

Patrick Wright's observation in his brief Marxist, cultural chapter on Butts in 1985 supports the notion that Butts's vision was not in opposition with Eliot's "mythological method," specifically in the sense that she recognized the need to hold on to and give order to a past she saw as slipping away. He states that hers is a "writing full of panic at the realization that the world it craves can, for very good reasons, no longer exist anywhere *but* in texts; and in bizarrely Gothic, cranky and hallucinatory texts at that."[10] Sensing the displacement and loss of her own world and social order, Butts's writing and her characters have no choice but to "go weird," and she cannot "secure her transparent green world without going to extreme lengths of artifice."[11] Yet, no matter how accurate Wright's observations may be about her style, Butts's "artifice" of myth and ritual in her work offers her what she so clearly longed for in her life, a return to a pastoral ideal of a green world (similar to E. M. Forster's greenwood),[12] which she perceived as an integral element of her youth. The very "weirdness" of her characters and their games reflects the tension between the modern world and the ideal world which they see receding because of technological progress and urbanization. Their desire for ritual suggests a last grasp at preserving what the rapidly changing world has forgotten or erased from memory. In *The Waste Land,* Eliot, like Butts, sees a world unable to recognize the realities behind the ancient symbols and myths of its past; therefore, its entire existence is stunted, parched, emotionally and spiritually sterile. Butts, like her contemporaries and critics to follow, saw Eliot's interpretation of the Grail legend as focusing on the contemporary world's sterility and sense of spiritual decadence. Certainly, the hope of regeneration notwithstanding, his lady of situations, his typist, his pub characters, his drowned Phoenician sailor, his Tiresias in *The Waste Land* all reflect what has become of a society without a spiritual center: love has been reduced to a sterile routine; regeneration now functions in a machine-like manner rather than through the natural processes of love and nature.

Although Butts addresses these issues in *Armed with Madness,* particularly in the characters of Felix, Clarence, Lydia, and Philip, she shifts her focus away from the moral decay of the urban landscape to the sacramental elements of the natural world's primitive past. Here her characters reenact a ritual that may offer answers to what she saw as Eliot's "despair and disillusionment." Through immersion in past ritual and authentic kinship to nature, as well as their initiation into its mythic offerings, her characters manage, if only temporarily, to ward off the effects of the society from which they have retreated. This focus on authenticity and initiation leads us to discover in Butts a complexity involving the Grail legend and ancient rites that is somewhat different from Eliot's.

Butts appears to diverge from Eliot's view in two distinct ways: first, although she recognizes what the "city" represents to her contemporary society, she finds solutions in the natural world, a place offering a healing of wounds and an opportunity to know ourselves and our origins. Only those who have a legitimate ancestry in the land or who possess a natural kinship to the secrets of this green world can be true questers. They alone have the opportunity to discover some spiritual truth about the cycle of existence, as in the fertility and vegetation cults examined by Weston, Frazer, and Harrison. Second, the quest focuses on an authentic participant or initiate who is female; while Butts's central female character at least offers a generative influence, Eliot's females suggest a negation of regeneration or a spiritual sterility as reflected in a barren society; his lady of situations in "The Burial of the Dead," his pseudo-Cleopatra or his pub character, Lil, in "A Game of Chess" are all examples of this sterility. In *Armed with Madness* Scylla fills the role of the "female principle of life" along with her spiritual counterpart Picus. Although Scylla has the same potential for falling into disaster as do Eliot's characters, her major focus is on a physical and spiritual love, authenticity, and a very real connection to the sacred elements of the living presences of the land.

Butts's characters sense the same despair that Eliot describes, but they choose to remove themselves physically from the wasteland of modern urban society to begin their "sacred game," a ritual which connects them to a simpler past, to a quest for spiritual renewal. Their ritual play transforms itself into a kind of living sacrament. Butts learned from the anthropological and mythical studies of Frazer, Harrison, and the Cambridge Ritualists that "modern man's fears may spring from causes far different from those of his ancestors in the ancient past, but the symptoms are similar, and the method Eliot suggests that artists use as a weapon against the threat of anarchy has its roots in ancient ritual."[13] Although both Butts and Eliot utilize myth in an attempt to order the chaos of contemporary society, Butts believes she emphasizes regeneration where Eliot accentuates spiritual devastation. Where Eliot finds a resting place in myth, Butts creates and redefines the ritual act.

Drawing perhaps most significantly on the Cambridge Ritualists, whose ideas were comparable with but went beyond Frazer's, Butts appears to highlight their specific connections between ritual and myth. Shelley Arlen tells us that although the Ritualists worked with many of the same ideas as Frazer, they went somewhat further in using an "organic theory of society derived from Durkheim and Spencer to study the function and structure of religion in society."[14] Jane E. Harrison, as the acknowledged leader of the Ritualists, saw ritual and art as deriving from "a common psychological and spiritual human impulse,"[15] and, unlike Frazer, who was not willing to connect primitive religious ritual with all art, Harrison identified a "bridge" (ritual) between art and religion. In doing so, Shelley Arlen contends, her work, along with the theories of the Ritualists in general, appealed to and inspired much of the writing of the twentieth century and contributed significantly to the school of myth criticism:

> Literary critics interested in the psychological underpinnings of art's creation and its relation to religion have continued to value the Ritualists for their discussions of myth and ritual. It is no coincidence that T. S. Eliot (who became a confirmed Anglican) and Northrop Frye (himself a minister), were influenced by their theories. As Eliot and Frye contend, modern alienation, the hunger for something nameless, finds sustenance in myth which gives life order and meaning. For many literary critics, structuralists, and psychologists, it is the Ritualists' plumbing of the irrational, unconscious aspect of man's mind that continues to fascinate, regardless of whether the Ritualists are considered historically correct in their theories of origins.[16]

The blend of theories from Frazer, the Ritualists, and Jessie Weston contributed much to the critical and literary theories that were to follow; however, the distinctions among their ideas are very relevant to Butts's view. For Butts, as for so many modernists, the connections between myth, ritual, art, and religion develop as extremely important issues for her work and for her characters' survival and success. Jessie Weston explains in *From Ritual to Romance* that "I should wish it to be clearly understood that I hold the Grail story to have been primarily dramatic, and actually performed."[17] Similarly, Harrison's "ritual theory" in *Themis* explores how myths evolved as explanations of rituals, and in her *Ancient Art and Ritual* she examines the connections between primitive rite and modern art. In their belief in the primacy of the rite over mythology, the Ritualists claimed that the rite was actually an acting out or doing. Harrison explains the "[t]he Greek word for a *rite* . . . is *dromenon,* 'a thing done,'" and the word *drama* also means "thing done"; in making that association she asserts a key relationship between art and ritual.[18] Harrison and the Ritualists present a more pervasive influence on Butts's work than does Frazer. Like the Ritualists, especially Jane E. Harrison, Butts was interested in primitive origins, looking for structure and definition in her own, personal natural world. The religious impulse of art that Harrison delineates clearly is an integral part of Butts's vision. In their reenactment of a past ritual, Butts's characters find themselves participating in a "sacred game," a game raised to the level of sacrament. In *Armed with Madness* the participation in this modern Grail quest by Butts's characters can be interpreted as a re-doing of primitive drama to explore how art, as Harrison argues in *Ancient Art and Ritual,* can "help or hinder spiritual life."[19] The impulse to blend emotion with rational, intellectual activity in Harrison parallels Butts's approach and helps define her own views on the function of art in the modern world.

Drawing significantly on Robert Ackerman's *The Myth and Ritual School: J. G. Frazer and the Cambridge Ritualists,* the first book-length analysis of the Cambridge Ritualists,[20] Martha Carpentier, in her 1994 article on Harrison, claims that Frazer could connect ritual only with peasant plays, not modern art, because he separated primitive ritual from "civilized" man. She argues that Harrison is the originator of the "ritual theory" which linked primitive origins with the origins of drama in ancient Greece:

> Unlike Frazer, Harrison's thinking was neither rationalist nor hierarchical, thus allowing her to find "bridges" between "savage" and "civilized" creativity that Frazer never allowed. Thus Harrison had a far greater influence on the younger generation of modernist writers, such as Virginia Woolf and D. H. Lawrence, a fact that is not often enough acknowledged.[21]

Butts's sensibilities, religious impulses, and overall vision seem to rest closer to those of Harrison too. By having her characters "act out" an ancient rite, Butts connects them to a more primitive, magic time that relied more on instinct and emotion than did the rationalism of her own time. Butts knows that some answers to the "dis-ease" of the present may be found in the past, or as Harrison explains, our desires to understand the savage and his psychology are significant "for our own sakes . . . since we realize that our own behavior is based on instincts kindred to his," and also that "by understanding his behavior, we may understand, and it may be better, our own."[22] In Butts's attempt to redefine her world and to offer temporary solutions to the problems and alienation of her post–World War I society, she, like Harrison, contributes to modernist ideas of the function of art to heal and to come to a better understanding of our own selves, motives, and desires.

In spite of the subtle differences among the Cambridge Ritualists, Harrison, and Frazer, the main idea Butts establishes in her own work is that a return to the connection with an earlier state can offer a stabilizing influence, a temporary stay against the inevitable "Tide" of progress. Butts's instincts of the primitive, which she personally experienced at her home in Salterns, are the source of her inspiration and a "bridge" between the world of the past and the "civilized" madness of urban society. In *Armed with Madness* Butts looks for structure and definition not in organized or dogmatic religion but in the natural world with which her major protagonists have an authentic affinity.

This blending of anthropology, Christian legend, and ancient pagan ritual makes Butts's work modernist and complex. Some understanding of the intricacies of Butts's intentions might be clarified by a reading of Leon

Surette's discussion of Eliot and Weston. Surette contends that Eliot's *The Waste Land* can be read as an initiation rite in addition to a Grail quest and explains that Weston tells us that the "Grail legend is a distorted and fragmentary survival of a forgotten initiation into the Mystery of life involving a frightening encounter with death, and into the Mystery of death involving an erotically formulated encounter with the Divine."[23] Much of this description could apply equally well to Butts's *Armed with Madness* (and much of her other work), which combines the Grail quest and ancient vegetation and fertility ritual with the idea of the occult initiate. In this context, Butts examines the necessity of sexual fecundity if the land and the king are to be revived. As we shall see in *Armed with Madness,* although sexual preference is not an issue for love, since her characters experience both homosexual and heterosexual relationships, it does become significant if fertility and regeneration are to be accomplished. In this sense the sexual quest in Butts's novel parallels the spiritual quest.

This focus on the quest for spiritual truth originates for Butts at an early age. She tells us in *The Crystal Cabinet* that after reading a poem by Kipling, which had moved her, her mother broke in and interpreted Kipling's notion of romance in light of the earthly love of Lancelot and Guinevere, not the higher love signified by the Grail. Butts reacts:

> To the brutal lucidity of youth this seemed one of those disappointing moments when, about poetry and other things, grown-up people had just got it wrong. Whoever supposed Kipling would bother about Lancelot and Guinevere? Mother seemed to think that those kinds of stories were the best stories in the world. Lots of grown-up women seemed to. When the really only interesting thing about King Arthur was the Grail. . . . If Kipling meant anything at all about King Arthur, he meant the Grail, and not like Tennyson. The real Grail, which was the most wonderful thing to think about in the world and Mother had got it wrong.[24]

Clarification of the significance of the Grail and its offer of spiritual truth, then, becomes the core of her novel and a means of resisting the spiritual depravity of civilization. Butts turns to myth and legend to find solace from the fragmentation of her own society and to seek what Frazer, Weston, and Harrison suggest might be found in the continuum of primitive ritual. When Alicia Ostriker states that Yeats, Eliot, and Pound turned to myth as a means of "defying their culture's rationalism and materialism," and of expressing their "conviction that civilization has declined from an earlier state more coherent than the fragmented present, in which the spiritual life represented by myth was culturally more central,"[25] she not only, in effect, describes Butts's vision but also separates Butts somewhat from other female writers who, as Ostriker contends, "do not share the modernist nostalgia for a golden age of past culture."[26] Butts recognizes the underlying terror of such a belief in spite of its ability to offer order to chaos, yet she clearly asserts a nostalgia and a stronger need for understanding a more primitive time to help define her own.

Although contemporary reviews and a critical article from 1951 argue that "[a]s an attempt to integrate the Grail myth into modern literature, it *[Armed with Madness]* is a failure,"[27] it might be suggested that *Armed with Madness* succeeds as a distinct modernist retelling of the Grail legend. If the quest fails in the novel, it is because, as Butts tells us, the sacred game of her modern knights is like the "whole Grail story, the saga story *par excellence* that has never come off, or found its form or its poet. . . . There was something in their lives spoiled and inconclusive like the Grail story."[28] Butts indeed thrusts the comparison of her novel with the Grail legend on her readers, but, as Marianne Moore comments in her 1928 review of *Armed with Madness,* Butts takes a "compassionate view" of this "informed, formless party. . . . But Miss Butts is not palming anything off on us. We may make what we may of it. . . . It is sympathy she offers us in Carston's reply when the vicar wonders 'whether a true picture of the real is shown by our senses alone.'"[29] What Butts manages to accomplish in *Armed with Madness* is a fascination with and a kind of "sympathy" for a community of acquaintances who, no matter how "weird," as Patrick Wright has indicated, pursue their sacred game with a desire to mend and heal the wounds each has acquired from the wasteland of existence. Some succeed in a way different from others; some fail, but the longing is genuine.

Isolated in a country house on the rugged southwest Cornwall coast in England, the characters in *Armed with Madness,* a community of grail knights (five men and one woman, along with the steady, unchanging character of their nurse, Nana) set out to play a sacred game involving a cup, a dried-up well, a spear (obvious Freudian symbols which the author, like Weston in her work, clearly recognizes) and a quest of mythic proportion. Because the game follows no rules (unlike traditional ritual), since it reflects the chaos of the world from which they have attempted to escape, it ignites emotions and launches them on an adventure of ritual and mythmaking. In this game the knights strive to redefine and reevaluate morality in an attempt to alleviate the "dis-ease" of their present existence. In tune with W. B. Yeats's apocalyptic vision and Frederick Nietzsche's "transvaluation of values,"[30] Butts's narrator perceives that "everywhere there was a sense of broken continuity, a dis-ease. The end of an age, the beginning of another. Revaluation of values" (9). Through immersion in a past ritual and in the sacredness of nature (with a distinct awareness of its Wordsworthian sense of good and evil, power and helplessness), these young questers struggle to restore some order to and to make sense of the wasteland that followed World War I. They labor not to wallow in emptiness; instead, as Jascha Kessler explains, their response to such overwhelming loss is "Let us therefore stop our hand-wringing and our self-pitying whining, our effete nastiness and rottenness, our miserable existence in the Wasteland, and look for Life."[31]

The sacred game, then, initiated by Picus by throwing a cup into the arid well and later having Felix fish it out with a spear, gives the group an excuse to seek out a living sacrament in order to fulfill the truer meaning of ritual: "an expression through prescribed acts of the wish or need to exert power either forbidden or unattainable in ordinary life."[32] Butts, beginning the game by having Picus drop the cup in question into the well, opens interpretive complexity to involve the Freudian, female significance of wells in addition to the well of the Orphic Tablets, which links the initiate to his/her divine origins. Memory of the past, of one's ancestors, of the original union between Earth and Heaven creates a complex quest of seeking that divine origin, a quest which translates, no matter how it has been clouded by what Butts calls "fashionable psychology,"[33] into a "sacred game."

We know from *The Crystal Cabinet* that Butts had found the Orphic Tablets while reading in the British Museum as a young student.[34] Harrison clarifies the text of these tablets in her *Prolegomena,* where she explains that the two wells mentioned in the tablets are the Well of Mnemosyne or Remembrance and the forbidden Well of Lethe, Forgetfulness. The Well of Remembrance, according to Harrison, is an avowal of origins, and the origin claimed is divine. The text of *The Petelia Tablet,* which makes these associations, reads as follows:

> Thou shalt find on the left of the House of Hades a Well-spring,
> And by the side thereof standing a white cypress.
> To this Well-spring approach not near.
> But thou shalt find another by the Lake of Memory,
> Cold water flowing forth, and there are Guardians before it.
> Say: "I am a child of Earth and of Starry Heaven;
> But my race is of Heaven (alone). This ye know yourselves.
> And lo, I am parched with thirst and I perish. Give me quickly
> The cold water flowing forth from the Lake of Memory."
> And of themselves they will give thee to drink from the holy Well-spring,
> And thereafter among the other Heroes thou shalt have lordship. . . .[35]

Harrison and Yeats, as Carpentier claims, strove to "restore a sense of mysticism and magic to modern life, to rediscover the momentary union with divinity."[36] The text of the Orphic Tablet claims this mystic memory for mankind. Butts's characters in *Armed with Madness* long for a return to that source, to drink from the "Lake of Memory" and re-establish their place as children of Heaven. Since so much has been pared from these characters, in their confusion and loss of memory of an ancient past and perhaps a divine origin, they revert to a longing for childlike protection from the external world. Like children playing at knighthood, their quest is distorted because society has been uprooted, dislocated. Armed with the madness of that world, they become caught in a dream world of unreason and illusion and retreat into their own rituals and quests as a kind of revenge on the world they choose not to confront.

This choice is a conscious one for all the questers because there exists a tension between their community in Cornwall and the call of life in the city, a tension which sends them on a frantic and childlike search for meaning. Northrop Frye, in writing about Blake's treatment of the archetype, captures the essence of what Butts is saying in *Armed with Madness*. This quotation is especially appropriate since William Blake was such an influence on Mary Butts (she choose a Blake poem title for the title of her autobiography) and since it addresses the issues of war and how war affects and mimics childlike thinking. Although Frye is writing specifically about Blake, the quotation strengthens the connection between the thinking of Butts and Blake. Frye says that there was a time when

> In childhood happiness seemed to be based, not on law and reason, but on love, protection, and peace. But we see now that such a view of life was an illusion derived from an excess of economic security. . . . And after all, from the adult point of view, the child is not so innocent as he looks. He is actually a little bundle of anarchic will whose desires take no account of either the social or the natural order. As he grows up and enters the world of law, his illegal desires can no longer be tolerated even by himself, and so they are driven underground into the world of dream, to be joined there by new desires, mainly sexual in origin.[37]

Having been stripped of their economic security and a sense of things being right with the world, Butts's characters fit Frye's description of Blake's longing for a return to childhood security—for Butts herself, that innocent time in childhood when the countryside of her family home and Blake's drawings, vividly displayed at Salterns, affected her view of the world. Frye explains that Blake's characters Urizen (reason or law), Orc (the bound spirit of passion), and Los (work or constructive activity) reflect the conflicts between "innocence" and "experience." When the dream world, in which childish passion predominates over reason, becomes an unbearable strain, it breaks loose and projects itself on society in the form of war, and the line between law and war is blurred. Robbery, murder, and aggression become virtues rather than crimes. Work then takes the energy wasted in war or thwarted in dreams and translates it into experience; in doing so, "it becomes increasingly obvious that work is the realization of a dream and that this dream is descended from the child's lost vision of a world where the environment is the home."[38]

Scylla, the major female character of *Armed with Madness,* and her companions have lived through the experiences of war, have had their privileged social and economic security ripped from under them, and continually long for what they have lost. Like children who need protection, which they bring with them in the person of their childhood nurse, and a return to a happiness which ultimately is an illusion, they explore their own rituals and quests as insulation from the outside world. Scylla explains to Carston, the American outsider, that she and the other British members of the group use "[s]wank . . . and instinct. To cover quite intolerable pain. You see we know between us pretty well all there is to know" (31). They live in a reality whose adventures, as Scylla observes,

> are like patterns of another adventure going on somewhere else all the time. A very different sort of affair, a state suggested if you like in a good work of art. The things down here seem hints of it, but there is nothing to make us sure that it is a reality. . . . Because we have no money, and the wrong lovers, and our instinct for power is starved. For we come of families which have never been without power before. And the name for all this is our subconscious minds. And between Freud and Aquinas, I've managed to tell you about it completely wrong. For another of its names is intellectual beauty, and another, the peace of God. (31)

In *Armed with Madness* the modern knights' adventure is a desire to relocate a center and to regain some power over their lives. Freud and Aquinas cloud things with reason and the sense that truth is a known entity; for Aquinas, especially, truth follows rational considerations set forth by the Catholic Church. Butts would not have been satisfied with a purely rational and dogmatic approach to faith or to truth. Instead of the intellectualization and authoritative approach to the search for a hidden reality, Butts's characters, through a known ritual or legend, struggle to redefine intellectual beauty in a world devoid of peace and protection.

Of the principal players in *Armed with Madness,* Ross seems the sanest of the group, an artist who "never wanted anything that he did not get," and who sees human life as something "to eat and drink, to embrace and paint" (9). Ross retains his aloof, artistic vision throughout the confusion of the human game; he has "some sort of stable tip in invisible affairs" (111), but won't tell what it is. Instead, he tells them that they can "look at his pictures" (111). As a result, Ross remains in the background, symbolic of the fixed, yet fluid, element of art. On the other hand, Felix, Scylla's brother, "was scared. Fear made him brittle and angry and unjust. Without faith" (9). He finds it necessary to venture back into the demimonde of Paris to seek out Boris, a White Russian whose loss and isolation reflect his own. Felix sees Scylla as a demon participating in the quest in order to arrive at some kind of vision. As he explains to Carston, "what he [Felix] wanted was not vision, but fashionable routine" (21), and he participates in the quest more as a worldly and confused spectator than as a true knight. He is young and wants what has "been lost out of the world" (79), but does not know how to believe in the way that Scylla, Ross, and Picus believe in the spiritual quest.

Clarence is a serious artist, "discovered and produced by Ross" (22). Described by the group as "a bit too handsome, like a super-chorus-boy" (111), Clarence, unlike the others, is not armed with his madness. Instead, madness surrounds him in his jealousy of having lost Picus to Scylla; he is Blake's Orc set loose. Clarence is the only member of the group who has been to war; he is wounded physically and psychically by the world's insanity and, like many of Butts's characters, is undecided sexually. As a representative of the Waste Land, this modern Fisher King views Scylla, not as redemptive Earth goddess or saving knight, but as a monster who must be exorcised or sacrificed for the good of the community, which he identifies with the return of his lover. When Clarence succumbs to his madness, he attempts a ritualistic martyrdom or crucifixion of Scylla by tying her to a statue of their lover Picus. Fashioning arrows with the feathers of a gull he has killed, Clarence, in his own wounded and confused state, shoots at both statue and woman.

Clarence's attempt to shoot Scylla while she is tied to Picus's statue recalls an idealized painting of the martyrdom of Saint Sebastian, willing to die for the love of his God. Or perhaps this is an endeavor to crucify or martyr Scylla at the altar of love. Clarence's response to Scylla and Picus's love reflects a blending of the sacred and the profane, as Scylla translates into a symbol of love in its highest form, the giving of one's life for love. In Clarence's eyes, Scylla has to be made into a scapegoat who must be sacrificed in order to preserve the status quo, to protect Clarence's world from the intrusion of what he views as a profane love. Like St. Sebastian, however, Scylla survives the arrows and lives to forgive her enemy.

Like the redemptive healer she comes to represent, Scylla moves from "absolute contempt of Clarence" (145) into "a state a *clarté* the other side of forgiveness" (146), and she is rescued by the rational American, Carston, and her mythic trickster counterpart, Picus. Clarence has not survived the quest because he confounds the search for truth with petty jealousy and a very real, personal madness. Like the Fisher King, Clarence reflects the depravity and plight of the external world which has taken its toll on him. Without the assistance of the seeking knights, Clarence's world is doomed to waste, and as Jessie Weston emphasizes in *From Ritual to Romance,* the misfortunes on the land are essential to the Grail story.[39]

In the character of Carston, the American outsider, Butts infuses her work with a knight who, perhaps reminiscent of Lancelot, comes to the group to learn and observe how the malevolent forces of war have disconnected their society. Robin Blaser asserts that "Carston, as a character, always presents a near stereotype of the American who has lost all memory of the past: he belongs to the new, the direct, the simply sexual, until late in the novel; it is he who resolves as much of the Grail trick as is possible, a true modern Grail knight in that he asks the right questions."[40] But first he must fall in love with Scylla and labor to understand the group's immersion in this sacred game. However, the American never fully comprehends because, as Butts herself once commented to Robert McAlmon, "You clean, pure, young American. You are a gentleman, one of us, but you don't know the depths, the depravity of Europe. There are sinister forces, there is a black cloud gathering to overwhelm us all, and we must combat it with the good, the pure, the sweet, the true."[41] Carston, although he longs to understand and to be taken into the confidence and protection of the group, finally realizes that he is not equal to their spiritual adventure and that this is not where his fate lies. He recognizes at the end of the quest that he never will be one of them and insists, "I don't want to be" (159).

At the center of this sacred game stand Scylla and Picus. As their names suggest, they are creatures from a mythic past. Here Butts adds another layer of meaning. Scylla is both monster and healer, or, as the narrator explains, "They called her Scylla from Drusilla, altering it because they said she was sometimes a witch and sometimes a bitch" (5). A complex character viewed as the six-headed, man-eating monster of *The Odyssey* by her spiritually bankrupt and confused brother and by Picus's rejected lover, Clarence, Scylla also recalls the myth of Scylla, daughter of Nisus. In this myth Scylla is willing to deliver her father and the kingdom into the hands of King Minos, with whom she has fallen helplessly in love, only to be treated with contempt and revulsion and finally rejection.[42] In both myths Scylla does not fare well. However, Butts's Scylla has an immense capacity for love, as did the daughter of Nisus. Scylla of *Armed with Madness* heals with that love; Scylla of myth, daughter of Nisus, destroys, but in both instances love is the central issue. Butts incorporates both myths but converts the idea of the destructive force of love to a positive one. Her character views love as a natural development parallel to that of nature, and her capacity for forgiveness develops as an extension of that love, battling "sinister forces" with "the good, the pure, the true."

Scylla, along with Picus, is the spiritual core of the novel; she has an authentic connection to nature and its magic, a very human Earth goddess situated among them, offering spiritual redemption. As Carston recognizes, she represents, like the ancient bearer of the grail, "the female spirit of life" (30) and is herself among them a "living cup" (38). Although Scylla, also the center of sexual symbolism, disrupts a love affair between Picus and his wounded lover, Clarence, she remains the focus of the entire community of knights as jealousy, ritualistic crucifixion or martyrdom, and finally love develop in this bizarre and very modern quest. Through the pairing of Scylla and Picus, Butts reverses the sterility of the wasteland myth. Because the homosexual joining of Picus and Clarence offered no opportunity for regeneration, it becomes inevitable that Scylla and Picus must unite literally and symbolically to combat the negativity (e.g., Eliot's wasteland) which has reduced love to sex.

As symbols of the Grail legend in its pagan or Christian interpretation, Scylla (the cup) and Picus (the lance) offer the opportunity for redemption or healing. The Lance and the Cup, Jessie Weston says, "are sex symbols of immemorial antiquity and world-wide diffusion, the Lance, or Spear, representing the Male, the Cup or Vase, the Female, reproductive energy."[43] In their various interpretations, Weston elaborates, the "Lance and Cup are, *outside* the Grail story, 'Life' symbols, and have been such from time immemorial . . . why, then, should they not retain that character *inside* the framework of that story?"[44] Between her knowledge of Weston and of Freud, Butts employs numerous interpretations of the subconscious along with the ancient associations of fertility and renewal. In fact, in Butts's novel, these symbols do retain the symbolic character Weston describes, and, in spite of their ambivalent actions and interpretations by other characters, Scylla and Picus become the center of a life force completely in contrast to the arid world of the city.

In the character or name of Picus, we find "the Woodpecker who was Zeus" (30). Here Butts imbues her novel with the work of the Cambridge Ritualists and especially that of Jane E. Harrison. Harrison's sense of ritual and *mana,* an "unseen power lying behind the visible universe,"[45] provides Butts with the focus for the character of Picus, the initiator of the sacred game. Blaser has noted that Butts carefully edited the original phrase describing Picus cited in Suidas and given and translated by Harrison, what Blaser terms "a brilliant example of the new anthropology and of the new reading of the ancient world": "Here lies dead the Woodpecker who also is Zeus."[46] Blaser continues by describing what Butts does in editing the phrase:

> Scylla's version is carefully edited, removing the word "dead" and changing the tense to the past. The original suggests an ancient mythic event in which Zeus displaces or assimilates an indigenous Pīcus. The quotation has obviously been adapted to the magic of the narrative. Picus "lies" both because he is present and, in the tradition of Pīcus, the magician and trickster, he is lying in the matter of the cup. Picus who "was" Zeus is now the Picus of their own lives, setting off the recurring pattern of the search for the Grail.[47]

According to varying accounts of Ovid and Virgil, Picus was a famous Latin soothsayer who made use of a *picus* (a woodpecker) in his augury. The entire legend of Picus is founded on the notion that the woodpecker is a prophetic bird, sacred to Mars. When Circe's love for Picus is not requited, she turns him into a woodpecker, who, however, retains the prophetic powers which he had formerly possessed as a man.[48] These powers, the "watching of the birds we are accustomed to call the 'science of augury,'" are, Harrison points out, in origin "pure magic."[49] Like the mythical Picus, Butts's Picus moves strangely like a bird, has a psychic, mystical connection to the natural world, and possesses a *mana* which distinguishes him (and in some sense alienates him) from the other grail questers.

Picus is a trickster, both wise and foolish, and enjoys the practical jokes he inflicts upon his fellow knights. Once again, Butts layers meaning. As an archetypal motif, David Leeming notes, the trickster functions as "profoundly inventive, creative by nature, and in some ways a helper to humanity. Jung sees in him a hint of the later savior figure."[50] Jung, in *The Archetypes and the Collective Unconscious,* states specifically that the trickster "is a forerunner of the saviour, and, like him, God, man, and animal at once."[51] Picus, by spreading strife, by creating and confusing the sacred game, in a sense establishes the opportunity for the knights to invent a way out of their predicament, to redefine their lives. In effect, he initiates the game to force their hand and to make them act rather than whine.

In his role as an element of nature and as a god, Butts's Picus also takes on other levels of symbolism. As Jane E. Harrison says of the mythical version in *Themis,* "Finally Picus enshrines a beautiful lost faith, the faith that birds and beasts had *mana* other and sometimes stronger than the *mana* of man," and "of all living creatures, birds longest keep their sanctity."[52] In fact, Harrison explains that Picus was a medicine-king and an indigenous weather-daemon, doing work similar to that of Zeus until Picus actually becomes a title of Zeus. Then he knew that "he was really Zeus,"[53] thus connecting Picus even more closely to the natural world and its primitive origins. Just like the god Zeus he becomes identified with in myth, Butts's Picus is the dynamic catalyst who sets events of *Armed with Madness* in motion. He plants the Grail cup in the well, gives it to his goddess/woman Scylla, and later hides the cup in Carston's room. He initiates and encourages the quest as the community attempts its moral search for truth in its private world.

Armed with a magic madness as their only shield from the insanity of the outside world, the grail knights seek an answer to the origin of the cup. In their purity of purpose, such madness, defined by a mad world, oddly suggests sanity and becomes a kind of armor protecting them from the external world. In this sense they address the knight in each of us because they have not succumbed to despair. In the various seemingly unholy ways they handle the cup, the suggestion is that these are steps in discovering its true symbolism. Ross uses it as an ash tray, Picus for whiskey and soda. We discover it has been the spittoon of Picus's father's girlfriend, who has caused the suicide of Picus's mother. It even, perhaps, has a history as a container of poison, as Mr. Tracy, Picus's father, informs them, or as a sacred mass cup. Mr. Tracy appears as a rather diabolic figure, an incarnation of a Victorian age that is past its prime. He is a philandering Zeus figure to Picus, the irrational power begetting the trickster son who is next in the sacred line. Carston notes that Mr. Tracy was "something built by centuries of experience, and no longer in flower" (74). By identifying the cup as a container of poison, Tracy tries to contaminate their Grail quest but fails, as does all that he represents. Beginning the game like "Chaucer who loved everything for what it was. A sword for being a sword, or a horse" (68), the questers must learn to appreciate the cup's worth from the ground up. They must accept it for what it is physically before they can understand its spiritual significance. When Picus presents it to Scylla, he recognizes her role as healer and mediator of the group. Consciously or unconsciously, he and Scylla achieve the next level of understanding of the Grail; they know of the possibility of its being a means to the world's salvation and that it needs a "female spirit of life" to bear it and to act as its agent to bring renewal to the wounded world.

However, a certain purity of desire must attend the questers, or the quest must inevitably fail. Picus and Scylla, in their physical and spiritual love, manage to hold off the intrusion of the outside world. She becomes Leda, the lover of a bird who is also a god, and it is only at Gault Cliff, immersed in the natural world where they can consummate their love, that she "turn[s] the corner where love sees" (58). Here their lovemaking transcends Picus's previous love affair with Clarence, which Picus has discarded, and becomes a rite, a love that is "as much a creation as any growth in nature" (68).

Surrounding and embracing the entire quest is the woodland, every bit as alive as the people who occupy it. The companions view the woods as some magical place inhabited by pagan spirits, and Carston recognizes the moment he sees Scylla that "[t]he wood and the woman might be interchangeable" (12).

When Scylla is alone with Picus at Gault Cliff, she refers to the wood as "Baldur's wood" (57), making a connection with Norse mythology, which Butts had avidly read as a child, and suggesting that the wood plays the role of the collective unconscious possessing a knowledge or "pattern" deeper than what appears: "they [the companions] had something else to occupy their attention, something that the wood knew" (55). In the myth of Balder, Frazer explains that Balder is the handsomest and most-beloved of all the immortals. Balder, having foreseen his death in dreams, feared it, and the goddess Frigg extracted an oath from every object on earth—except the mistletoe plant, which seemed too young—to swear an oath not to harm him. But Loki, tricking Frigg and the blind god Hother, arranges to have Hother throw a twig of mistletoe at Balder.[54] With Balder's death comes the death of innocence, and in the modern world its replacement, Butts implies, is madness.

Clearly, events in the novel parallel this myth. Blinded by his madness, Clarence attempts to kill Scylla with an arrow; if successful, he would remove innocence, this divine "spirit of life," from the quest. Paradoxically, the wood represents the potential for destruction while also offering a retreat from the outside world, and the suggestion is that here in the world's "subconscious mind," beneath the insanity, true peace can be found if one can understand its dangers along with its beauty: "another of its names is intellectual beauty, and another, the peace of God" (31). Scylla and Picus commune with this natural world and are the authentic initiates plumbing the legend for its truth.

What remains, then, is to view the characters who are still caught in the wasteland of the city. Lydia, a friend of the questers who was and is in love with Clarence, marries Philip, a "gigolo, in a shaky business, in London, without capital, after the war" (115). When Scylla visits Lydia and Philip, she realizes that to speak of the cup would be a kind of sacrilege because their world would taint the quest. After reprimanding Scylla for being "alone with all those men" (119) in the country, Lydia and Philip reveal their immersion in the urban wasteland in a desperate attempt to draw Scylla back into that world. Together they cry, "We feel it since we married. It does not do, it does not do, to go against society" (119). This encounter, along with Felix's return to the demimonde of Paris and his affair with Boris, reveals the sharp contrast between what is taking place in the country and the decadence and a lack of vision present in the city. Lydia's jealousy and desperation and Felix's confusion and despair exemplify all that is wrong with a society stripped of a soul.

The complications of the quest, the jealousies, the return temporarily to society to visit representatives of the wasteland, and the crucifixion scene, all suggest that the game has failed. Ross feels they "aren't worthy" (43), but Scylla knows that "[i]f the cup is anything at all, if it was once an old cup of the sacrament people called 'big magic,' if it's anything or nothing, we can't hurt it, and it can't hurt us. We have our courage and our imagination" (44). Like Butts herself, Scylla sees the answers in the sacredness of myth and ritual. In her essay *Warning to Hikers,* Butts writes, "Contact with nature is very much what a man has when he participates in any rite or sacrament. Rites and sacraments are a kind of drama, a ritual play taken from universal natural events. They are about the health and ill-health of the soul, about marriage and birth and death. Things which happen."[55] Here the influence of Jane E. Harrison once again pervades Butts's thought:

> Magic, sacrament and sacrifice are fundamentally all one; they are all the handling of the sacred, the manipulation of *mana,* but usage has differentiated the three terms. . . . Sacrament is concerned rather with the absorbing of *mana* into oneself, magic deals rather with the using of that *mana* for an outside end. Moreover sacrifice and sacrament tend to go over to the public, ceremonial, recurrent contacts effected collectively; whereas individual, private, isolated efforts after contact tend to be classified as magic.[56]

Drawing from Harrison's observations, Butts presents her characters as participating in all three elements of an ancient or primitive past, thus blending, as Weston does, ancient mysteries with Christian legend. Picus is a magical character imbued with the magic of myth, the Grail knights attempt to create a sacrament in their reenactment of the quest, and Clarence endeavors to achieve a sacrificial purging of his own personal threat. Therefore, the ritual of the companions' Grail quest is a rite of reawakening to restore the pagan's imaginative, curative influence to a broken community, and in this sense they try to perform a magic transformation of their external wasteland.

Finally, at the request of Picus, Clarence returns the cup to the well, the womb of mother Earth and conduit for the divine, from which they had initially fished it. Carston and Picus rescue Scylla from Clarence's sadistic madness, and Picus heals her wounds with his magic, "Hush, love. I've got to do magic and make you well. Better magic than at Gault" (150), reminding us of Harrison's association of the augury of birds found in the origin of magic. This marks the end of the adventure for Clarence and Carston; however, Scylla and Picus, the "living cup" and her spear, have seized a truth of love from their spiritual journey. By having the cup returned to the well, Butts suggests that her knights will remain protected by its magic until answers become clearer and the knights purer, after they have defined their search and have brought forth a newly focused community. Scylla reaches out to Clarence, as he contemplates suicide, and returns him to their "home circle" (158). Carston, however, must move on to new adventures.

The "things which happen" in *Armed with Madness,* where every phrase is loaded with meaning, focus on returning health to the soul. The companions use the cup of the Sanc-Grail to represent the growth and expansion of their consciousnesses and their personalities and all conflicts that this growth entails. The rite of seeking the truth of the Grail cup opens the way for the future. These are modern questers, living, loving, fighting, sacrificing for the dawn of whatever lies ahead. They strive to combat the ill-health of the Waste Land by seeking to understand and interpret events that occurred long ago. The ritual which they perform over the course of the novel is the natural result of their actions and their efforts to achieve an understanding of the world around them. Rites and sacraments offer this opportunity.

At the very beginning of the novel, Butts tells us that what the knights were seeking was "[t]he meaning of meaning? Discovery of a new value, a different way of apprehending everything" (9). By focusing on the reawakening of old gods and legends, Butts modernizes the Grail quest and offers a hope of illumination and understanding once we learn to re-connect the past to the present. As Barbara Wagstaff tells us in the afterword to this edition of *Armed with Madness,* part of the madness of the twenties was "trying to live the truth of myths and legends, which madness arms Scylla and Picus" (320). And in this arming, style reflects content. Several contemporary reviews of *Armed with Madness* comment on the fact that when reading Butts, once one enters her world, one then must accept it as "a world unto itself" so that, as readers, we accept the truth of the happenings: "Aldous Huxley and William Blake walking hand in hand, with what results one can perhaps imagine,"[57] or, as another writer states, "as if one experienced mind as an actual mechanism, within his own person."[58] Mary Butts herself stressed the necessity of obliqueness in writing about the Sanc Grail—like the knight's move in chess that she referred to often in her writings, like a translation of experience rather than a direct interpretation or telling of the experience. *Armed with Madness,* like much of Butts's work, fits such obliqueness in both form and content.

Armed with Madness proposes a modern ritual, a retelling of an ancient legend of a search for truth. The legend acts as an outline that stands apart and records the struggle between entropy and order. The narrative follows a linear path for over one hundred pages, then shifts, somewhat abruptly, from numbered chapters to individual headings, most with names of characters as titles. Style here reflects content. The "ordered" text shifts by jumping from character to character, all the while continuing the plot line but at the same time inventing a disorder within the prevailing structure. The framework of myth sets the plot in motion, and the traditional chapter headings give the illusion of order. Suddenly, the structure changes, and we sense the disorder existing inside the external form.

Myth and legend structure *Armed with Madness,* but Mary Butts's characters give overall shape to her aesthetic in general. If her novels are viewed in sequence, there is something of an ebb and flow, a rise and fall in character development that carefully mirrors the plots. The same characters appear and reappear (most often with the same names) from novel to novel, and the repetition suggests the ritual form, the continuation of a particular aesthetic imaging. Specifically, Scylla, Picus, and Felix reappear in *Death of Felicity Taverner,* but in lesser roles. Boris, who is nothing more than a "find" of Felix's in *Armed with Madness,* is the lost soul of *Imaginary Letters* and the surprisingly violent savior of *Death of Felicity Taverner.* Although the importance of their roles shifts from novel to novel, each character retains his or her own significance throughout. The recurrence of characters imitates the prescribed actions of ritual and links narrative structure to symbolic meaning.

In *Armed with Madness* the characters are both pure and impure, but the desire and longing are true in each. The old vicar tells Picus and Carston that "[t]his story as I see it . . . is true Sanc-Grail. The cup may have been an ash-tray in a Cairo club. But it seems to me that you are having something like a ritual. A find, illumination, doubt, and division, collective and then dispersed" (140). By highlighting the spiritual depravity of a world lost but yearning for spiritual reawakening, Butts has modernized the Grail legend. She finds her center in the natural world and its connections to its primal past.

CHAPTER FOUR

"Visible Pan": Imaginary Letters *(1928),* Death of Felicity Taverner *(1932),* Warning to Hikers *(1932)*

"Blot out the landscape"

The Greek god of "flocks and shepherds, forests and wild life, and fertility," part man, part goat, Pan is the "playful, lascivious, unpredictable, always lecherous" son of Hermes and the nymph Dryope.[1] When Mary Butts uses the term "Visible Pan" in her fourth novel, *Death of Felicity Taverner,* she brings into focus her vital excitement about the visible seductiveness of nature and its beauty along with humanity's role in the wild and unpredictable essence of the natural world. In *Imaginary Letters, Death of Felicity Taverner,* and *Warning to Hikers,* Mary Butts offers us a way to explore the tensions between human beings and nature, ancient ritual and modern civilization, and the unpredictability of people, who are at once human and animal, nature and god. She examines the sexual complexities of contemporary society and the loss of a sustaining past. If *Imaginary Letters* reveals the desperate need to connect with another human being, *Death of Felicity Taverner* and *Warning to Hikers* emphasize the significance of returning to the essence of nature and its beauty. In "Visible Pan" Butts defines the importance of cooperation between the seen beauty of the natural world and the human inhabitants who embody the fertile vitality represented by the escapades of the god Pan. For Butts, life is a sacred game that is both frightening and playful, serious and lascivious, yet able to be fulfilled if nature and humanity work together.

Imaginary Letters, dated "Autumn, 1924," at the Hotel Foyot where Mary Butts lived in Paris, was not published until 1928 by Edward W. Titus

Press.[2] It appeared with "copper plate engravings from the original drawings by Jean Cocteau," and a publisher's note states that it "is the first book not written by himself that Cocteau consented to illustrate."[3] Although Boris appears at the end of *Armed with Madness* as a "find" of Felix's, *Imaginary Letters,* an epistolary novel of letters never sent (and never intended to be sent) to the mother of this White Russian émigré, launches the character of Boris Polteratsky. In these letters, the narrator, a young woman living in Paris, attempts to clarify and interpret her feelings about the young Russian. Driven by a fascination of the mixture of cruelty, pain, beauty, and madness in her relationship to the homosexual boy who is not her lover, the narrator finds he offers her a "state of imagination" which somehow initiates the creative process, or, as she puts it, he is "the cause of art in others (*IL* 235).

Boris is a "monster of vanity and pride. A high-bred, honourable boy. Capricious, selfish, insensitive. Shy as a rabbit, helpful and shy. Lecherous, drunken, bold and chaste. He arouses equally unconquerable affection and despair" (*IL* 235), qualities which reflect the life of the lost in Paris and London of the twenties. Like many of that generation, in Butts's portrayal, the sons of Russian aristocracy have been stripped of a privileged way of life, a life which they have not yet learned to abandon. As a result, they enter the demimonde of Paris and London and wallow in pain and shallowness by giving and offering sexual favors to those who are prepared to take them in. Mary Hamer notes that "Boris is a symptom, a sign of a distress that is universal, only one of many such little displaced boys 'spat out' by 'the war that confounded all shores', to run about Paris."[4] Mary Butts, like the female character of this novel, understood the feelings of these lost boys and sought to discern their pain and their cruelty. In a sense, she saw them as defiled by grown-ups and stripped of their innocence. Butts portrays these young men as survivors, willing to endure humiliation and pain in spite of their losses. Robin Blaser claims that "her life threw her among homosexual and bisexual men. She understood their distance from women, the underworld of their thought, even to madness. She understood the unrequited, the youthfulness of all sexuality and its terror."[5] *Imaginary Letters* is an endeavor to comprehend the character of the Russian boy Boris and his own terror of existence as it relates to the woman who has chosen to care for him.

The female character is willing to take from the relationship whatever he chooses to offer. She seems clearly aware that because of her insights into his world, his pederasty, his suffering, and his mixture of sensuality and cruelty, she draws from him a kind of inspiration which begins the writing process; it is a strangely symbiotic connection which benefits both partners. If she can understand his suffering and loss, then perhaps she will be able to penetrate her own. Played out at the level of theme and tone, Butts's female endures the anguish of such a relationship because the struggle, the battle, the pain assure her of existence. As long as she can feel and relate to pain, she remains alive, and Boris supplies exactly what she needs. He both reflects and exacerbates her pain. In this sense, Butts's letter writer reflects one of the major concerns of European modernism in the wake of World War I, namely, the importance of pain and death in the development of self-awareness.

Boris can be both good and evil, an essential mixture which establishes a fascination with the character of Boris throughout much of her fiction; his situation, in fact, mirrors that of Butts and her social equals. Patrick Wright's assessment of Boris is that he "is an epitome of dispossession in the Butts style. For him everything is either in the past, in memory or in the blood: a whole betrayed nation and racial ('Slav') character stacked up behind a name."[6]

The sense of dispossession or dislocation permeates much of Butts's work. Many of her characters, like Boris, are part of a spoiled and privileged set whose loss somehow transcends mere superficiality because they have a sense of tradition, homeland, and a true memory in the blood of a style and a way of life that has been irretrievably lost through war, change, and progress. There is a real struggle to preserve the money and the privileged lifestyle; however, Butts and her characters yearn for a more noble purpose to sustain them, to maintain a stamina for believing in enduring traditions and symbols. Because of her background, her personal loss, her family's dysfunction, Butts interprets the immediate world from her own perspective but longs for an understanding of a higher truth and sacredness. Echoing the *fin de siècle* sadness of the previous century, Butts also exhibits Wildean "art-for-art's-sake" aestheticism in her attitudes; yet, like W. B. Yeats, she quests for some meaning, some recognition that life is ultimately worthwhile and that truth is something to be sought after. Pain, suffering, and exploration of alternate lifestyles and ways of thinking about the world are, at least, an affirmation of existence and, at most, a doorway to the imagination and its creative source.

The desire to understand the conflicted relationships of the young, dislocated men, as well as her own ambiguous relationships, informed much of Butts's life. Writing about homosexuality with a curiosity prevalent at the time, she, as Bryher records, "understood, pitied, and did not judge them [the new kind of underworld, debris of a civilisation]."[7] Instead, with a motherly sympathy, which she did not expend on her own daughter, Butts "wrote of them without sentiment, knowing that they would take from her as mercilessly as from a stranger, but seeing them as dropped playthings of the gods, always worth saving."[8] In Boris, we see her distaste for Bolshevism and her compassion for what Louis Adeane calls these "Russian emigrés, decayed aristocrats, college boys, and cosmopolitan queers, to all of whom she radiated maternal sympathy and with all of whom she intrigued, quarrelled and was reconciled with more than customary conviction."[9] These relationships, in fact, also contributed to her passion for living. An expanded look at Butts's journal entry (Paris, May 2, 1927), cited earlier, addresses the joining of sex and healing and explains her connection to men who somehow live outside the norms of accepted society, whether it be through homosexuality, madness, or simple terror of existence, and whose pain is a source of inspiration, fascination, and wonder:

> What do I love, outside writing and clothes and opium and the weather and my friends? I have always had since I can remember an incomparable pleasure in finding someone psychically sick, and learning about it, and seeing if there is a way out. This feeling very much mixed up with sex—bed not necessary, but it makes things work better. That is any power I have seems to work better in that relation. I've always wanted to make my lovers well, sense powers liberated in them, fears in the dustbin, raw life taken in and coming out translated.[10]

The notion of "psychically sick" seems to be at the center of much of Butts's passion and her work.[11] The interest in healing can be equated with the power of her art to transform experience and by doing so to offer the author the power of creation, "raw life taken in and coming out translated." As long as Butts's letter writer in *Imaginary Letters* can keep the relationship viable, she maintains the inspiration to write. Once the relationship goes bad, the letters and the inspiration come to an end. Since the letters are written in the present, we have a sense of the effects of the ongoing relationship; however, in her final letter, the would-be lover of Boris recognizes the end of her interval of inspiration:

> Madame,
>
> It is over now. It is exceedingly difficult to describe to you how. Against my will, and, I think his; against our practical interest, our romantic interests, against what we might have realized out of them, we have come to the end (which, for all I know, may be a beginning, and is certainly the beginning of something else). . . . Every history of every love affair is important. For one reason that it reflects the exact states of emotional tension in its age and its group. (*IL* 263)

The end of the relationship marks the conclusion of this record; now the creative artist must look for the "beginning of something else" to inspire and fuel the imagination. As so many writers have remarked, the creative process consists of building, tearing down, and rebuilding once again. In doing so, the creative result translates and "reflects the exact states of emotional tension in its age and its group," perhaps Butts's way of preserving and defining the historical moment. Frank Baker's memory of her confirms this sentiment: "What Mary Butts had in high degree and held inviolate was a fearless sense of her own historical significance to her times. And certainly she had never been afraid of asking difficult questions of life."[12] Some of those "difficult questions" Butts confronted through the interrelationships of her characters. In *Imaginary Letters* the relationship (for Butts and for her letter writer) holds a mirror to their world and its dissociation and is the focus of inspiration. Through the process of writing, the connection between the letter writer and Boris acts as a temporary stay against the terrors of the outside world. As long as they are together, even without sex as an intimate link, they sustain each other. Boris clings to his female friend, and she says, "I was not to go away, ever, because without me he would do worse things and mind them less" (*IL* 242).

Whatever Butts means by "psychically sick," in *Imaginary Letters* she establishes and defines the character of Boris who will go through various stages of development in her novels as he later becomes involved with the Taverner family. Boris's fundamental sense of loss and of not belonging create a need for healing, which Butts's letter writer is ready to supply. It may also serve as a source of power for the letter writer. Her attempt to understand and to tolerate his behavior is one way for her to deny her powerlessness as a woman in a predominantly male hegemony.

Theorists of gay studies will find much to explore in the relationship between Boris and his female friend. Eve Sedgewick, for example, discusses the classifying process of various categories of male homosexuality and concludes that "we, as women, learn yet another way in which we are powerless, unless we can finally master the unmasterable map of male sexuality."[13] The mastery of such an "unmasterable map" is precisely what Butts's letter writer attempts; however, what she derives from such a relationship is not totally without benefit for her. She draws an odd sort of intellectual and creative strength from the association. Yet, her desire to understand the boy's actions and pain is sincere:

> There is always the long way out of the wood, the cast round when you have made a map of it. The way that implies the patience I am without, and the only pleasure, the satisfaction of the mind when it is on the track of what *is*. . . .
>
> What they [the letters] have done, I know, is to fix a little in this flying world your fleshly and my ghostly son, the black and green boy, who comes less and less often to see me now. The ray, the shadow, the memory, the mirror in which I have looked, seen and understood, imperfectly, many things. (*IL* 265)

In examining such a relationship between women and gay men, Butts was certainly ahead of her time. With the development of gay studies and queer theory now a part of literary investigation, analyses of this early-twentieth-century novella should recognize the originality and prophetic quality of Mary Butts's psychological and creative insight, especially since the complexity of feelings that comes from the female letter writer involves serious emotional pain.

Boris's vacillation between cruelty and need does, however, suggest something Butts seems to be exploring at the core of a very different kind of love and longing. Blaser tells us that "[t]hese letters are, in fact, addressed to the imagination where love usually has his seat,"[14] and a very unique seat it is. Butts, however, goes beyond the historical moment; in the process of her letter writing, her narrator demonstrates and provides insight into the imagination as the creative source of art. Quoting from the song "Adieu; farewell earth's bliss" in Thomas Nashe's play, *Summer's Last Will and Testament,* "Brightness fall from the air, / Queens have died, young and fair,"[15] Butts, in the inspired moment, alters the line to interpret Boris's predicament, one which she also desires to comprehend:

> "Queens survive, young and fair." Not that he is what a "queen" has come to mean now, but the line indicates his fanatical pédérastie.
>
> When the day comes when my looks are finally gone, and my appetites (I hope) with them, I shall write the best book that has ever been done on the half vital reality, half fashionable snobbery of our age, the romantic and sensual passions of men for men.
>
> Think that it is romantic, is sensual; is mixed with the will towards the creative life at the needle point where it pricks the unknown. Is sensual, jealous, angry, preoccupied with rendezvous and beds; in hotels, apartments, parks, bars; will follow the fleets to ports, scour the "grands magasins," prowl the suburbs for roughs, if dangerous the better. Is a recognized medium for advancing the career. Is comic, detestable, admirable. Has its prostitutes, its ascetics, its victims, its saints. I think I may add with justice, its dupes. (*IL* 239)

Whether Butts sees herself, or her character, as a "dupe" of these men, whose consciousnesses are clearly uprooted and damaged, driven by some remote longing in memory to feel a passion for life, can perhaps be answered in the way she herself chose to live her life. Butts's own life was as unconventional as the lifestyles of these young men who lived in a society where, as Stephen Barber points out in his discussion of Virginia Woolf's relationships with gay men, "being queer in modern Britain meant, in her [Woolf's] shorthand, 'being at risk,' 'being despised.'"[16] Leaving her husband John Rodker and abandoning her only daughter in the year of her birth for the physically and psychically very wounded Cecil Maitland, Butts submerged herself into the world of what Bryher identifies as the "debris of a civilization." Perhaps sensing the same loss and disconnection she felt with regard to her home at Salterns, Butts chose men whose needs reflected her own and who, in some uncommon process of heightened consciousness, become a source of inspiration for art. They offer a necessary pain from which to build, a memory in the blood which only the suffering and deprived can share, or as Bryher determines, "She was exploring the new type of emotion for which we have not yet words, we shall grow them in time, and to understand is first a judgment on the self."[17]

This judgment becomes intertwined with Butts's life. As noted earlier, at age fourteen Butts lost her father, whom she identifies in *The Crystal Cabinet* as the source of her introduction into the world of knowledge. Mrs. Butts never understood the relationship between Mary and her father, their attachment to the family home and its surroundings, or their passion for reading and learning. With the arrival of a new stepfather who had a "cheerful contempt for the arts" and a mother who declared that "men did not like women who 'knew things,'"[18] Butts's emotional attachments became even more detached and confused. One can only speculate on how this type of upbringing affected someone who lived when psychoanalysis was still in its infancy, who disdained the work of Freud and Jung as "fashionable psychology," and who needed to be nurtured and to give nurture to those she perceived as wounded.

A fascination with homosexual men seems to have supplied a need or filled an emptiness in Butts's own existence—one answer to a frustration and alienation she felt as a woman. An intellectual child, sent to Scotland to one of the "few schools which at that time gave a girl the same education as a boy,"[19] Butts felt her emotions and intellectual life were confused by a mother who had the wrong insights about life in general and about the role of women in particular. This perhaps left her with a very tenuous sense of being female. Butts's comments on the sensibilities of her own sex in *The Crystal Cabinet* reveal a double concern. On the one hand, in her chapter on Shelley she writes, "And women—their business was to be 'Free and sincere'. 'Good and kind'. Then they were not just people who didn't matter so much as men, who mustn't be allowed to learn things."[20] Yet, later after being labeled a "freak" by her classmates at St. Andrews for liking poetry, she makes a curious statement about how this has affected her:

> But a freak is what they called you here, in a process of long-continued jeering whose result was to set me into almost a life-enduring mould of mixed timidity and contempt. Over-sensibility and not always secret insolence, one of whose further results was a dislike and distrust of my own sex, and an inability to debate easily and unresentfully it has taken me years to overcome. If I ever have.[21]

Homosexual men offered elements she had lost as a child—a "masculine" presence, a love of art and society, willingness to express emotions, a shared sense of alienation, and "feminine" qualities with which she could identify. In addition, they represented an unrequited love, a love that is finally unattainable yet always an ideal to be sought. Having been stripped of the nurturing she needed while still young, Butts found herself wanting to nurture, to give what she herself had lost and was missing. In her longing for the father she had lost and the mother she felt she never had, Butts's relationships with homosexual men seemed to satisfy some of that need, the marriage of the male and the female in one person who also needs nurturing and mothering.

Harcourt Wesson Bull, a close friend of Mary Butts's from 1928 until her death in Cornwall in 1937, and Quentin Bell, Virginia Woolf's nephew whose friendship extended from 1928, when he was eighteen years old, until 1931 (he had "once visited her in Cornwall after that"),[22] offer other insights into this inclination of Butts's. In an interview with Robert Byington some time between 1963 and 1974, Quentin Bell attributes these connections with young men to her generosity: "There was something generous about her . . . something big about her. . . . She was congenial, in some way. . . . I suppose she flattered me. Which, of course, is never disagreeable. . . . She was very kind. She made one feel important. She made one feel one's good company."[23] Byington continues by musing on Bell's comments: "It occurred to me that I had just heard as succinct an explanation of Mary's appeal to younger men, uncertain of themselves, just beginning their careers, etc., as I was likely to."[24] Harcourt Wesson Bull, on the other hand (indeed, a much closer friend of Butts than Bell), in identifying Sergei Maslenikoff as the inspiration for Boris in *Imaginary Letters,* attributes this interest in homosexuals and the need to care for them not only to an amusement with their ways but also to her estranged brother, Tony. Bull suggests that "because of Tony" Butts felt compassion and a wish to mother, worry, and suffer over these boys. In fact, numerous memoirs comment on Butts's concern over her estrangement from her brother, and they also note his vicious attacks on her, along with the attack of his friend William Plomer, who wrote a scathing caricature of Butts as Lydia Delap in his novel *Museum Pieces.*

Robin Blaser speculates on why Butts was excluded from the Bloomsbury Circle and cites Virginia Woolf's account of Tony's feelings in her *Diary:*

> The entry for March 18, 1932, quotes him [Anthony Butts]: "I cannot say anything of my sister—She is a bad woman—pretentious—I can see no merit in her books—pretentious. She corrupts young men. They are always committing suicide." . . . And Mrs. Woolf comments: "Tony is ashamed of Mary, who thus defiles the Butts blood." Many of these details are simply repeated by Goldring in *South Lodge.*[25]

Bull states that she spoke often of the youthful, loving sister-brother relationship, that she adored Tony, "felt the change in that relationship most keenly—and substituted others for him all the rest of her life."[26] For whatever reason Butts sought out these relationships, their suffering and cruelty, she seemed to need them to sustain her and to act as a spark of inspiration for her art.

In her search for the words to define these emotions, Butts turned to ritual as a kind of psychological lifeline to the reality she believed existed in an ideal, Platonic realm outside the external reality she encountered daily. Like Boris who needs his female savior, Butts desired a pattern grounded in the external world in order to prevent her from moving too far away from reality, or she too would "do worse things and mind them less." Returning to a structured past of ritual and myth offered connections to both the inner and outer worlds that were of utmost importance to her. Hence, by the time she introduces the character of Boris once again in her fourth novel, *Death of Felicity Taverner* (1932; reissued 1992), she evokes primitive ritual as an answer to some of the confusion and pain felt so deeply by her characters.

The novel, about which she says, "Never had such trouble with a book before,"[27] tells the tale of an ideal woman, Felicity Taverner, the cousin of Scylla and Felix. Although Felicity is already dead when the novel opens, she is at the center of the plot that involves a complicated struggle between the family and Felicity's husband, Nick Kralin. To Scylla, Picus, Felix, and family, Felicity's purity (and symbolically the land itself) must be preserved. Nick, however, invades their idyll with a plot to blackmail the family and a plan to sell the land. When Felix brings Boris into the family concerns, the plot shifts to include ritual and myth. In *Death of Felicity Taverner,* ancient ritual functions as a way of justifying murder; Boris has an opportunity to repay the Taverners for their openness and generosity and finds a vindication for his own role in the mystery of Felicity's death.

This material is shocking, yet Butts seems to be creating something of an allegory with this novel. Ironically, Felicity cannot find felicity in a world that does not understand her and that finally destroys her. Hers is a very fragile happiness, easily bruised or wrecked by the insensitive world. Felicity lacks the wisdom of Woolf's Mrs. Ramsey; her predicament echoes Yeats's dictum, "The best lack all conviction / While the worst are full of passionate intensity." We, however, observe Felicity only from the point of view of Butts's narrator or through the eyes of Scylla, Picus, Felix, and her mother and her brother Adrian. Whatever dark side Felicity possesses is something of an organic outgrowth of the natural world with which she is identified or a product of the evils of the urban world; her transgressions serve to make her human and ground her in a world where she really does not belong. Mrs. Taverner and Adrian are insanely jealous of her ability to radiate goodness. Felicity's husband, Nick Kralin, through greed and a sense that nothing has meaning, longs to destroy happiness. Felicity's simplicity and goodness, Butts posits, cannot survive in a world full of "passionate intensity" focused on destruction of the past and its values.

Boris and Kralin are interlopers in a world different from their own in many ways, yet similar in its alienation from the sacredness of its land. Kralin takes on the role of evil incarnate and is more than a mere interloper; he symbolizes all that is wrong with twentieth-century society. In his efforts to taint Felicity's memory, Kralin taints the land. In Kralin, Butts's allegory indicates that the sacred and the profane may merge at times, but the profane cannot be allowed to overcome or destroy the sacred. Mrs. Taverner, Felicity's snobbish mother, and her son signify a past of small-mindedness and dark secrets, while Scylla and Picus retain their mythic qualities, and Felix, along with Boris, represents those lost in the underworld of civilization.

Enriching her novel once again with the work of Sir James Frazer, Jessie Weston, and the Cambridge Ritualists, Butts manages to transcend the literal and create the lifeline she craved in order to sustain her in a world so difficult to comprehend. In her *Prolegomena to the Study of Greek Religion,* Jane E. Harrison tells us that the function of the *pharmakoi* (human scapegoats) was "to purify the city."[28] Although the notion of human sacrifice involving death of the scapegoat varies from culture to culture, as Frazer and Harrison so meticulously record, human sacrifice of scapegoats did take place as a means of ridding society of evil. In general, ritual sacrifice, as René Girard elaborates, served to "protect the entire community from *its own* violence," and "[t]he purpose of the sacrifice [was] to restore harmony to the community, to reinforce its social fabric."[29]

In *Death of Felicity Taverner,* Butts retains several characters from her preceding novel, *Armed with Madness,* and combines the mythic elements of the authentic healer in the characters of Scylla and Felicity Taverner with that of the scapegoat in the form of Felicity's husband, Nick Kralin—a villain, a Jew, son of a Bolshevik, a blackmailer, a capitalist, and the embodiment of all that jeopardizes the community and threatens what the mythic goodness of Felicity stood for.[30] The fear of technological progress, the deprivation of a true sense of beauty, and the menace of commercial development of the land sacred to the Taverners are at the nucleus of Butts's concerns over the loss of or separation from what she calls "the 'bosom' of Nature," the "great daimon, who is masculine as well as feminine, father as well as mother."[31] This "bosom" is the sacred land of her home in Salterns that Butts felt nurtured, raised her, and, in effect, acted as mother and father to her.

Following the mythic structure of *Armed with Madness, Death of Felicity Taverner* raises the dead Felicity and her memory to the level of the Grail—a memory to be treasured, preserved, and sought after for the truth and beauty she represented. The job of preserving her memory and her sacred land on the isolated, southwest English coast becomes the principal consideration of her cousin Scylla, Picus (now Scylla's husband), and Scylla's brother Felix. These knights, however, are foiled by Felicity's evil husband, Nick Kralin, who has managed to procure Felicity's diaries and papers, which reveal secrets about her own life and scandalous information about her mother, "the original bitch,"[32] and her brother Adrian, both of whom resented Felicity's innocence and delicate beauty, which were "not of this world." We also discover that before Kralin begins his game of blackmail and extortion, he has already procured options on the land surrounding Felicity's estate and plans to vulgarize the entire area by turning the pristine land sacred to the Taverners into vacation homes. He would "build a hotel and a row of bungalows along the low cliff, light the sea lane and drain it" (249), a kind of Club Med in the untrammeled south of England. The embodiment of all that is evil to the Taverners, a "scientific pornographist. All for style, nothing for content" (177), Kralin possesses what the questers term the "Grey Thing" (178), the sense that nothing has meaning, an awareness of "the ultimate senselessness of everything" (178), an idea completely foreign to the sensibilities of the Taverner clan. "Infanticide *a la mode*" (172), practiced by Felicity's Victorian mother, who is jealous of Felicity's innocent freedom of beauty denied her own age, and Kralin's crass commercialism and "Grey Thing" merge to bring about the death of this goddess/angel whose goodness, purity, virtue, and sensitivity were so rare on earth that heaven "wanted her back" (173).

Although Felicity's relatives eventually and reluctantly join forces to combat the vileness of Kralin, it is another outsider and fellow countryman of Kralin (although of a very different caste) who comes to their rescue. Boris Polteratsky, who like the Taverners has been stripped of a life of privilege and who hates all that Kralin epitomizes, takes on a significant role in helping to solve the mystery and in performing the ritual sacrifice. Boris, "[w]hom they had fed and loved, and by whom they had been selected to bear all things and endure all things" and whose "lurid extravaganza" would begin after only brief intervals of "reasonable behavior" (167), is needy and spoiled, yet in spite of his desire for economic security no matter what the cost, he eventually succumbs to the sincerity of the Taverners. The Taverners evince a lifestyle stolen from Boris; as a result, he is both drawn to them and hates them because he no longer possesses choices:

> The Taverners were the kind of people who, if they have to choose, choose a boat and a library rather than a car and a club; cherry blossom before orchids, apples before tinned peaches, wine to whiskey, one dress from Chanel to six "from a shop." Who listen to jazz and Mozart, not to Massenet: who cannot endure imitations of anything; who do not tire of real things once they have got them home to play with. They knew what in relation to Chardin has been called "all the splendour and glory of matter." Like him they were in love. . . . They knew that the twenty-four hours of the day and night are cinema, an *actualité,* a continuous programme, whose hero is the sun and whose heroine the moon, whose play is the modification of light, whose "pathos" is sunset, with sunrise for epiphany. (300–301)

Their way of life may be fading with progress, yet they manage to maintain an essential sense of a particular way of viewing life that only a history of financial security and sensitivity to the natural world can provide. These are country gentry who refuse to lose their sense of style and what is right in the world; hence, they fight with a ferocity of purpose to maintain the purity of the land as a representative of that world. Boris, on the other hand, has been violently ejected from his world and his land and can only love what he feels is real in the Taverners (their sense of tradition, lifestyle, a reverence for the past) and hate them for possessing what he no longer can possess.

Involved on the fringes of the affair which brings about Felicity's death, Boris decides that in spite of his longing to wallow in his personal loss (which helps him forget the ugliness of his situation), he must battle the evil intent of Kralin, a fellow countryman who reminds him far too much of what has been ripped from him. Once Boris immerses himself in the predicament, the novel expands to include the sacred and the profane, ritual sacrifice and fear of loss.

In her essay *Warning to Hikers,* written in the same year as the novel, Butts states, "Contact with nature is very much what a man has when he participates in any rite or sacrament. Rites and sacraments are a kind of drama, a ritual play taken from universal natural events. They are about the health and ill-health of the soul, about marriage and birth and death. Things which happen."[33] Both the novel and the essay link ideas of ritual and fear to develop a larger structure, what Butts terms a "sacred game." In this game, Scylla, her family, and Boris collaborate to restore and protect the harmony which existed before Felicity's mysterious death, and it is at this point that we turn to ancient myth and ritual to examine what evolves in this modern rendering of an intellectual detective story.

By blending pagan and Christian topoi, Butts arrives at the place Leon Surette identifies as a "powerful wave of academic research and speculation into myth as revelation that was a constant force in Europe from the beginning of the Romantic period to the present."[34] When Butts introduces Boris as a key player in the game, the notion of Kralin as scapegoat, a metaphor for a plague on the community, becomes evident. Scylla's spiritual strength and Felicity's chaste memory act as the impetus for Boris to assist these friends who simultaneously irritate him and command his respect. In Kralin he sees not only a serious danger to the community of the Taverners but also the destruction of a privileged lifestyle (and, for Butts, a type of racial degeneration), as well as the loss of a murdered family in Russia which Boris cannot forget. "Boris," the narrator tells us, "understood little of the public events of his Revolution, perplexed by what had happened as any young gentlemen not trained in politics might be" (314), but he knows that Kralin comes from the "untraditional part of humanity" (314), that "there *are* people in the world with nothing to lose. . . . Having nothing to lose—a nothing which includes an indifference in their inner selves—they are free to make things happen; bizarre or violent things, stupid or intelligent things; secret or open—with often an odd preference for the secret" (315).

Instead of allowing Kralin to destroy the sacred natural land of the community, Boris takes it upon himself to cleanse or purify their community through the sacrificial murder of Kralin. Since the novel opens in the spring, the time is ripe for the sacrifice, for as Sir James Frazer tells us the expulsion of evil generally coincided with a change of season[35] in order to insure the fertility of the earth.[36] Boris and the Taverners see Kralin as the embodiment of disharmony and destruction of the sacred earth. In contrast, Felicity, as an ideal borrowed from paradise, had the "occupation . . . to be lovely and exquisite and kind. . . . To learn things and never show them off. It was her business to understand things and to love" (182). Because Felicity's vision extended beyond the seen world, she was "over life-size" (189); "She'd seen the world going to its present senseless devil, anaemic with stupidity and spite, and she had meant to do something about it. . . . She'd become more dangerous than she knew" (188). Since her death occurs in winter and since the Taverners associate the land with Felicity's physical being, "To them it is part of her—'part of her body'" (330), Felicity comes to represent the very earth itself, which needs cleansing, and an assurance of fertile rebirth. Butts illuminates this idea by telling us that the virtue, the "largest thing," shared by all Taverners, especially Mrs. Taverner, is a passion for the beauty of England (285). The purity of Felicity's memory, then, is necessary for the renewal of the sacred presence of the land and the community which inhabits it, or as Louis Adeane notes in a 1951 review, "the seekers find the Grail—but only within a material category, the land and the local pattern of culture which is preserved being merely a representation of Felicity herself."[37] However, Adeane's negative response of "*only* within a material category" fails to recognize the ritual function of Felicity as redemptive earth goddess, whose body symbolizes rebirth to the community and reflects ancient rites and practices which position the novel on the spiritual level of the quest rather than in a mere "material category."

The passion for preservation of the land and insulation of the community enlarges the emphasis on Kralin's innate baseness and his alien position in the community. In his study of the scapegoat, René Girard supports Butts's metaphorical use of Kralin, the Jew and outsider, by explaining that during a time of crisis in a culture or community, the "appetite for persecution readily focuses on religious minorities."[38] Anti-Semitism or persecution of any minority faith, Girard tells us, grew out of fear and extreme social disorder, whether internal or external.[39] Butts would certainly have been affected by the anti-Semitism so prevalent in modernism,[40] but her Kralin is only partially Jewish and becomes a threat because he lacks spirituality and because his vision is urban and far removed from the sensibilities of the English country gentry. He serves as a perfect metaphor for all that Butts and her Taverners fear. He is an intrusion into a lifestyle they desperately strive to preserve, and as one contemporary reviewer has noted, to Felicity's family—because he has failed to love Felicity as she deserved—"Kralin becomes a murderer."[41] As Butts and her characters see things, these are desperate times which call for desperate measures. By accepting the actions of Boris, they choose to combat evil with evil; he becomes their violent substitute for the female healer. The murder of Kralin metamorphoses into sacred ritual; therefore, the scapegoat as a mechanism for her novel fits perfectly as a symbol or metaphor for what must be purged from the community. The obvious path to this purging leads to the past and to identifying a *pharmakos* as a symbol of that which must be expunged.

In his study *Human Sacrifice in Ancient Greece,* Dennis D. Hughes cites a fourth-century extract by Helladius which locates a source for the term *pharmakos* in Athens during the spring festival of Thargelia: ". . . Pharmakos is a proper name and . . . he stole the sacred bowls of Apollo, was caught by the companions of Achilles, and was stoned to death, and . . . the things performed at the Thargelia are imitations of these events. . . ."[42] If we identify Kralin with *pharmakos,* we can extrapolate the notion that, since he stole things sacred to the goddess healer and is caught by Boris and his companions, then ritual sacrifice becomes significant to Butts's novel. Just as Hughes suggests that the events at the spring festival of Thargelia are an imitation of the events of Helladius's tale in ancient Greece, so is the ritual murder or expulsion of the blackmailer/ thief/threat to community in the character of Kralin a similar symbolic purging in a modern setting. Instead of preserving the sacred presences of the land which he has inherited from his wife, Kralin taints Felicity's goodness/goddess purity and imperils the good of the community, its renewal, its fertile offerings of life.

Sir James Frazer tells us that in many instances the *pharmakoi* were led from the city before the ritual or symbolic murder was effected, often by stoning.[43] Similarly, when Boris finally decides that Kralin must be sacrificed, he leads him to a cave on an isolated island, a "secret place" (353) away from the community. Symbolically, Kralin will be swallowed up within the womb of mother earth, and his death will serve to insure the preservation of the land. In collaboration with the forces of Nature, Boris hits Kralin and rolls his body into a pool within the cave, and "when it had sunk, weighted its chest with some stones" (357). Before leaving, Boris extracts "seven pounds, ten shillings in notes" from Kralin's body, which he identifies as "[t]he payment of the executioner" (358), and emerges cleansed by returning through the "Sacred Wood, along its green pebbled path to the house" (359).

The Christian parallel to the pagan concept of the scapegoat in which the victim becomes the Savior enlarges the metaphor even further. Girard tells us that the "sacred cannot function without surrogate victims";[44] therefore, Christ the sacred is also Christ the victim. Since Christ, also a Jew, took on the sins of all mankind, his sacrifice extends beyond a local community and sustains the spiritual life of mankind. Although this parallel is not to suggest that Kralin is a Christ figure, paradoxically, Kralin, although portrayed as evil incarnate, does take on traits of a savior through his sacrificial demise. His death preserves the memory of Felicity, saves the reputation of the Taverner clan, and temporarily impedes the modernity which will eventually destroy the sacred presences of the land. These fictional events reveal, as Barbara Wagstaff has observed, Butts's "passionate interest in Christianity as a mystery religion, a practice, a living *with* the sacred presences of places and things which the pagan world knew."[45] The modern idea of "savior" combines pagan rite with Christian belief to discover connections with "universal natural events"—all serious concerns of Butts. The "ritual play" translates in modern terms to act as both poison and remedy, scapegoat and savior.

Because Scylla and company do nothing to prevent or to expose Boris, they then become accessories to the ritual sacrifice, the ancient community participating in the sacred rite. Violence and the sacred are thus linked, or as René Girard puts it, "I may as well [say] 'violence *or* the sacred.' For the operations of violence and the sacred are ultimately the same process."[46] Since Butts frames her story in the sacred world of ritual, violence is viewed as necessary for purification, and the death of Kralin raises him to the level of a modern savior: "that which is on the verge of destroying the community becomes the means to save it."[47]

In *Death of Felicity Taverner,* Butts's characters manage to preserve, if only temporarily, the beauty of the countryside which supplies the spiritual well-being of the community. Jane Harrison observes that the *pharmakos* who has been identified with the ills of the city "is killed then, not because his death is a vicarious sacrifice, but because he is so infected and tabooed that his life is a practical impossibility."[48] Kralin's life contaminated with the "Grey Thing" must be expunged before he pollutes the health of the soul. In Felicity and her memory, Butts and her Taverners locate symbols that are so necessary in Butts's own decadent world of post–World War I society. It is, therefore, the image of nature's sanctity and the preservation of family tradition that Butts incorporates into her work to combat what she saw as evil within her own world. By symbolically eliminating or removing all impurities through a reenactment of primitive ritual initiated by awakening ancient communal instincts of self-preservation, Butts fuses the sacred and the profane.

This notion of the sacred and the profane winds its way through most of Butts's work. In her essay *Warning to Hikers,* she elaborates on the sacred elements of the countryside and the necessity of preserving the countryside from the city-dwelling "hikers" who violate its sanctity. Frank Baker identifies this violation as "[t]hat same ravishing which Blake had seen when the age of industrialism began."[49] The very real interlopers on this purity correspond to the horror of the proposed actions of Nick Kralin. Here in reality city dwellers have developed an unnatural "cult of nature" which acts as an intrusion on people who possess an innate and real sensibility to the natural world:

> Love of nature is the Bunk. You are either used to it, part of it and generally unconscious of it, except for some detail or of your own well-being, or you are an outsider. People, even of true sensibility, who "love" the country, who leave for a holiday full of rapture and anticipation, are not insincere, but they are treating it as an opera or a picture gallery, with the extra advantages of a first-class nursing home. They are treating it as a mixture of régime and art. This is unavoidable, natural, not dishonourable, but still the cult widens down until it reaches the people of fake sensibility; the people who have discovered that the country is good for children; all the people who think they should like something which they have never learned. Until the cult become craze reaches the mass of our people, the unique barbarian we have been breeding for generations, and who are beginning to stream out at the tail of our motor-cars. . . . Beauty, or even pure air, is not a friendly thing, not until it has passed into you so completely that you cease to notice it; so that when your consciousness of it returns, it will be like the sight of a lover who has never gone away.[50]

These city-dwelling barbarians, as we saw so clearly in *Death of Felicity Taverner,* are a threat to a way of life which was an essential part of Butts's country-gentry ancestry. Unlike those who were raised on the land and who have a unique attachment and a kind of blood relationship to it, the town-born is a fake. He is viewed as a "man who is dying, or a man who is outside tabu, as a man who has lost his dance,"[51] or as Frank Baker recalls in his memoir, Butts saw these intruders as

> people unable to live in the rhythm of the natural forces they seek to bring to submission by unnatural means: the television set, the transistor, the yap-yap of the news announcer, the advertisement hoarding—all those ephemeral products of the mass mind which ignore the timeless heritage forever expanding the seemingly short span of a man's life.[52]

Only those who have that innate sense of Nature, of its terror and beauty, can understand and appreciate its quality, can recognize the "visible Pan" (354) where Nature presents itself to the select few. Only those raised alongside Nature, whether peasant or aristocrat, are able to see its inner sacredness in its external trappings.

In spite of her country-gentry snobbery, Butts's work and her thought were far ahead of her time. With a 1990s sensibility, she reflects environmental concerns, the extremities to which these issues may be taken, the prejudices and hatred which pervade our own times; yet, ironically, these hatreds are precisely what disturb and upset her about what she views as the future. In response to a questionnaire presented to numerous writers, artists, thinkers, and poets in 1929 in the *Little Review,* Butts sounds very contemporary. When asked, "What do you fear most from the future?" her reply is "'Envy, hatred, malice and all uncharitableness' become a new morality,"[53] a very prophetic response in light of how the twentieth century has developed. However, in the two final questions, "What is your world view? (Are you a reasonable being in a reasonable scheme?)" and "Why do you go on living?" her answers, as usual, offer those Blakean contraries or Yeatsian opposites suggesting both hope and despair:

> 9. In moments of depression count myself a reasonable being in an unreasonable world. Am sure that in default of a "miracle"—which I don't consider impossible—the worst is coming to our civilization. Have a private view of the universe which does not seem to be reasonable, or "scientifically true," but which works for me, refreshes and delights me. I go by that, watch events and try not to twist them to fit.
> 10. Mainly out of good and extreme curiosity, on which depends a wish to see if the "miracle" referred to above will come in my time, or is susceptible at all to human encouragement.[54]

Vacillating between social worlds of the Paris demimonde and the country gentry with whom she was raised, Butts's sensibility is a very curious one. No matter how contrary or extreme her views seem, she radiates a sincerity about nature, ritual, the ancient past and its magic, and a sense that a return to this past with its worship of the natural world offers a healing and a solace from the terrors of "the machine of civilization."[55] In *Warning to Hikers* Butts is an activist fiercely protecting what she deems sacred from modern society.

This fierce sense of protectiveness is perhaps best described in her poem "Corfe," written some time in the 1920s about Corfe Castle in Dorset and included in Louis Zukofsky's *An "Objectivists" Anthology* (also published in 1932). Corfe Castle, its history, and its ability to survive the ravages of time and mankind represent what Butts is saying not only in *Warning to Hikers* but also in *Death of Felicity Taverner:* whatever the cost the *natural* must be preserved. The imagery of "Corfe" resonates with nearly all Butts's major themes, and its language supports the narrative development of her novel; history, myth, and ritual are our weapons against unwanted change:

> I
>
> Corfe, the hub of a wheel
> Where the green down-spokes turning
> Embrace an earth-cup of smoke and ghosts and stone.
> The sea orchestrates
> The still dance in the cup
> Danced forever,
>
> . . . .
>
> But when I remember you Corfe, I remember Delphi
> Because your history also is a mystery of God.
> "And God is no blind man and God is our father's"
> But like lovers
> Your cup is full of the courts of other princes
> Disrupting you.
>
> . . . .
>
> III
>
> God Keep the Hollow Land from all wrong!
> God Keep the Hollow Land going strong![56]

Echoing the Romantic sublime, Blakean contraries, a Yeatsian apocalyptic vision, and the voice of T. S. Eliot, Butts manages in "Corfe" to cover the territory which is of such great passion and concern to her. Anticipating the destruction of nature and its essence of "visible Pan," she offers a call to preserve what she deems most precious and sacred. In section 1, Butts introduces Corfe as the center of the natural world, "the hub of the wheel," embracing and containing the past, the present and eternity—all time. When her "sea orchestrates / The still dance in the cup / Danced forever," it recalls

Yeats's dance in "Among School Children" and perhaps anticipates Eliot's "still point of the turning world" (which would not appear until "Burnt Norton" in 1935). In this section, Butts creates a way for nature to act as the center of the eternal, eliciting ancient memories, "I remember Delphi," and equating the history of those memories and the worship of nature with "the mystery of God." The obvious intrusion of the modern world disrupts that stillness "full of the courts of other princes," while the "sacred wood" in its sublime possession of light and dark, fear and beauty initiates its royalty, its "players" or "princes"—those with a kinship to the land who are authentic participants in its secrets. By playing out its "shift of potencies" on a "night without a moon," the "sacred wood" moves from darkness to light as the "black ball" is thrown in and the "gold ball" is thrown out. Here we see Butts's optimism based on the natural world and the influence again of Frazer and Harrison as the shift in vision moves from despair to hope in the cycles of the natural world—birth, death, rebirth.

In section 2, Butts gives us humankind, treading down the hill but unable to "wear it down." Certainly echoes of Gerard Manley Hopkins' "God's Grandeur" come to mind. His sanctity of God's natural world clearly reflects that of Butts, but from a more orthodox position. By section 3, Butts now pleads that "God keep the Hollow Land from all wrong! / God keep the Hollow Land going strong!" Referring to a personal experience which she relates in *The Crystal Cabinet,* her initiates to the cult of nature echo the plea, and the allusion to Blake's poem of the same name transforms his crystal cabinet into "a glass world made out of grass," a natural world where all the secrets of eternity may be found. Speaking directly to her God, her creator of this incredible natural world, Butts begs for the destruction of progress and its intrusion by arming the "sacred wood" against its interlopers and against the technology which threatens its existence:

> Blot out the landscape and destroy the train.
> Turn back our folk from it, we hate the lot
> Turn the American and turn the Scot;
>
> . . . .
>
> Make many slugs where the stranger goes
> Better than barbed wire the briar rose;
>
> . . . .
>
> Taboo the barrows, encourage ghosts.
> Arm the rabbits with tigers' teeth
> Serpents shoot from the soil beneath
> By pain in belly and foot and mouth
> Keep them out of our sacred south.

The word "our" is key to understanding Butts's position. Here Butts gives us in poetry what she clearly delineates in prose in *Warning to Hikers*. This is the "sacred wood" of the country gentry: Butts and her characters whose kinship to the land is real and who seek to preserve its beauty and sanctity. Any false attempts to intrude will be easily foiled because only those who understand the darkness of nature as well as its beauty know how to cope; all others will be easily frightened away. Butts then joins her novel *Death of Felicity Taverner* to her poem and her essay.

Ultimately, the land is of primary concern, and Boris, who seems hurt and dislocated in *Imaginary Letters,* functions in *Death of Felicity Taverner* as the instrument to aid the initiates on their quest and to prevent them from being personally tainted with the crime. Together, Boris and nature effect the cure. Butts's narrator in *Imaginary Letters* senses that Boris is weak and needy, yet the Boris of *Death of Felicity Taverner* has shed his weakness and turns fearless as he brings the plot to conclusion in this later tale. Unlike *Armed with Madness,* both *Imaginary Letters* and *Death of Felicity Taverner* follow a straightforward narrative. The epistolary form of the letters progresses in linear, chronological fashion. With a concession to several flashbacks, the plot of *Death of Felicity Taverner* basically follows linear form and engages us with these characters we already feel we know. Beginning in the tradition of an intellectual detective story with Felicity's death, the plot progresses smoothly until Boris enters the novel with feelings of resentment for the Taverners' way of life. When he decides that Kralin represents evil to him as well as to them, he creates a twist in the plot. Again, Butts interjects a sense of distance between story and reader. No longer a pure detective story, *Death of Felicity Taverner* shifts to ritual form, and the form gives external order and meaning to events that follow. In this way, Butts removes the murder from the reality of aggression and horror and shifts readers' sensibilities so that they may view it as an inevitable outcome of ritual form: art, not reality. Once Boris makes his decision, the narrative moves swiftly to conclusion.

If *Imaginary Letters* begins with a desperate longing for love and compassion, the hatred and malice she so feared in civilization develops in *Death of Felicity Taverner.* However, Butts is exploring and expanding the meaning of ritual, as Jane Harrison saw it, and is transforming its structure to serve her narrative framework. In his memorial lecture on Harrison, Gilbert Murray explains that "[s]he [Harrison] would try to penetrate the real purpose or meaning of a horrible practice like omophagia, or the tearing and devouring of live beasts, and almost forget the fact in the idea, or in what she supposed to be the idea, which informed it."[57] In a similar manner, Butts raises the murder of Kralin to the level of ritual sacrifice to play down the horror of the act; in effect, the purpose of "purging" helps her and her characters to "forget the fact in the idea, or in what she supposed to be the idea, which informed it."

Finally, in *Warning to Hikers* Butts ends her environmentalist plea with a phrase from John Keats's "La Belle Dame Sans Merci" that sums up what she sees as the results or repercussions of the civilized world's intrusion on her sacred land. Without such outrage and concern, Butts felt, there would be "Quiet in the woods. They can be very quiet when a wind from nowhere lifts in the tree-tops and through the pine-needles clashing the noise of a harp runs down the trunks into the earth. *And no birds sing.*"[58] It is a very real and believable plea in a century that has observed progress continue to destroy her "virgin earth." Deprivation of the richness and music of nature would place her completely in the position of Boris. Instead, the Taverners, and Butts herself, cling to their "memory in the blood" as primary sustenance and meaning.

From the moment we meet the Boris of *Imaginary Letters,* we sense the significance of his role because Butts's letter writer intimates that her relationship with Boris is the spark which initiates and drives her creative abilities. When he reappears in *Death of Felicity Taverner,* Boris transforms from a metaphorical object/muse into a more symbolic instrument of fate, a character who will indeed act on the concerns Butts details in her essay *Warning to Hikers.* These three works are linked in theme and symbol. The muse simply metamorphoses into the active instrument of justice, as Butts sees it, violent and troubling though its actions may be. In *Warning to Hikers* Butts tells us that in the "sanctuary" of nature, humanity leaves a "dirty little trail"; however, "[m]an's baseness can renew and rebuild itself, but not inside the precinct of the sanctuary. It must be withdrawn for that into its own breeding-place."[59] Boris and Kralin, in effect, withdraw into their "own breeding-place" when they confront each other; killer and killed both become at once savior and scapegoat. Butts's Nature has its "own breeding-place," and it can renew itself, defend itself, and terrorize people with its "earthquakes and tidal waves." These are the "dreadful works he [man] calls God's act or hand."[60]

We visualize these terrors in Nature's instinctive defense of itself in section three of "Corfe" when Butts has Nature cast its spell by preparing rabbits, snakes, lobsters, and bees for battle. In its struggle against the unnatural intrusions of humankind, Nature, along with Butts and her characters, turns violent, dark, and unsettling, in keeping with the themes we encountered in *The Crystal Cabinet.* Keying in on the fierce protectiveness of nature, Butts identifies Boris's pernicious actions as an organic outgrowth of a true defender of the natural world. Whatever the cost, the land and the way of life must be preserved, and Boris and the Taverners are willing to accept this violence because they see it as a natural, inherent response; they embrace violence because it serves a higher end. Like the natural world, Boris and friends see their actions as ritual, "[c]hanges and transformations and vengeances appropriate to the situation."[61] The three works considered here and "Corfe" unify a darker and more troubling aspect of Butts's fiction by combining, transforming, and elevating murder into ritual preservation.

CHAPTER FIVE

"Brightness Falls": Three Collections of Short Stories

"a shift of potencies"

Our spiritual consciousness acts through the will and its instruments upon material objects, in order to produce changes which will result in the establishment of the new conditions of consciousness which we wish. This is the definition of Magick.

—Aleister Crowley, *Confessions* 125

Mary Butts published three collections of short stories: *Speed the Plough (1923), Several Occasions* (1932), and *Last Stories* (1938), issued posthumously at Bryher's instigation.[1] The stories, filled with daimons and demons in the form of witches, goddesses, and searching young men, echo the ideas presented in her longer works. Criticism of Butts's short stories, both that of her contemporaries and more recent reviewers, is often as cryptic as her work; however, many critics concur that her genius lies in her ability to write in the short story form. Gerrit Lansing has written in a letter: "It is arguable that in the form of the short story Mary Butts's genius found its most felicitous and satisfactory expression."[2] John Ashbery's comments in his preface to the 1992 American edition of her stories once again become relevant. Ashbery discusses why her stories make her seem our contemporary with "her startling ellipses, especially in conversations; her drastic cutting in the cinematic sense; and her technique of collaging bits of poetry and popular song lyrics . . . into the narratives," her treatment of characters who can be "*wired* in a very 1990s way—the homosexual ones, for instance, whom she treats with a sympathy and openness astonishing for the England of her time," while leaving us with "an impression of dazzle, of magic."[3]

Reviews of her contemporaries range from the high praise of J. C. Squire, who considered Butts "one of the very best" of the contemporary artists,[4] comparing her with James Joyce, Henry James, Katherine Mansfield, and Marcel Proust, to Rose Macaulay's mixed appraisal: "that touch of brilliance which makes one overlook a good many weaknesses. . . . She is often crude, very often strained, exaggerated, untrue; sometimes . . . decidedly vulgar, continually lacking in lucidity."[5] In an almost incomprehensible review of *Speed the Plough and Other Stories* in 1923, Glenway Wescott identifies one of the most significant flaws of her short stories when he claims that they "present no solution and no surcease";[6] ironically, this observation provides one of the keys to her modernism. In Rhys Davies's review of *Last Stories,* he claims she had "the vision of a seer . . . she tried to convey the activities of forces unknown to the ordinary senses; magical forces."[7] No matter what opinion reviewers had or have of her stories, and whether or not one feels that her genius rings truer in the complexity of her longer works, there seems to be a consensus that both the stories and their effects offer a sense of magic.

Mary Butts studied and practiced magic with a serious interest in how it could affect and alter experience and consciousness and was interested in its mystical purpose of attempting to establish contact with higher spiritual realities. When she met Aleister Crowley ("The Great Beast") in the early 1920s, the intensity of her interest in magic deepened. Although Butts was already familiar with magic and the occult, he instructed her in some of his own magical practices. She, however, was not overly impressed with him and commented in 1921 that "Alastair [*sic*] is an assistance, not a road nor a card."[8] Crowley's basic definition of *Magick* as a means to create a new reality appears in his book *Magick in Theory and Practice,* his manual for those who wish to practice this perilous art. He claims that the definition of Magick is "the Science and Art of causing Change to occur in conformity with Will."[9] Although Crowley calls Butts a "large, white, red-haired maggot" in response to her relationship with Cecil Maitland, he acknowledges her assistance in the completion of his work on *Magick* and expresses his gratitude to her for her help in "indicating a large number of subjects which I had not discussed."[10] Her contact with Crowley's ideas, then, not only enhanced his thinking about magic but also apparently became incorporated into her own thinking and writing about magic and its consequences in both the real world and the fictional world of Butts's characters.

We know that Butts met Cecil Maitland in 1919, who then introduced her to Aleister Crowley and his occult group, and that she spent the summer of 1921 with Maitland at Crowley's abbey in Cefalu, Italy. Robert H. Byington and Glen E. Morgan note that Mary and Cecil were "initiated into Crowley's cult, participated in any number of bizarre, sometimes orgiastic, rites, and departed for Paris and London in the fall visibly shaken and exhausted by the experience."[11] In spite of the difficult and somewhat mysterious circumstances surrounding this visit, Butts was influenced by Crowley's thought, and she and Maitland practiced black magic in their apartment in Paris.[12] Although Butts eventually severed the relationship with Crowley, her curiosity about the practice of magic and the ceremonies surrounding the occult remained a major interest and concern.

By the time Butts was introduced to Crowley, she had already read Jane Harrison's *Epilegomena and Themis* and would have combined Crowley's idea of willing change with Harrison's view. Harrison saw magic as arising "primarily from a *dromenon,* a rite which emphasizes, and aims at inducing, man's collective desire for union with or dominion over outside powers."[13] Butts was also in agreement with Harrison that the Great Mother preceded the male divinities, and she looks to the goddess when she searches for her primal past, for the secret wisdom lodged in racial memory.

How one brings about change, according to Butts, has to do more with the supernatural and the past than with the present. In an article written for *The Bookman* in 1933, Butts examines the supernatural in English fiction, explaining her sense of the occult and the supernatural, whose "success depends on evocation, a state . . . of wonder in its rarest sense, of *clarté,* of a universe enlarged."[14] Butts never tries to prove a case; she merely offers us a glimpse into the universe she conjures in her own magical and supernatural world. Virgil Thomson called her "the storm goddess" who could "stir up others with drink and drugs and magic incantations"; he also observed that "[t]here was no evil in her; her magic was all tied up to religion and great poetry."[15]

As a great admirer of the ghost stories of popular writers of her times, particularly M. R. James, Butts senses the reality of supernatural influences in stories like "With and Without Buttons," and especially in "Mappa Mundi" from *Last Stories,* in which a young American boy in Paris completely disappears, leaving only a shadow of himself to haunt those who understand the underworld of Paris.[16] Like many of her stories, it is a cautionary tale, a parable warning those unfamiliar with what she terms "the other side of the shadows" to be careful of their footing in this city of "profound reserves." In this sense Butts is what Frank Baker calls a "psychic writer,"[17] always exploring two worlds, both very much a reality to her and her characters. As she was later to explain in *Traps for Unbelievers,* magic "has something to do with a sense of the invisible, the non-existent in a scientific sense, relations between things of a different order: the moon and a stone, the sea and a piece of wood, women and fish."[18]

The desire to wield magical power generally comes from a female character, one who is at once woman and goddess. Butts's search for this goddess capable of affecting change is, in effect, a quest for the storehouse of racial memories. Through these memories the character moves easily between two worlds, rending the veil separating them. The interconnection of racial memories and numinous forces allows the character to call up her goddess heritage at any given moment. One example of such magic appears in "Widdershins," a curious story from *Several Occasions* that purports to have a world-wounded, over forty, male mystic as its central figure. Butts's narrator tells us that Dick Tressider was a martyr of reality who "needed" magic but did not understand that "what he wanted was magic." He has a desire to hold on to the "moment of pure being, the co-ordination of power," but he is not quite able to pull it off: "What he wanted to happen was for some man to say a word of power which should evoke this state, everywhere, not by any process, but in the twinkling of an eye. This is magic."[19] Dick has been a soldier and has seen what happens to "civilized man"; his longing is sincere, and he manages to have an out-of-body experience on his way to visit his friend Daphne, but his desire seems somewhat forced, too self-conscious, and he is frustrated and unsuccessful in his quest.

The word *widdershins* is a variation on *withershins,* which the *Oxford English Dictionary* defines as "a direction opposite to the usual, the wrong way"; "in a direction contrary to the apparent course of the sun (considered as unlucky or causing disaster)." Interestingly, "Widdershins" was first published in Ford Madox Ford's *Transatlantic Review* in March of 1924 under the title "Deosil." This word, a variation of *deasil* and in direct opposition to *widdershins,* is defined as "righthandwise, towards the right . . . in the same direction as the hands of a clock or the apparent course of the sun (a practice considered auspicious by the Celts)."[20] The title's change to one of opposed meaning by the time it appears in *Several Occasions* in 1932 suggests that Butts had a change of mind about Dick Tressider's journey. Dick is ineffective and tries far too hard to induce a state which comes naturally to a female with mythic origins.

When Dick arrives at Daphne's, she is preparing for a night on the town. Her name and dress suggest, however, that she is part of myth and nature and magic. Daphne, dressed in green and white with crystal at her ears and waist and a wreath of bright green laurel leaves on her head, is "like a tree in glory" (200). Because she blends her natural self with the painted self of society, Dick wants to swear at her and even hit her; he thinks she is turning in the wrong direction toward a false paradise. When Daphne invites him to join her at a party on Saturday, Dick responds, "I'm afraid I should be out of place. You would find my change of values too complete" (202).

Daphne, however, draws on her goddess heritage and the implication is that she can move from one world to the other with ease; she is not limited to a single time or place, nor is she confined by either place. She tells him, "There are several Paradises, Dick. Me for this Paradise" (202). The suggestion from Dick's point of view is that Daphne has succumbed to Apollo's wiles; she has accepted his lures and has turned to an earthly paradise. From Butts's view, however, we sense that Daphne knows more than Dick. Even though Daphne paints her face, when she dresses herself in the colors and forms of nature, the laurel leaves on her head "were like the leaves of no earthly laurel" (201). Butts intimates that Dick, wounded, lost, and longing, must find a way, which Daphne knows innately, to live in both worlds—the world of reality, or the earthly paradise, and the world of magic and myth.

As we have seen, the notion of the goddess and her female heritage plays an important role throughout Butts's work, and perhaps more specifically in the short stories. Christine Downing in *The Goddess: Mythical Images of the Feminine* explains this affirmation within the feminine:

> Recognition of the many goddesses that inform one's life also helps protect one against inflationary identifications and against the sense of being swallowed up by some fatally determining mythic pattern. The goddesses also seem to find ways of reminding us that they are indeed numinous forces, never reducible to our attempts at psychological interpretation.[21]

Butts's females/goddesses clearly identify with their past, or as Downing puts it, "I sensed that the pull to Her was a pull to an ancient source."[22] Butts discerned this from the beginning of her childhood. She was not a feminist by today's definitions, but she realized and acknowledged early on that, as Downing states, "To be fed only male images of the divine is to be badly malnourished. We are starved for images which recognize the sacredness of the feminine and the complexity, richness and nurturing power of female energy."[23] Butts drew on this energy and this primal past as a way to fight the demons she found in everyday life, and many of her stories are clearly avowals of that role of women. Her female protagonists look to a feminine archetype in which they find a numinous source and center. They call up a heritage that offers a universe at once organic, sacred, and whole.

In "With and Without Buttons" (*Last Stories* 1938), "Brightness Falls" (*Several Occasions* 1932), and "From Altar to Chimney-piece" (*Last Stories),* the magic of the goddess source decidedly plays a significant role. Although the females in each story are extremely different, the idea of magic (the ability to make things happen, or as Crowley claims, "causing Change to occur in conformity with Will") is clear and concise. "With and Without Buttons" is perhaps one of Butts's stories most influenced by M. R. James's ghost stories infused with the supernatural. It is also one of Butts's more playful tales in the sense that the characters are not completely aware of their power and find themselves surprised with the outcome of the prank they play on their neighbor.

Trenchard in "With and Without Buttons" is a man who possesses a "faith of disbelief" (22). Entrenched in his notion of "pseudo-rationalisations," he cannot hear the penetrating sound of "earth breathing silently, a female power asleep" (23). His next-door neighbors in this remote village of Kent are two sisters who determine to try his faith of disbelief by planting gloves (with and without buttons), found in a box in their shared attic, throughout his home, pretending that they arrived via some supernatural force.

This story is a willing of change, a playing at magic. The sisters think that they can alter Trenchard's belief, and by the end of the story he is truly overwhelmed by the otherworldly experience. What is significant here, however, is that the sisters call up these forces without realizing their own power. Once they plant a single glove, the gloves begin to appear at various places by themselves. The sisters also uncover a tale about the ghost of a woman whose decaying petticoat flies through the attic and haunts the house of Trenchard and the sisters. By the end of the story, what began as a prank to dispel Trenchard's disbelief ends with a certainty of supernatural forces. There is the stench of the other world called up by the petticoat and there are the gloves, some with buttons (closed to supernatural notions) and some without buttons (open to ideas)—all lying side-by-side.

The suggestion here of the skins (gloves) and the stench they leave behind—the story ends with the line, "But, oh God, it was the smell of it . . ." (38)—is part of what Butts identifies as "'Elementals." This is an ancient belief in the "animal-thing, seen, heard and smelt, but impervious to touch and infecting like a poison"[24] Butts compares such elementals to Ariel and Caliban, spirits that evoke in humans the "fear that there is animal life outside the animals he knows, less than human life and more, and infinitely malignant."[25] In "With and Without Buttons" the skins of the gloves become elementals revealing the supernatural life outside the "skins, furs, shells and feathers of our earth,"[26] very convincing not only to Trenchard but also to the sisters.

By willing a change, the sisters perform a kind of magic. They invoke the powers of their sex, from witches to goddesses, and succeed in proving to Trenchard, and surprisingly to themselves, that these forces exist in the real world. It is a will to power, what they identify early in the story as "the power women sometimes want to have over men, the pure, not erotic power, whose point is that it shall have nothing to do with sex" (24).

The secret power of women is also the focus of "Brightness Falls." Taking her title from a song by Thomas Nashe, "Adieu; farewell earth's bliss," in his play *Summer's Last Will and Testament,* Butts manipulates the various interpretations of Nashe's song, examining the transience of human life and pleasures. She further suggests a "fall" from the air of something supernatural and otherworldly. Butts's male narrator begins, "There is no head or tail to this story, except that it happened. On the other hand, how does one know that anything happened?" (203). These comments set the tone for the entire story, since we are never exactly certain what takes place. Here Butts's male narrator struggles with the relationship between men and women and claims that ultimately men "hang together against our women, and not wholly from rational reasons. All one finally discovers is that, when they urge us, the loveliest and wisest become all one with the slut" (203).

Max is married, happily it seems, to Parmys, and he states that "over our marriage there was some occult link" (204), "[l]ike a separate quality—detached. It gave us some strange moments, which were perhaps our best. It was like a place, slightly to the right or left of where you are going, that marches with you; that is occasionally lit up from inside" (205). However, this link, which ignites their passion initially, begins to worry Max when Parmys tells him it is the "key" to their love. From this point on, we know that Parmys is witch and goddess; she loves "chinese balls" and "witch balls" and claims to see herself and whoever is with her when she looks into them, knowing there are places "about like that." Parmys' interest, however, focuses on her moon goddess friend, Cynthia, with whom she spends her evenings dancing and going to parties in the "eye of the world" (206).

Cynthia, of course, is one of the names of the goddess Artemis, the goddess of the hunt, the moon, unmarried women, and chastity. Her parallel on the dark side of the moon is Hecate, and by using the name Cynthia and identifying her as a "queen and huntress" (211), Butts invites associations that indicate the uncertainty between good and evil. Parmys and Cynthia lead a secret life that Max can neither understand nor penetrate. Their relationship is surrounded by mystery, and as Max explains to the narrator, they are "overspiritualized women," and he believes them to be mixed up in some form of witchcraft, "spells, magic; all women's occupations" (204). Max admits that his "mind is not sufficiently trained to examine and explain" these sorts of things, and, as a result, he has, in a way he cannot comprehend, failed her. We come to understand that Parmys is shielding Cynthia from some inadvertent action Cynthia has taken with a strange character called Dr. Corandel, who has been hunting Cynthia. Parmys feels compelled to protect and care for Cynthia in spite of "all her high manners" because Cynthia is "innocent of heart" (210).

With the introduction of Dr. Corandel, and the seemingly meaningless play on his name with Coromandel, the spice coast at the southeastern tip of India, we are reminded of the narrator's opening statements, "There is no head or tail to this story, except that it happened. On the other hand, how does one know that anything happened?" (203). We do learn that Cynthia has been having an affair with Dr. Corandel and that Parmys doesn't approve of it "for some reason that was probably a mask for jealousy" (211). From this point, when Max next encounters Cynthia, he no longer sees her as "a queen and a huntress" (211); Cynthia and Parmys, however, retain their psychic connection and continue to commune with their goddess/priestess past. Beside Cynthia's "extreme distinction and beauty," Max notices that "Parmys looked coarse; and again that was because Parmys was like an archaic goddess stored with raw power" (213).

Stirring up their goddess/priestess power is the focus of the story. There is a sensuous interchange between Parmys and Cynthia, and Max tells us that they needed him to "mind them." What exactly takes place, we never fully understand. The magic, supernatural power they possess, as witches and goddesses capable of changing and shaping experience, somehow seems to lift them out of this world, and Butts's notion of living in two worlds at once comes into focus again. Max narrates the experience:

> I saw her [Parmys] take her left wrist, putting her arm round her, holding in her right hand Cynthia's right hand. "Look now," she said, "look again. It is here." Her voice was like strings of gold and silver, love and something detached, or even matter of fact. . . . They took a step forward; indeed, through all of this were walking very slowly across the grass, into the wind, I beside them. But this is true also, that I couldn't stay beside them, because they were half in, half out of another world. Also, they changed. Before there had been Parmys resolute, and Cynthia distressed; now there were two shapes, abstractions. (214)

Although Max manages to walk "up to and along with a place I could see in flashes. Up to and along with" (215), he remains divided from the magic of the experience. Parmys and Cynthia are attempting to use their power to effect change, to perform magic and correct the situation between Cynthia and Corandel, but although Max sees part of what they see, he cannot explain it. Since Max is the narrator of the event, we also cannot see what takes place, and the mystery of these two "charming" and "enchanted" children, "drenched with some abnormal radiance" (216) remains indecipherable to us as well, but we sense it is what Butts identifies as "one description of a state evoked, of consciousness enlarged."[27] By the end of the story, Parmys and Cynthia appear physically refreshed by the experience, and we know that we have been invited to skim the edges of a mystical and magical experience without understanding what that experience was or how to conjure it for ourselves. Parmys and Cynthia invoke their goddess past to move temporarily out of reality, to let their brightness fall over the event so that they can maintain the upper hand they possess as initiates of a secret power they are just beginning to discover.

The suggestion of the occult and secret rites is the focus of another enigmatic story "From Altar to Chimney-piece" (*Last Stories* 1938), a story Jascha Kessler calls her "Jamesian story about evil."[28] This frightening tale carefully blends biographical events with occult secrets, the sacred and the profane, to filter a darker view of Butts's contemporaries and their activities. In the story, set in Paris, Cherry, Butts's young, female character ripe for any encounter, takes on the role of witch, similar to that of Judy in *Ashe of Rings*. She is no longer the mysterious but beneficial daimon with connections to that other world; instead, like Judy, she calls up the dark powers of her race as she captures and attempts to destroy Vincent, the story's narrator. After a long, slow introduction, uncharacteristic of Butts, we learn that Vincent is near forty, a Cornish gentlemen, and "a piece of middle-aged war breakage" (244),

> lacking at any time the power to seize life by the throat and strangle it into submission, he was one of those who work joyfully for whatever in their age is best. The stuff out of which the "perfect, gentle knight" was made; and at the time, in war or medicine, in government or agriculture, in works of organisation or mercy—a man who needed, for his full development, a law, a worship, if possible a congregation and a church. At best, a hero. (239)

In this passage Butts reveals some of her major concerns for what is missing in civilization just as in *Traps for Unbelievers* she expresses her concern for the loss of any central "belief or practice of religion, organised or private."[29] Religion, "what has up to now been considered as necessary as air,"[30] has gone out of fashion as have the values of this "gentle knight," and for Butts it is essential to reconnect with ancient deities, Christian or pagan or both.

During the second half of the nineteenth century, Darwinism had caused a serious spiritual crisis and from that crisis an interest arose in replacing what was lost. Madame Blavatsky, the Theosophical Society, Rosicrucianism, and the Hermetic Order of the Golden Dawn, for example, provided for some a satisfaction for the spiritual cravings that had developed. By the early twentieth century, the renewed interest in spirituality was a vital element of modernist thought, and investigation into the occult, with its promise of secret wisdom, became part of the world of artists and poets. Butts, in "From Altar to Chimney-piece," offers a glimpse into a society trying to understand the loss of spiritual values and moving in directions contrary to what she feels the practice of occultism and spiritualism should be.

Mircea Eliade's word for such loss is "desacralization." In his discussion of the sacred and the profane, Eliade claims that "desacralization pervades the entire experience of the nonreligious man of modern societies and that, in consequence, he finds it increasingly difficult to rediscover the existential dimensions of religious man in the archaic societies." These archaic men, tended to live "as much as possible in the sacred or in close proximity to consecrated objects."[31] Eliade claims that for "primitives as for the man of all pre-modern societies, the *sacred* is equivalent to a *power,* and, in the last analysis, to *reality.*"[32] Interestingly, Butts, in delineating her concerns for modern man, examines what occurs when man is not imaginative enough to understand the role of the sacred and profane in his existence. What happens, Butts suggests, is that he could become a "crank," merely playing at the specifics of the ritual game. He has lost his connection to the past and interprets the valid aspects of magic and ritual in terms of some "pseudo-science" for which meaning has been lost and distorted.

All these concerns reach a culmination in "From Altar to Chimneypiece." After Vincent becomes enchanted by the youth and exuberance of the young, free-spirited American girl living in Paris and surrounded by mystery, his life begins to unravel even more. Vincent has passed his own youth on "Vimy Ridge, in hospital and on the Somme" (242) and foolishly believes he can recapture some of that youth by marrying Cherry and bringing her back to his homeland. Cherry, however, has become involved with a secret cult group, who meet regularly "between Montparnasse and the Boulevard St. Germain" (248), at the home of Miss Van Norden, an old woman sorceress who "knows nothing of her circle" and who "sees herself as the *salonnière*—her house full of young men of genius. And how it amuses them!" (260). Miss Van Norden is modeled, of course, on Gertrude Stein. This portrait is Butts's comment on Stein's salon in Paris as a pretentious ritual worship of art, "[a]ll gossip or the latest experiments in the Arts" (253). In a letter to Hugh Ross Williamson in 1932, Butts discloses her feelings about Gertrude Stein's writing and how her society, according to Butts, reflected the destructive elements of modern society:

> I've finished today a song story (50 pages), whose real title is 'The Gertrude-Stein-Song'. . . . In fact, its *all* true, but nicely arranged. Of course, I had to hide who it was,—fairly well—but I'd like to learn that depraved old creature not to monkey with the English language! As you may gather, I think the story is a Wow. . . . Its all about the Surrealistes and their cult of the cruel and the obscene, all about 'le culte du Moi' and living entirely in your sub-consciousness, and what happens when you do. . . .[33]

Her words indicate Butts's dislike for popular artistic movements and emphasize the importance of Butts's sense of style. As mentioned in chapter 2, by the 1930s Butts had become disenchanted with Joyce and his attempts to "reproduce half-conscious thinking"; Stein had taken stylistic experimentation even further, and Butts did not approve. For Butts, the practice of one's art was as sacred as her reverence for the natural world. It may be acceptable to tamper in minor ways with language in order to explore consciousness, but her feelings about Stein's "experiments in the Arts" tells us that, according to Butts, Stein had gone too far, thus diminishing art rather than enhancing it. Still, "From Altar to Chimney-piece" is a brutal evaluation of Stein and her salon. It stresses the emphasis that Butts placed on the value of creating art that is true and honest, an art that may be difficult but one that rewards with the expression of a distinctive imagination.

Once Cherry convinces Vincent to make a visit to her, Cherry's young American and French friends meet in a sort of mindless ritual dance:

> The art of the latter was based partly on a mystical reliance on the subconscious, partly on extreme Communist theory. In essence a belief in magic—"*Le Moi est le Verbe, et le Verbe c'est Dieu.*" In practice, a measured brutality, a logic of destruction all somehow made elegant, flashed with "chic" blythe qualities of the french [*sic*] mind, its instinct for proportion—even in the realm of chaos and old night. While for reasons Vincent could not make out, the French who knew everything and the Americans who knew nothing, met, at the house of the old woman in a kind of uneasy dance. (248)

None of the participants seems comfortable with the dance as they move around the room, looking "up at the celebrated collection of pictures, or down to the tables at books and manuscripts and *objets d'art* . . . counterclockwise" (252). To Vincent, it all seems too "automatic," yet in the room he senses there is a shared secret, "even a mysticism" (254), something known to all but him.

Once Cherry turns down Vincent's proposal of marriage, he, still believing that she "would have restored full life to him" and that he could have taught her not to fear life, visits a "Frenchwoman of distinction who knew everything that happened in Paris" (257). From her he learns that the young Frenchmen at the old woman's house are a "very bad lot indeed" (257), attempting to copy the "principles and practices of Revolutionary Russia" (257). From her novels, we know Butts's sympathies are not with the revolution, and these young men, then, are described as "horrible," "playing obscene practical jokes; they had a cult of cruelty—psychological cruelty; and those whose nerves would stand it made a study and a practice of physical torture. . . . They had a system of blackmail which helped them to live . . . a protest against bourgeois morality" (257). In addition, what made their actions and beliefs intolerable to Vincent and to Butts, we assume, "was their spirit of which they boasted of cold scientific inquiry" (257) and "[i]n Art, a cult of the arbitrary use of words to express the private dream" (257–58). If Butts is characterizing and criticizing Gertrude Stein and her salon in this story, she adds a critique of Aleister Crowley's approach to life and his examination of the occult as well; in fact, Jascha Kessler sees the story as "the cathartic by which she purged herself of her former fascination with the labyrinth of the Magus."[34] Indeed, the ugliness of the story must have served to help her move out of the destructive black magic practiced by the enigmatic Crowley and his group.

The wise Frenchwoman in the tale explains to Vincent that the women who link themselves to the group, who "pretend to understand and adore what they are about," are the kind of young woman "who likes to be hurt" (258), and this is how Cherry is involved. To her and her friends, Vincent is an idiot, a joke, and when she lets Vincent see this side of her, he no longer sees her as Artemis the hunter; she now appears to have the look of the hunted.

The hunter in this tale is Blaise Boissevan, one of the worst of the young men hanging around the salon and fairly reminiscent of Crowley, the Great Beast himself. Blaise and these evil young men make it their business to seduce young daughters of the bourgeoisie, get them pregnant, and then "there must be an abortion," leading the young women to suicide or death. The Frenchwoman tells Vincent that of the young women she knew, one was in a madhouse, one a cripple for life, and another "like one hypnotised" (259). Blaise had sent one of them out on to the streets to solicit for him, and she later killed herself, leaving a letter praising him and saying "they were all pioneers of a new civilisation" (259). We sense from this description of Blaise and his followers that Butts is penetrating the depths of this underworld and re-creating some of the "profligacy and vice" she had encountered at Crowley's Abbey of Thelema where the doctrine "Do what thou wilt shall be the whole of the law."[35]

Blaise, whose young women "usually die one way [or] another" (259), practices spells, and some of them are based on a desecration of the communion Host. Once we learn this, the title "From Altar to Chimney-piece" falls into place. On his final visit to the old sorceress, Miss Van Norden, Vincent notices on the cabinets a series of shining objects which he recognizes as "frames, supports, stands for the ciborium, the box—in this case a round of hollow glass, fixed on to the disk—to hold the wafers of the Host," now "made into delightful chimney-piece ornaments" (264).[36] The old woman explains that they are from Spain and the only remnant of their sanctity is the Greek letter Chi painted in blue: "She picked up one and began to rub it on a filthy handkerchief of khaki cotton, on which she spat.

The old paint was dry and cracked and the signature of Christ rubbed off at a touch" (264). Here Butts's concerns for spirituality and its deterioration into degradation and profanity reach their culmination. Ritual has been desecrated, desacralized by those who "play" at magic, black magic, but without a true understanding of spiritual connections. Butts's goddess, who in this tale wants a master, is led astray by such magic, and the story ends with Cherry "gone off somewhere" with Blaise, and Vincent finally understands. However, as with most of Butts's stories, we are not entirely clear what Vincent has come to understand. We only know we have been offered a glimpse into the darker side of the moon where the sickness of the brilliant children is "part of the world's sickness" (262), or as Butts explains in *Traps for Unbelievers*, "man is not God, and it is no use pretending that he is."[37] Vincent sees in them the curse of their civilization and wishes "his own wounds had won a better world for them, a world wherein they would not have found it possible to invent the form of life they had" (262), again the Christ image so typical of war literature appears. As in *Armed with Madness* we see children playing at reality, re-creating values and re-inventing meaning. In this tale, it has turned as dark as one could expect of a world controlled by lost children.[38]

This theme replays itself in a somewhat different fashion in "Friendship's Garland" from *Several Occasions*. Here the magical becomes linked to nature and its mystery. Cesca, the narrator, and her friend Zoe are once again children caught in a society that is sick, nasty, and vicious. Identified as "they," or "[i]ntelligences without imagination," the members of this society see Zoe and Cesca as the "hunted and innocent" (273). This story is a metaphor for modern life, pitting the material against the spiritual, experience against youth, corruption against innocence. The temple of this wasteland of modern society is a gathering place called The Craven where there is "no nature at all. These things are not natural, marble like cheese, red velvet, and plaster gilt" (275). Zoe and Cesca are hounded by members of this group who "could not love themselves" (273) and who make it their life's work to insult, to shame, "[t]o be rich—to be *rangé*—to be cute; to cut your friends—to suffer for nothing—to be a cad" (279). Carlo and his sister are the priests of this temple and make life miserable for Zoe and Cesca. Zoe is strong and can fight against these forces; Cesca knows how to "make herself invisible" (274), and this ability becomes her redemption.

After being badgered by Carlo and his sister, Cesca wants "a sanctity to turn on like a tap. I felt myself growing old, my face greasy and stretching under its make-up" (280). Cesca must become "invisible" to this world in order to escape it, and thus Butts must find a way out. She does so by calling up a vision once Cesca returns home and finds a mystical satisfaction in the trees just outside her room. Seeing the room as if it is on fire, Cesca looks outside to view the leaves that were "fiery green tongues," reminding us of Pentecost and tongues of fire and thereby suggesting a sense of renewal and rebirth. She becomes "conscious of the movement of the earth through space" (281), and the next time she looks into the mirror her face is "half old, like a child recovering from a sickness" (281). We view Cesca's epiphany, a magic willing of change, as protection from the wasteland she longs to escape. Like Daphne running from the rape of Apollo, Cesca becomes one with the tree and its sanctity: "I saw that it was also myself" (282), and she undergoes a rebirth. Her final glimpse into the mirror reveals she has been transformed by the sacred in the natural world, "I looked like a child that has been dipped in dew" (282).

This is a simple and direct story without the convolutions of some of Butts's other works. We see sick, evil society pitted against the innocence of youth, nature, and myth. One reviewer of *Several Occasions* included "Friendship's Garland" in a group of Butts's stories that "will take their place beside *The Waste Land, The Poor Man,* and *Those Barren Leaves* as documents of revelation,"[39] revelation and insight into a very wounded society searching for a way to deal with the reality of existence. Because Cesca, as ancient druid and creature of myth, is one with nature's sanctity, she is able to extricate herself from the viciousness and artificiality of The Craven and all it represents. Good and evil are clearly delineated here as Butts turns to earth's magic to bring about a spiritual change.

"The Saint" and "Madonna of the Magnificat" also examine evil, but show an evil that is an inevitable, and even necessary, part of spirituality, not the ugly darkness suggested in other stories. Instead, it is sin for clarification and knowledge, not for destruction and corruption. These two stories appear in the same early collection, *Speed the Plough,* and although they treat the subject of sin, they are lighthearted and affirming.

In "The Saint" a sixty-year-old woman has devoted years to the church and its beliefs; she has lived an exemplary life. However, as the story opens she is listening to a sermon about the fate of the devils and begins finally to question the role of sin in the Christian faith: "She had an image of life as particles sucked into the charity of God's breath, all but certain black specks her church and the preacher called the evil spirits, the enemies of souls. He was describing the choice they had made, to be outside God, Who was sorry for them, but could not, because of His justice, exercise His power" (266). In a Miltonic vision of the "angels falling out of heaven in a glittering rain" (268), the old woman wonders about the suffering of these creatures of God. She sees their children, "the imps of darkness," participating in their suffering, begins to weep for their eternal damnation, and finds comfort in a "picture of the devils' return into the kingdom and charity of God, but she found that there was no authority for this, and it tormented her" (268). Her torment extends to an Egyptian goddess whose "lights had been taken away" by the candles of the church, and this crisis of faith, of "pity and love," leads her toward a magical moment of "rapture": "The love of Christ she knew, and since Christ is God, and God is Love, that one might love God's enemies, as well as God. She went into the state of rapture, until the idea of the soul in pure union passed out and became a need for action" (269).

Rapture is a state the mystic St. Teresa of Avila experienced frequently, and she claimed it to be, as Evelyn Underhill writes, "absolutely irresistible: we cannot hinder it."[40] In this mystical vision, reminiscent of St. Teresa's, the old woman realizes that she must create change in her own life and consequently in her immediate world. Identifying with all who have sinned and suffered on earth, she attempts to extrapolate from their experience to the eternal suffering of God's "angels who suffer in exile" and who are damned for eternity. She turns her prayers not only to suffering humanity but also to these fallen sinners, who are a very real part of her world. Suffering humanity must be accounted for, and in order to understand such suffering, she determines, after a long drought in nature mirroring the drought and pain in her soul, that "[h]er prayers were no more than thunder drops. She understood that her love must make her one with the beings for whom she suffered; that to do that, she must sin" (269).

This sin is her magic, change in conformity with will. In her duties of caring for the altar vessels, she decides to steal a communion cup used only when a Bishop comes to celebrate and puts a piece of cement in its place. While she is deciding what to do with it, it becomes the "devil's cup," but this does not deter her; she must understand the nature of sin in order to understand the suffering of the world and the powers of darkness. The woman must draw from her ancient source, her *mana,* what Butts identifies as "that which gives a man or a woman potency in every act or situation."[41] Suggesting Freudian symbols, the cup becomes the life force not only of God's purity and truth but also a female symbol of life and fertility. Symbolically, the woman gives birth to a new self; she moves from one who blindly accepts faith and never strays to one whose experience is broad enough to encompass all of humanity and its facets. She sells the cup for "one-fifth of its value" and "by what she had done, she knew she had related herself to everything that there is in the world" (271). Her loneliness subsides, and she believes she has finally seen truth, a "universal God."

Balancing ideas of evil from the Gnostics to Plotinus, Butts offers a vision of connection with humanity as a whole. Without sin, one cannot understand sin; thus, the act of sinning is an enlightenment, a glimpse into the wholeness of experience. By the end of "The Saint," we are reminded of another mystic, St. Catherine of Siena, whose experiences moved her to action. In a final conversation with her Vicar, who mourns the loss of the cup and becomes despondent over its fate, the old woman senses he is wrong "to despond" because the "loss had brought him much sympathy" (272), and that now it is time to take action. She offers the money she has received for the cup for the establishment of a "School for Mothers" that the entire community was anxious to have. By converting her sinful action into good, the woman completes her voyage of discovery. She has mixed the sacred and the profane and in doing so has joined with all of humanity. Extending her vision into the darkness, she finally sheds the loneliness she had felt as a "good" Christian.

The sacred, the profane, tabu, *mana,* magic, sin, and natural curiosity are all parts of Butts's most irreverent and at the same time most playful story, "Madonna of the Magnificat." In *Being Geniuses Together,* Robert McAlmon tells us that Mary Butts and Zelda and F. Scott Fitzgerald once returned on the same channel boat to Paris. The Fitzgeralds "dearly loved" Mary's short stories and particularly "Madonna of the Magnificat." McAlmon insisted at the time that "Mary Butts's story was a stunt, and not worthy of her," but the Fitzgeralds were not convinced this was true. Later, when they had gone on deck, McAlmon records Mary's response: "'The precious lambs,' she said. 'Just babies, Bob, my pet. Of course you are right about that story. I did it as a space filler. The publisher thought the book too short.'"[42]

Whatever Butts's intentions were for this story, it is many things at once: confusing, irreverent, satirical, challenging to people of faith, disturbing, anachronistic, and bizarre. Using the account of the Annunciation in the Gospel of Luke as the envelope for the story, Butts attacks an article of faith by bringing into question the virginity of the Blessed Mother. The story begins with Mary in the "thirteenth year of her virginity" when her angel appears. Taking the announcement in her stride, her response is "'Am I to have a husband so soon?' And then: 'Need I marry Joseph?'" (283). The angel merely takes a red lily from a bunch that had previously been passed to Mary through a slit in the storehouse window, turns it white, replaces it, and vanishes: "She ran into a corner. The lily was visible in the dark" (283).

Mary tells her mother of the experience, who then rushes to tell Joseph and her relatives of the event. (Elizabeth is included in the group she hurries to tell. In the gospel, Elizabeth lives outside the city of Nazareth, miles from the Lower Galilee.) There is much turmoil, questioning, and speculation, but Joseph takes Mary aside "into a corner and thrust her back into it, speaking very close, his small hard body against hers. 'Little girl, I do not mind.

We will call it by a right name and be married at once'" (286), calling into question Mary's truthfulness and her virginity. Her lily falls to dust and she runs off with Nico, a young boy who had offered her the lilies and had thrown through the window slit a handful of rotten dates and a dead puppy.

We are not certain what to make of these events, but when they run off together on the hillocks, Nico argues with Mary, telling her, "You can't have the Messiah, you've been about with me" (288). Nico's claim complicates the narrator's opening announcement that Mary was in the "thirteenth year of her virginity." Without denying that she had "been about" with him, Mary responds that her family does not suppose him to be a man. Nico suggests they visit Panthera, a Roman officer who "knows everything."

Panthera listens to the story of the angel, takes her on his knee, wonders if she is "really a virgin," tells her about Rhea Silvia, whose twin sons from the god Mars become founders of Rome, and explains to her that the heroes of most countries have had "for a mother a girl like yourself" (290). Mary asks, "Is God ever good to them?" and his response is that "[t]hey had what God gives when he comes personally" (290). Panthera offers to be the father of her child, but she responds, "Not now," and she calls Nico to return to Nazareth with her. Nico, however, is angry because she has spoiled his chance to go to Alexandria with the Roman soldiers and threatens, "I shall say how you got your baby. I shall say it's the soldiers. I shall say it's Captain Panthera. They'll believe that" (292). She convinces Nico that her baby "must have his chance," they return home, and Joseph tells her he will "worship him" and take care of her. The old men accept her story, call her the Mother of God and Butts's story ends with the words, *"And Mary said""* (293).

Once again Butts fuses the pagan and the Christian in a story that is central to Christian doctrine. The supernatural presents itself, of course, in the form of the angel, but this story appears to be more about humanness than about the supernatural. Only once when Panthera questions Mary about seeing an angel does Mary suggest that there is "another kind of seeing," and we are not certain what she means. The reality of the religious doctrine becomes confused with what we have come to understand of Butts's style and beliefs. What is this other kind of seeing in a story about God's angel announcing the coming of the son of God? Perhaps in making Mary, the virgin, a namesake, Butts wanted to challenge Mary's passive acceptance of the miracle. Frank Baker asserts that Butts was proud of bearing the name of the Mother of God but thought of herself more as a "Daughter of the Gods," and her second husband, Gabriel Aitken, once presented her with a Christmas card in which she was the Virgin and he was the Angel of the Annunciation, "offering her the slightly drooping lily of purity."[43]

In "Madonna of the Magnificat" Mary is a young teenager with a mind of her own who accepts the situation only after she has thought and questioned what her role in the experience will be. Although there is divine intervention in her life, Mary's decision is that of an independent young woman struggling to maintain a sense of self. "Madonna of the Magnificat" is a difficult story filled with symbols that presuppose the reader's knowledge of the gospel. Butts's style intrudes extensively here as we find no dialogue between Mary and the angel, and in the rapid-fire interrogation by the elders, we find no attribution to the speaker. These stylistic peculiarities add to the confusion of the tale as well as to the confusion of Mary's predicament. However, there is no vitriol, no sarcasm, no ridicule. The implication is that Mary will be part of a miracle, but like the women visited by gods, she must learn to live her own life as well and must prepare for the divine on her own terms. This is a Mary of the modern world—a woman not afraid to question, to seek, to break tabus, and to learn from the change that magic brings into her life.

The stories examined here are merely a selection from Mary Butts's three collections, but they exemplify her ability to create magic through art. In many of her short stories the focus shifts from the rural countryside to the urban environment of London and Paris. Yet even here Butts and her characters attend to some aspect of myth, ritual, or mysticism to help define their world or describe their escapes from the predicaments and alienation of modernist civilization. The magic of these stories, even in the city, remains the magic of nature and origins. The stories leave us with the impression of an urbane and clever craftsperson whose artistic accomplishments celebrate diversity and narrative inventiveness. The author is at once, witty, skillful, consistently fascinating, and even subversive. Oliver Conant, in his 1992 review of the two recent issuings of her selected stories, complains that the writing is uneven, occasionally unintelligible, and can seem "precious or pretentious in a bright, schoolgirl way." However, he claims her "modernist neo-Gothic" style "can stand comparison with those of her famous contemporaries," while the "very best stories speak memorably to the reader of their author's moment, the modern moment, with all its excitement, its promise, its disillusionment."[44] Conant might have noted the range of a broadly educated woman exploring universal terrors and recasting them into artistic achievement that was ahead of its time.

For a 1990s society raised on the technological magic of television and movies, Butts's stories, on nearly every occasion, make us ask, "How did that happen?" Yet we never quite disbelieve that *some*thing did happen and that the experience pushed the veil aside just enough to glimpse an existence that transcends the external world and that is ultimately connected to the place where myth, ritual, and mysticism began. Paul West compares Butts's artistic quality to a hummingbird that we cannot quite see because of its constant motion.[45] Like the hummingbird that leaves us wanting to see more, Butts and her stories startle us in a very contemporary way. Each time we return to them we sense that we have experienced hummingbird magic, and we long for just a bit more.

Conclusion

"Like a black ball thrown in
And a gold ball thrown out
And the players are princes"

In *No Man's Land,* Sandra M. Gilbert and Susan Gubar argue that "male writers from Pater to Wilde to Yeats, along with many of their descendants, linked a new perception of what they saw as the archaic power of the feminine with the reactive urgency of the modern aesthetic they were themselves defining. . . ."[1] As a woman, Mary Butts linked into that "archaic power of the feminine," and she marked her own place within the modern aesthetic by identifying the value of the *natural.* Butts knew that separation from the natural world, as well as from one's own essential nature, was a wound that could be healed only by a return to a past when humanity and the unknown effectively interacted. Butts's artistic vision springs from the sense of disconnection (dis-ease) in the modern world and from the desire to tap into the "archaic power of the feminine" to achieve connection. The drive to reconnect initiates the creative process.

In *Madwoman in the Attic,* Sandra Gilbert and Susan Gubar note in their discussion of the word, *author,* that the power to create art is a taking of authority,[2] an authoring of control. By contouring her art to seek interaction with the sacred, Butts achieves inner authority. She and her fictional characters wield such authority when they use myth and ritual as the framework to reinforce their spiritual well-being; these structures from the past are a generative force that leads Butts's characters to a heightened consciousness. In effect, if one learns how to maneuver within this "sacred game," expressing independence and imagination, one arrives at an inner harmony or insight that resonates with historical and mythic symbolism. These motifs, embedded in the texts, deepen and complicate the conflicts as Butts's characters move through the drama of their tales.

When we explore Butts's interpretation of nature and humanity's original connections to the natural world, we move toward a definition, an authoring, that includes what is natural for human beings in general. Nature protects and renews itself and is not susceptible to societal ebbs and flows; it fights to sustain itself against all intrusions of people, science, technological progress, and urbanization. Sensing a duality in the word *nature,* Butts seems to have recognized in her life and in her art that to be "psychically sick" was to be out of tune with what is natural. Once we move too far from origins (myth, ritual), we lose our natural essence; we lose our souls. To be *natural* is to fight for self-preservation. As a woman who had to fight for her education and her place in society (and who seemed to do so with an independent verve), Butts identified, for instance, with homosexual men and, in her own nurturing way, joined forces with them. In her eyes, these men were moving toward what they knew to be their true natural condition and deeper legitimacy. Her heroes and heroines labor to sustain the quest for knowledge of their true nature, i.e., for who and what they are. The natural in themselves and in the external natural world is their source of power, a haven from the intrusions of societal contrivances that labeled homosexuality a deviation and that impinged upon their freedom. For Butts, homosexuals and other "outcasts" are fighting to preserve their basic nature, to finish the game.

If nature, as related to the land, is a metaphor for human authenticity, then Butts's vision falls carefully into place. The bohemian world lifted her from the external controls of society and presented her an opportunity to live her life in a manner less affected by that society. Similarly, her characters, through the external ordering offered by myth, ritual, and mystical questing, symbolically rise above or move outside of the confines of their fictional realities. The more one understands the rules, the better one plays the game.

Although Butts herself did not formally promote a feminist or political agenda, her life and her art are testimonies to a feminist vision that found its power by examining spiritual and natural sources. By the time Butts died in 1937, literary fashion had begun to move away from the abstractions of high modernism. Butts had already discovered her own style and her own voice by utilizing the external structures of myth, ritual, mysticism, or fairy tale to frame a personal vision about the world she inhabited and the world she could see developing in the future. As C. G. Jung has suggested, "The most we can do is to *dream the myth onwards* and give it a modern dress."[3] Butts's art is her dream in "modern dress."

Butts searched for answers by defining the problem and the solution very specifically. Precisely because Butts struggles with issues of origin, she marks out her own version of modernism. Her voice is one that is not only ahead of its time but is also relevant today. Through her artistic individuality, an individuality that never wavered in its certainty about solutions to the "dis-ease" of her contemporary society, Butts established her place within the modernist aesthetic that was experimenting with language and was attempting to define itself and its place in literary history. Butts's art is a statement of certainty within the uncertainty of her time; even when events in her work turn dark, there is a sense of play, a transcendence offered by the overriding structure of the game. Her response to Pound's dictum to "Make it new" was to do so by reinventing and reconnecting with the old. The "archaic power of the feminine" inspired her and taught her how to create her art while, at the same time, offering a remedy for the wounds of society. Anne Baring and Jules Cashford note that "the goddess myth can also be seen in the attempts of many human beings to live in a new way."[4] Butts was a prophetic writer who knew that looking into the future meant a careful consideration of the past; her art heals with the belief that one takes control by drawing strength from the past. For Butts, the "new way" of interpreting myth was at least an attempt to conquer fear and confusion. There is still much to unearth in the work of this female modernist. My hope is that this study lays the groundwork for other literary investigations into the variety and depth of Mary Butts's art.

• • • • • •

In 1932 Mary Butts wrote a review of *The Vision of Asia: An Interpretation of Chinese Art and Culture,* a book she called "wise and good and of extraordinary interest."[5] In discussing the mystic's search for salvation, Butts finds that only in the "farthest East he has found what he is looking for, which our world is dying for want of, a *restatement* of final realities serviceable both to the heart and head of every man of good-will."[6] Butts's life and her work are an attempt to restate final realities, to suggest that the other world, the unseen one, is as much a reality as the one in which we spend our daily lives.

Sensing that we are beings of varied and rich mental experiences, Butts recognized the power of our conscious minds to perform the magic of change. She found in the natural world her *mana,* her potency to live life as she chose. Barbara Wagstaff notes that during the time Mary Butts lived there was something in the air, a power, not unlike the 1960s in America, that for some was disastrous.[7] Butts lived life like a free spirit, yet she never lost her sense of the sacred and gave her best energies to her writing.

When she returned to nature by moving to Land's End in Cornwall at the end of her life, Butts became something of an Anglo-Catholic, formed a friendship with Father Bernard Walke of St. Hilary's, and assisted him in maintaining his church. She wrote numerous reviews and prose essays to pay her bills and wrote historical fictions, two of which were published during her lifetime—*The Macedonian* (1933) and *Scenes from Cleopatra* (1935). She left an unfinished manuscript of *Julian the Apostate.*

When Butts died, she was in negotiations with T. S. Eliot for a volume of her short stories to be published by Faber. On 22 March 1937, Angus Davidson, Butts's literary executor, sent thirteen complete stories to Butts's agent, Leonard Moore, who was then to forward them to Faber. Davidson also sent a list of the thirteen stories to Eliot, saying that the stories would soon follow. Nathalie Blondel tells us that, although a letter from Eliot to Angus Davidson, dated 24 March 1937, acknowledged receipt of this letter, there is no record of the stories ever arriving at Faber or of Eliot's rejection. Blondel speculates that a rejection by Eliot would have been unlikely "(. . . since he suggested their publication originally). Had Faber published a volume of Mary Butts's stories, there is no doubt that her reputation, albeit posthumously, would have been secured."[8] Sadly, it was not.

By returning to the sacred world of nature that she had worshipped most of her life, however, Butts, according to Frank Baker's account, was able to find a kind of solace in her final years. Baker recalls asking her how to live through moments of negation and black despair. Her response was "[r]ead, read, read. . . . Read. Always read. When the heart fails and there is no health in anything, turn to your books. Always read at such times."[9] And read she did, to keep herself afloat and to enlarge her world, and her writings offer the same to us. They expand our world and our experience as we glimpse a soul who asks for "[n]othing but spiritual development."

Appendix

By the early 1930s Mary Butts's flamboyant lifestyle had reached a calmer place. She was living in Cornwall close to the natural world she had inhabited as a child, and her life had now come full circle to end where she had begun. During this time Mary Butts, deserted by her second husband, Gabriel Aitken, found a form of peace and produced two historical novels (in addition to one unfinished historical novel *Julian the Apostate*) and *The Crystal Cabinet.* I have chosen to include brief commentary on *The Macedonian* and *Scenes from the Life of Cleopatra* in an appendix because, as I noted in the introduction, I believe that Mary Butts was moving in a new direction with her writing at this point in her life. She no longer relied upon the frenzied style of her earlier works and moved to a unique reconstruction and reinterpretation of standard historical figures. Thomas McEvilley, in his preface to the 1994 reissuing of these novels, observes that "they seem to represent an emphatic rejection of the world around her. Or perhaps a sense of returning to the root, of completing the circle."[1] Although Butts's emphasis remains on the spirituality of Alexander and Cleopatra, in writing historical fiction she seems to have found a way to deal with her inheritance, a concern throughout her life and her writing, which she associated with her father and her great-grandfather Thomas Butts.

Ruth Hoberman has written chapters on both *The Macedonian* and *Scenes from the Life of Cleopatra* in her book *Gendering Classicism: The Ancient World in Twentieth-Century Women's Historical Fiction.* I refer readers interested in this aspect of Butts's art to this excellent book.

Hoberman writes that "[p]aternal inheritance is an obsessive theme in Mary Butts's work and one reason Butts chose to write historical fiction, for the very act of writing historical fiction is a way of asserting inheritance over the past."[2] By the time Butts came to Cornwall, she seems to have reconciled the struggle she had had to face as a young woman growing up in a world that in many ways ignored the burgeoning intellect of exceptional females. Her life and her writing were a testament to how she chose to fight. Hoberman rightly contends that Butts's "vision of the connectedness of all of history and her own role as filler in of the pattern underlies her sense of her role as novelist, most specifically as historical novelist."[3]

Stylistically, in both novels Butts's voice assumes an authority even stronger than that of her earlier fiction. She writes as a contemporary of Alexander and Cleopatra, and, although the narrative voice shifts from character to character, we are never at a loss as to who is speaking—a typical difficulty of her earlier style. We do, however, recognize stylistic effects that separate clauses from their referents and sentence fragments that do not always clearly connect to sentences before or after. Yet, in these two novels, Butts shows tremendous control of language, and the narrative flow is consistent and carefully orchestrated to lead readers into the rhythm of the life of the characters. Form and content unite to create the historical moment.

In *The Macedonian,* originally published in 1933, Mary Butts shows her scholarly as well as her inspired literary talents. The novel is structured in ten parts, beginning with Alexander's birth and narrating significant highlights of his life from early youth through his campaigns to his death. The choice of events, as Hoberman points out, "seems to be following the mana—going wherever the energy is most intense, where human motives seem least relevant, the incursion of nonhuman forces most probable."[4] This is especially clear in the chapter that recounts Alexander's visit to Siwa, where he visits the temple of the god Amen-Ra and senses his connection with the divine as the son of the god.[5] In this recognition Alexander tries to understand what has joined him: "It was not a person. It was something that shaped equally the Universe and an acorn, and It called him friend."[6] Butts's emphasis here is that Alexander is not a god but contains an energy, a spiritual force, that makes him stand out among men even if Alexander refuses to distinguish between himself and god. His recognition and acceptance of such a force, such moments of transcendence, single him out as leader, both spiritual and physical.

The identification of this force within Alexander is the focus of Butts's narrative and expands the vision she explores in all her fiction. When we first hear of Alexander it is as the forthcoming child of Olympias and Philip. Butts clarifies the distinction between the two worlds of mother and father.

Olympias represents the barbarian, pre-Olympian, pre-Homeric view of the world where the distinction between human beings and gods is blurred, what Aristotle identifies as "her ecstasies and her savageries, her barbarian lawlessness and unreason and desires and certainties" (18). Philip, however, represents the rationalism of the Greeks; he is man, not god. In creating Alexander, Butts uses her writing to forge the connection between the two worlds. Alexander is part of both worlds. The fact that Alexander must struggle between godhood and rational thinking shows a balance and a consistency within the form and structure of Mary Butts's writing and her vision. Ruth Hoberman argues that Butts finally rejects the rationalism of male hegemony and that "Alexander's religious feeling aligns him with his mother, Olympias, whose *enthousiasmos* contrasts sharply with the rationalism of her husband and his friend Aristotle."[7] Hoberman claims that at Siwa the stamp of Jane Ellen Harrison's *Prolegomena* clearly marks Butts's acceptance of the non-analytic mind and thinks back to the "haze of the primitive 'one,'" a rejection of male hegemony and an affirmation of "[t]hose for fusion. . . women and conquered peoples—those the Greeks are intent on defining as 'other.'"[8] She concludes her chapter on *The Macedonian* by stating that by "insisting that mana, not man, shaped history, she [Butts] was aligning herself with formlessness and jouissance against plot, purpose, and male hegemony."[9]

Although I agree generally with Hoberman's comments about Butts's style and use of mana, I would argue that precisely because Alexander struggles with both aspects of his personality, embodied by mother and father, he is a projection into the future of a world that Butts longs for—a way to fuse both worlds, of finding men who embody and internalize elements of both rather than rejecting one in favor of the other. When Eumenes tells Ptolemy that what Alexander wants is "to make the earth and its various peoples plastic, interpenetrated one with the other; capable of exchange of resources and excellencies. To put an end to this silly nonsense of Greek and Barbarian" (18), his voice speaks as the author's would. Butts may reject male hegemony and what it stands for, but in Alexander she indicates the power and greatness of one who finds a balance between the two extremes. Since he is infused with both extremes, this mixture defines his greatness. There is no need to call him great; instead, Butts shows him as great. Butts finds power not in the separation of male and female pasts but rather in the melding of both and in masculine acceptance of its primal matriarchal past as an influence on the present.

By creating such a character as a part of history, Butts indicates that if society, like Alexander, were to desire the pre-Olympian oneness, then it would become empowered by the struggle. In the sense that I refuse to see

Butts as rejecting rational or Olympian thought or as identifying rational thought primarily with maleness, I believe I diverge from Hoberman's argument. Butts valued the classical past, and part of that past included the Olympian gods. What I do agree with is Hoberman's assertion that Butts's intent in writing historical fiction, in addition to laying claim to her father's inheritance, is also "to rewrite the past and find there images of power that transcend gender."[10] Understanding what it means to "transcend gender" is key to understanding Butts's writing. Alexander personifies the union of reason and spirituality, or, as Butts reminds us several times in describing Alexander, "it took two to make a heart's desire." For Butts, this union translates into truth. Her poem "Pythian Ode" from 1924 states, "Truth is the heart's desire. . . / Truth is a mean between extremes. / Be comforted." Alexander represents such a mean, a norm for greatness.

• • • • • •

In Mary Butts's 1935 appendix to *Scenes from the Life of Cleopatra,* she recounts the various interpretations of Cleopatra's character from Chaucer to Bernard Shaw and defends Cleopatra's position as a woman and queen about whom "there is not a shred of evidence to show that she had amorous dealings with any on earth other than Caesar and Mark Antony . . . she (who was theoretically the source of Law) could not help herself. . . . She was a girl, in a desperate situation, whose actions were *ipso facto* legal" (341). Because we know that Mary Butts's scholarship was extremely rigorous, we accept her account of Cleopatra and mentally reject other interpretations of her character. Butts's suggestion is that "men—historians or not—do not like to think, and so refuse to believe, in an active woman alone, enjoying the use of power" (343).

Mary Butts struggled with the writing of this novel in Cornwall and was grateful for correspondence with Jack Lindsay, who was also writing a book about Cleopatra *(Last Days with Cleopatra)* and who shared ideas and information.[11] That he saw their two books as "complementary" was extremely encouraging to Butts at this time, and he told her when it came out that "I think you have done a really important bit of work in bringing out the atmosphere and meaning of Cleopatra, and I look on the book as almost vital contribution to that understanding of the graeco-roman world which is near to my heart."[12] When *Scenes from the Life of Cleopatra* appeared in 1935, it received a great deal of attention because it carefully and in a scholarly manner presented a narration of events while obviously taking Cleopatra's "side," as Nathalie Blondel points out.[13]

Oswell Blakeston commented in 1971 that he remembered some admirers of Butts's work exclaiming on its publication, "Oh, I never realised

Cleopatra was so like Mary Butts."[14] The identification with Cleopatra was obviously clear for Butts herself. In 1933, just two days before *The Macedonian* was published, she writes in her diary,

> Can I now write the life of Cleopatra I have so often told myself. Yes—if this is the key—(were my family ruined to show me this?)—that she could no longer stand the degradation of the Lagidae? If that is the key to it all . . . *if I'm right,* I can do it. . . . I feel as though all the pieces of a puzzle were falling into place. It explains Caesar, her ridding herself of her kin, her cultivation of herself.[15]

Butts acknowledges here that she shared with Cleopatra the confusion and frustration of family history and justified the lifestyle chosen by each woman to survive. Nathalie Blondel says, "However disproportionate the decline of the Ptolemies to that of the Butts family in historical significance, she clearly felt that a shared sense of humiliation gave her the necessary entrée into the mind of Cleopatra."[16]

Butts's Cleopatra, of Greek heritage and culture, is the inheritor of the Ptolemy line set on the throne of Egypt after the conquest of Alexander the Great. Strong, independent, and ambitious, she is extremely aware of her heritage, her sanctity, and her dual Greek and Egyptian inheritance. She knows her goddess connection and lives it openly. Her road to power as a woman, Cleopatra intuits once Caesar approaches Alexandria, is through the power of her sexuality and beauty. In a world ruled by men's military exploits, Cleopatra, even as a very young woman, utilizes the strength she possesses.[17] This is not a wanton woman seeking gratification; instead, Cleopatra is a strong and clever queen who understands her individual source of power both as a female and as a goddess, an avatar of Isis. All the while maintaining historical accuracy, Butts creates a unique image of the historical Cleopatra that is at once accurate and insightful.

As in *The Macedonian,* Butts depicts the conflict between Rome and Cleopatra in a variety of "scenes" beginning where *The Macedonian* left off and bringing us through time to Cleopatra in Alexandria. She is a young girl of fourteen, attended by her faithful "women of honour," Charmian ("the child of an ancient egyptian house") and Iras ("a Greek, daughter of a General whose family had a kind of hereditary attachment to the Lagidae"). Together, Butts tells us, they "presented a perfect image of the double nature of the kingdom and the civilization over which she [Cleopatra] was to rule" (138–39). And this kingdom mirrors the double nature of its ruler, woman and goddess. Because of Cleopatra's heritage, she assumes her divinity in a way that Julius Caesar cannot.

In Ruth Hoberman's thorough chapter on *Scenes from the Life of Cleopatra,* she again sees the presence of *mana*—the all pervasive energy—

as Butts's key to examining Cleopatra, an element overlooked by previous historical accounts. Butts, Hoberman contends, connects the spiritual energy of mana with the female body and further claims that "[t]hrough Isis, then, Butts connects mana to timelessness."[18] Cleopatra's moments of contact with mana, says Hoberman, are also "moments of bodily dissolution, conflating time and space in terms suggesting Kristeva's notion of 'monumental' time."[19] By conflating time and space, I would suggest, Butts also conflates the time of linear history with Julia Kristeva's monumental and cyclical time. By writing the history of Cleopatra, by perceiving her character as one with the energy of life, by showing Cleopatra as a reincarnation of the goddess Isis, Mary Butts reveals a fundamental source of power that has been lost to her own generation. Kristeva tells us that these two types of temporality are "found to be the fundamental, if not the sole, conceptions of time in numerous civilizations and experiences, particularly mystical ones."[20]

The mystical moment for Cleopatra comes as something of an epiphany, as it did for Alexander at Siwa. Since Cleopatra is, according to Egyptian beliefs, a reincarnation of the goddess Isis, hers is a truly authentic joining with the divine. Cleopatra relates her moment of mystical revelation or the moment when she gave herself to "the air and the light and the earth." She tells Caesar:

> I was born to it. . . . Then it is that I come out of myself, and Something—call it Goddess—becomes me and I That. That which was August in time had departed: that which is eternally August entered. When it has done that, my body is as though it had been in a different state, as though it were impregnated with a life that is not the common run of the blood. I move, distinct, elated, but not with myself. I do not want—I am—power. I am filled to the lips though I do not speak. I have seen things of which our actions are the translations." (220)

Cleopatra's experience reminds us of Mary Butts's seeings related in her *Crystal Cabinet,* and the connection between Cleopatra and Butts is strengthened. Through the acceptance of the goddess within, Cleopatra asserts her inherited position as the Goddess Isis and the association with Kristeva's monumental (eternal) and cyclical (repetitive) time of female subjectivity join with the Isis-Osiris-Horus/birth-death-rebirth cycle of Cleopatra, Caesar, and their son, Caesarean. Hoberman connects Caesar's epileptic seizures to "moments of mana—contact similar to hers," especially when he has a seizure during the birth of their son.[21] Yet Butts makes it clear that Cleopatra is goddess because she is the authentic inheritor of her race, not a godhood assumed by position or conquest.

The duality of godhood and female are central to all of Mary Butts's work, and in Cleopatra she has found a way for opposites to reside in one. The other figures, like Cicero (whom she characterizes as repugnant, manipulative, exploitative), Octavian (who is vile and conniving), and even Mark

Antony (whom Cleopatra loves), are far less significant than the descriptions of the queen herself. Narrative structure reflects this emphasis with a careful, somewhat cinematic shifting between various voices interpreting events as they happen and offering different points of view and perspectives through letters, conversations, and an omniscient narrator. Whenever the narrator's voice appears, it is in complete sympathy with Cleopatra and her dilemma as a young woman and as queen of Egypt. In a cinematic sense all is just a bit out of focus except for the role of Cleopatra. Reinforcing Butts's mirroring of her own world with that of Cleopatra, this narrative voice incorporates contemporary elements, language, and references, while propelling the narrative itself, and Cleopatra's authenticity mirrors what Butts struggles to make clear in all her fiction. The fact that Butts ends the novel, not with Cleopatra's death, but with a conversation between her and Mark Antony suggesting the impending end, extends Cleopatra's connection to timelessness. Cleopatra is at once part of the linear time of historical narrative, is an element of cyclical time as the reincarnation of the goddess, and remains also an opening up to the eternal. We do not experience her mortal death; instead, Butts ends with the power of her magic as she anticipates what is to come for both of them: "But what he remembered for ever, as if his gilt corselet had been stripped off him, was her breast against his. As though the touch of her body had turned its gold to air" (340).

Although Butts succeeds in establishing Cleopatra's role in history, she trades some of her earlier vitality of style for erudition and scholarship. *Scenes from Cleopatra* has more exposition and explanation than does *The Macedonian.* Yet, through her historical perspective, Butts manages to reexamine in a distinct way a figure whose role in history has been a source of mystery and confusion. If this one is more difficult than her other novels, it is because history assumes more knowledge on the part of readers. The classical past was essential to Butts for understanding the present, and for her those who write history are "there—to tell the story, certainly, to be painstaking, to be accurate; also to give a carefully balanced view of historic probabilities in a story of infinite importance on some of whose vital details Time has closed his jaws."[22] *Scenes from Cleopatra* and *The Macedonian* offer insights into "historic probabilities."

• • • • • •

Finally, I would like to comment briefly on Mary Butts's poetry, which has recently gone to the Beinecke Library at Yale and which remains uncollected. Kenneth Irby at the University of Kansas has been working on Mary Butts's poetry for years, and it is an area of her work that deserves separate attention of its own.

I have chosen her poem "Corfe" as an introduction to this study because it embodies the major themes of Mary Butts's fiction and her vision in general. Much of her poetry addresses the same issues as her fiction, and her fiction has been labeled poetic by more than one critic. Yet, because of its form, the poetry enlarges and expands the ideas in a different genre; in fact, much of her poetry can be clearly associated with specific works of fiction. For example, "Picus Martius" examines the connection between the woodpecker and the god Zeus, reinforces notions explored in *Armed with Madness,* and reminds us of the role of Picus in the novel: "Recognize a bird in a man / That it is feathers, air / Not flesh." Or later the advice of the birdcatcher admonishes: "'Steady, Ganymede! / Careful Leda! / That bird was a god / Was a man,'" and we remember the importance Butts places on the distinction between god and man. This poem first appeared in *The Hound & Horn* in 1930.

Another poem, "Pythian Ode," which appeared in the *Transatlantic Review* in 1924, hearkens again to ancient Greece and to the same concerns of the significance of the past on the present:

> When I think of you, Delphi, I am reminded of a fair young
> man smiling:
> And an old woman goddess:
> And an old woman goddess:
> And a cluster of women pretending to be bees.
> . . . .
> Truth is the heart's desire
> . . . .
> Truth is a mean between extremes
> . . . .
> So you became
> A little old town with a too large cathedral.
> . . . .
> Quod inferious sicut superius est.
> Be comforted.

In these few lines Butts echoes her concerns with truth, authenticity, the past, and the various ways to interpret reality. The Latin quotation perhaps embodies what she struggled with in her novels—that what is below is the same as what is above. We remember characters in her novels making such observations—that what we are experiencing is really only a reflection of what is going on in another place, another world.

Other poems are obvious imitations of her contemporaries. "Thinking of Saints and of Petronius Arbiter," which appeared in 1932, is clearly a take on T. S. Eliot's final section of "The Hollow Men." She writes,

Between a toy and a crucifix
Between a joke and a prayer
Lies the Bird-Catcher
Who caught the peacock of the world.
. . . .
Because love is
Because of what love is
(We who know what love is.)
And it is not possible to love
Any people but these.

Eliot's "The Hollow Men" had appeared in 1925. Mary Butts admired Eliot's work and perhaps the imitation was a form of flattery or perhaps she was extending Eliot's view.

Whatever the case, she also wrote a poem called "Two Ways of Not Seeing the World," reflecting, of course, the American poet Wallace Stevens's "Thirteen Ways of Looking at a Blackbird." Stevens's poem appeared in 1917. Nathalie Blondel does not give a date for Butts's poem, but Glen E. Morgan published it in *Antaeus* in the winter of 1973 along with several other previously published poems. I asked Camilla Bagg about this poem, and she could not remember when or where or whether it was published in Butts's lifetime, but she was certain that Mary Butts knew the work of Stevens. Glen E. Morgan asserts that the bulk of Butts's poetry was written in the 1910s or 1920s, but it seems safe to assume that Butts echoes Stevens since she so carefully imitated Eliot later on. This poem pits two observations of a "young gentleman" against each other in relation to how he views the antiquities of the past—one includes his mistress as compared with the wonders of "placed harps, urns, sphinxes, shrubs / To adorn this sensibility," and the second observes the same objects but "Bores us with his cultivated reactions / To the amusing in art." Again, we see Butts addressing concerns that are central to her work: only the authentic inheritor/initiate knows how to appreciate and incorporate the past into the present in any meaningful way.

Whenever the extant poems of Mary Butts are collected and published (there are approximately one hundred of them), it will be impossible to comment on them without taking into consideration her major concerns with the dual nature of existence, the reality of two worlds—the "seen" and the "unseen," her strong desire to interpret the past in relation to the future, the role of the "female principle of life," and the emphasis on authenticity of those who are initiates in a sacred game of life. Most of her poetry in some way emphasizes the power of mana—the energy or life force that is central to most of her major characters and especially to Alexander and Cleopatra. Her poetry supports and expands all these ideas.

Notes

PREFACE

1. Camilla Bagg, personal interview, 15 April 1998.

2. Camilla has written a detailed account of her dealings with the American academics, "A Literary Friendship," which will now be included in the Butts papers at Yale. I was allowed to read her original version but not granted permission to quote from it.

3. Although Elena Storer-Nitzberg participated in the conference, she subsequently took a Ph.D. degree in psychology and did not publish anything on Mary Butts. The 1984 conference, "The Writings and the World of Mary Butts," took place at the University of California, Davis. Barbara Wagstaff arranged for her papers and tapes of the conference to go to the Bancroft Library at Berkeley.

4. Camilla Bagg, personal interview, 15 April 1998.

INTRODUCTION

1. Douglas Goldring, *South Lodge: Reminiscences of Violet Hunt, Ford Madox Ford and the English Review Circle* (London: Constable & Co., Ltd., 1943) 151.

2. Bryher, "Recognition Not Farewell," *Life and Letters Today* 17.9 (Autumn 1937): 160.

3. Christopher Wagstaff, ed., *A Sacred Quest: The Life and Writings of Mary Butts* (Kingston, NY: McPherson & Company, 1995). A more extensive bibliography can be found in Nathalie Blondel, *Mary Butts: Scenes from the Life* (Kingston, NY: McPherson & Company, 1998). Blondel's biography, based on the twenty-one years of journals that Butts kept from 1916 to 1937 and on various family papers and correspondence, gives a full account of Butts's life and background.

4. Bonnie Kime Scott, ed., *The Gender of Modernism* (Bloomington: Indiana UP, 1990) 2.

5. Alicia Ostriker, *Stealing the Language: The Emergence of Women's Poetry in America* (Boston: Beacon Press, 1986) 2.

6. For example, in addition to Scott's *The Gender of Modernism,* see Rita Felski, *The Gender of Modernity* (Cambridge, Mass.: Harvard UP, 1995); Marianne DeKovan, *Rich and Strange: Gender, History, Modernism* (Princeton: Princeton UP, 1991); and Kathleen Wheeler, *'Modernist' Women Writers and Narrative Art* (New York: New York UP, 1994). See also Lisa Rado's collections of essays, *ReReading Modernism: New Directions in Feminist Criticism* (New York: Garland, 1994), and her *Modernism, Gender, and Culture: A Cultural Studies Approach* (New York: Garland, 1997).

7. Sandra M. Gilbert and Susan Gubar, *No Man's Land: The Place of the Woman in the Twentieth Century,* vol. 1: *The War of the Words* (New Haven, CT: Yale UP, 1988) 156.

8. Blondel, *Mary Butts* 13. Also the proceedings from the conference on Butts at the University of California, Davis, 23–24 November 1984, collected by Barbara Wagstaff, offer Robert H. Byington's views on Butts's background and her pretensions of aristocratic status, Tape 5.

9. According to various sources, Mrs. Colville-Hyde found her daughter with her husband in a compromising position. Mary Butts in *The Crystal Cabinet* explains that it was nothing more than an innocent affection for her stepfather. Butts examines the strained relationship with her mother, who accused her of indiscretion with her stepfather on her return from boarding school. The accusation apparently is one source of Mary Butts's intense dislike for and hostility toward her mother that never left her throughout her life, although most other sources suggest that Mary Colville-Hyde was not a bad mother at all and did the best for Mary that she could. Bryher in "Recognition Not Farewell" talks about "another story, too terrifying to be told" that never actually came to light. Robert H. Byington also addresses this in his paper at the 1984 conference on Butts. Yet the details of what actually occurred remain a mystery. That *something* happened to create a psychological wound within Butts is certain.

10. Camilla Bagg, conversation with author, Dorset, England, 1 June 1996. Mary had disdain for her mother's social class, her ideas about women, and her lack of sensitivity to books and the mind. Later, problems with her mother and her estrangement from her only brother, Tony, focused on her own wild living and her frequent use of drugs. Camilla Bagg, Butts's daughter, says that later the rift between mother and daughter widened because of Mary's problems with money and her concerns over her inheritance, which was controlled by Mrs. Butts. Apparently all three of them (Mrs. Butts, Mary, and Tony) were completely inept when it came to handling finances. As a result, what they did have, they squandered, and Mary was always asking for handouts from friends. See also Robert McAlmon's unpublished typescript, "History of Encounters," in the Beinecke Library for an account of Mary's desperate attempts to acquire money.

11. Blondel, *Mary Butts* 58.

12. Blondel, *Mary Butts* 90.

13. See Robert H. Byington's "Chronology," in *A Sacred Quest,* ed. Wagstaff 245–50. Byington states that Butts left Camilla with Poppaea Vanda, "the pen-name of a ballet critic, a friend of MB, with whom Camilla live[d] for the next five years."

14. Bryher papers, 12 June 1923 (Beinecke Library).

15. Nathalie Blondel, personal interview by author, Bristol, England, 3 June 1996.

16. Bryher, "Recognition Not Farewell" 163.

17. Qtd. in Blondel, *Mary Butts* 429.

18. Robert H. Byington, "Interviews with Virgil Thomson, Eugene MacCown, Quentin Bell and Hugh Ross Williamson," in *A Sacred Quest,* ed. Wagstaff 44. See also Quentin Bell's chapter on Mary Butts in *Bloomsbury Recalled* (New York: Columbia UP, 1995). See also the recently published essay by Mary Butts, "Bloomsbury," *Modernism/Modernity* 5.2 (1998): 32–45, originally written in 1936 but not published, where Butts critiques the Bloomsbury Circle, its members, and its effects on contemporary society, but interestingly defends Roger Fry (who was then dead). She also examines Wyndam Lewis's scathing account of Bloomsbury, *The Caliph's Design* (London: Egoist Press, 1919).

19. Blondel, *Mary Butts* 417.

20. Gillian Hanscombe and Virginia L. Smyers, *Writing for Their Lives: The Modernist Women 1910–1940* (Boston: Northeastern UP, 1987) 112.

21. Leon Surette, in *The Birth of Modernism: Ezra Pound, T. S. Eliot, W. B. Yeats, and the Occult Movement* (Montreal: McGill-Queen's UP, 1993), connects the occult, mysticism, and myth, a combination that is evident in Butts's work and which Surette finds in other modernists.

22. Feminist critics Alicia Ostriker, Susan Friedman, and Adelaide Morris examine similar concerns in H. D.'s poetry. Other modernist authors also address these issues, particularly the role of myth in art, with a point of view unique to each. David Spurr, discussing the function of myth in Joyce, Eliot, and Pound, argues that "What is a source of comedy in Joyce is an occasion for despair in Eliot." See David Spurr, "Myths of Anthropology: Eliot, Joyce, Lévy-Bruhl," *PMLA* 109.2 (March 1994): 267. Butts finds that myth, ritual, and mysticism connect her both to the past, which she believes must inform an understanding of the present, and to contemporary history.

23. Jascha Kessler, "Recovering Mary Butts: Beauty and the Beast," *The Bookpress* 3.7 (October 1993): 13. Kessler notes that D. H. Lawrence was only five years older than Mary Butts but that they were from different social strata and "nor did they have anything to do with one another personally." Kessler states that Butts and Lawrence did come to "similar conclusions about what had happened to the world, and they are congruent in imagining what might, indeed must, be done to remedy the present, if there was to be any hope for the future" (12). However, Kessler makes a clear distinction between their prose styles and, in effect, dismisses any extension of this comparison as differences in approach and clarity of style. See p. 12 of Kessler's article for further discussion.

24. See, for example, Alan Dundes, ed., introduction, *Sacred Narrative: Readings in the Theory of Myth* (Berkeley: U of California P, 1984), where he writes: "A myth is a sacred narrative explaining how the world and man came to be in their present form" (1). For Butts, the key word in this definition would be *sacred.*

25. Mary Butts, "The Real Wordsworth," rev. of *The Later Wordsworth,* by Edith C. Batho, *Time and Tide* 14.48 (2 Dec. 1933): 1448. See also Evelyn Underhill's classic work on mysticism, *Mysticism: A Study in the Nature and Development of Man's Spiritual Consciousness* (New York: World Publishing Company, 1955) 71. Underhill most clearly defines mysticism as "the science of ultimates, the science of union with the Absolute." Butts went so far as to believe that

it might be possible to induce the mystic state. In one of her journal entries at Aleister Crowley's Abbey in Cefalu, Italy, she states, "Talked about last astral journey with A[leister]. C[rowley]. The idea is to find an authentic means of inducing the mystic state." See Robert H. Byington and Glen E. Morgan, "Mary Butts," *Art and Literature* (1965): 170.

26. William James, *Varieties of Religious Experience: A Study in Human Nature* (New York: Modern Library, 1929) 371.

27. Hugh Ross Williamson, "Three Letters," in *A Sacred Quest,* ed. Wagstaff 148.

28. See Surette, *The Birth of Modernism.* Here Surette states that occultism "sees itself as heir of an ancient wisdom—either passed on from adept to adept or rediscovered in each new generation by mystical illumination" (7). The distinguishing factor between the occult and the mystical is the possibility of illumination through initiation in occultism, and the single rite of the occult is that of initiation (13–14). The words *mysticism* (Gr., μψστικοσ mystikos) and *occultism* (L., occultus) both originate in the secret or hidden, but mysticism evolved to a more open revelation of the "Absolute" than the sworn secrets of an adept of the occult. In occultism the initiate can be taught to receive the secret, ancient wisdom. Once an adept of the occult is illuminated, however, he or she may not reveal the illumination to the non-enlightened; it remains the secret wisdom of the chosen, incomprehensible to all but the select.

Finally, all these terms converge in a concern with an ultimate reality. Leon Surette contends that *occultism* regards *myths* as "records of contacts between the human and the divine" and is itself a secret understanding of ancient wisdom or universal truth (7). *Ritual* is a set of prescribed acts to understand or respond to the perceived actions of the gods, and *mysticism* is a journey toward union with the infinite God (7).

29. Lillian Feder, *Ancient Myth in Modern Poetry* (Princeton: Princeton UP, 1971) 15.

30. In her essay *Traps for Unbelievers,* Butts delineates her concern over the current fashion of disbelief and indifference toward religion. Butts here explains that magic has something to do with the invisible; it preceded religion, but religion was not derived from it. The ritual game was a primitive science whose perception of the invisible, if applied, could put man back on track in discerning the relations between disparate things. Butts knows that this perception has not died in man, and it reveals itself in the artist. See Mary Butts, *Traps for Unbelievers* in *Ashe of Rings and Other Writings.* All subsequent references to *Traps for Unbelievers* will be referenced to this text. (Kingston, NY: McPherson & Company, 1998).

31. Byington and Morgan 171.

32. Qtd. in Blondel, *Mary Butts* 249.

33. Kessler, "Recovering," 13.

34. Virgil Thomson, *Virgil Thomson* (New York: Alfred A. Knopf, 1966) 87.

35. Alicia Ostriker, "Thieves of Language: Women Poets and Revisionist Mythmaking," *Coming to Light: American Women Poets in the Twentieth Century,* ed. Diane Wood Middlebrook and Marilyn Yalom (Ann Arbor: U of Michigan P, 1985) 16.

36. Susan Stanford Friedman and Rachel Blau Duplessis, eds., *Signets: Reading H. D.* (Madison: U of Wisconsin P, 1990) 386. Joseph Blotner has noted that Virginia Woolf (consciously or unconsciously) used mythical figures, not to draw direct parallels between mythic personage and character, but as symbols which enhance the resonance of a work. Mrs. Ramsey of *To the Lighthouse,* Blotner observes, symbol-

izes the female principle. See Joseph Blotner, "Mythic Patterns in *To the Lighthouse,*" *Myth and Literature,* ed. John B. Vickery (Lincoln: U of Nebraska P, 1966).

37. Mary Hamer, "Mary Butts, Mothers, and War," *Women's Fiction and the Great War,* ed. Suzanne Rait and Trudi Tate (Oxford: Oxford UP, 1997) 235.

38. Shelley Arlen, *The Cambridge Ritualists: An Annotated Bibliography of the Works by and about Jane Ellen Harrison, Gilbert Murray, Francis Cornford, and Arthur Bernard Cook* (Metuchen, NJ: Scarecrow Press, 1990) 2.

39. Arlen 20.

40. Ruth Hoberman, *Gendering Classicism: The Ancient World in Twentieth-Century Women's Historical Fiction* (New York: State U of New York P, 1997) 51.

41. Julia Kristeva, "Women's Time," *The Kristeva Reader,* ed. Toril Moi (New York: Columbia UP, 1986) 191.

42. Kristeva 194–95.

43. Arlen 20.

44. Butts felt a hostility toward psychoanalysis and surrealism, as Louis Adeane tells us, because they "sprang from a feeling that they reflected a split between parts of the self within, and the natural order of the world without." See Louis Adeane, "Mary Butts," *World Review: New Series* 33 (November 1951): 24.

45. In *The Birth of Modernism,* Leon Surette explains that Harrison's "special kind of historicism . . . dominated the period" (58). Surette maintains that the mystical and transcendent cast of Harrison's remarks on the religious impulse represents "a powerful wave of academic research and speculation into myth as revelation that was a constant force in Europe from the beginning of the Romantic period to the present" (58). Surette sees this "wave" as contemporaneous with occult revival and the birth of modernism and clearly delineates the genuine thrust of interest in myth, occult, and religious exploration as centering devices for two centuries "out of tune" with their primal origins. Butts was influenced by the Romantic impulse as well as the "constant force" prevalent at the turn of the century.

46. Toril Moi, *Sexual/Textual Politics: Feminist Literary Theory* (New York: Methuen, 1985) 13.

47. Mary Butts, "A Glimpse of the Victorian Scene," *The Bookman* (May 1932): 119.

48. Marianne DeKovan, "The Politics of Modernist Form," *New Literary History* 23.3 (Summer 1992): 688.

49. J. C. Squire, "The Modern Revival of the Short Story: Miss Mary Butts' Success," *Daily Telegraph* 8 March 1932: 16. Squire's point is that one can compare Butts with numerous authors in a review so that one can "convey to people whether they will like a certain thing enough." Yet, as criticism, rough or superficial comparisons do not do much to advance understanding of this very complicated artist.

50. Malcolm Bradbury and James McFarlane, eds., *Modernism 1890–1930* (London: Penguin, 1991) 16, 25.

51. Hamer 219–20.

52. Bradbury and McFarlane 24.

53. Qtd. in Blondel, *Mary Butts* 100.

54. Kessler, "Recovering" 12.

55. Bruce McPherson, personal correspondence, 2 January 1998.

56. Qtd. in Blondel, *Mary Butts* 335.

57. Bryher, "Recognition" 160.

ONE: "I STROVE TO SEIZE THE INMOST FORM"

1. Robin Blaser, "Here Lies the Woodpecker Who Was Zeus," in *A Scared Quest: The Life and Writings of Mary Butts,* ed. Christopher Wagstaff (Kingston, NY: McPherson & Company, 1995) 165.

2. Nathalie Blondel, in her biography of Mary Butts, notes that Butts's "knowledge of Greek places her writing outside the educational experiences of her female contemporaries" (*Mary Butts: Scenes from the Life* [Kingston, NY: McPherson & Company, 1998] 22). Shari Benstock, who omitted Mary Butts from her *Women on the Left Bank: Paris 1900–1940* (Austin: U of Texas P, 1986) 25, in her discussion of the role of language in Modernism explains that the "men of 1914 were schooled in the classics, shared a knowledge of Greek and Latin . . . Joyce learned some Greek on his own. . . . H. D., Natalie Barney, and Renée Vivien learned Greek on their own in order to read the fragments of Sappho that became available in the 1890s, and the one woman Modernist whose writing consistently turns on classical sources of English words is Djuna Barnes, who received no formal education at all and who learned etymology by reading *The New English Dictionary.*" Mary Butts's childhood knowledge of Greek and Latin would place her closer to male modernists in her pursuit of language. In fact, she claimed in 1919 that "Only in Homer have I found impersonal consolation—a life where I am unsexed or bisexed, or completely myself—or a mere pair of ears" (qtd. in Blondel, *Mary Butts* 22).

3. Hugh Ross-Williamson, "Three Letters," in *A Sacred Quest,* ed. Wagstaff 148.

4. Mircea Eliade, *The Sacred and the Profane: The Nature of Religion* (New York: Harcourt, Brace & World, 1959) 140.

5. For discussion of feminist re-vision of the Romantic poets, see Anne K. Mellor, *Romanticism & Gender* (New York: Routledge, 1993), Margaret Homans, *Bearing the Word: Language and Female Experience in Nineteenth-Century Women's Writing* (Chicago: Chicago UP, 1986), and Marlon B. Ross, *The Contours of Masculine Desire: Romanticism and the Rise of Women's Poetry* (New York: Oxford UP, 1989). See also Anne K. Mellor, ed., *Romanticism and Feminism* (Bloomington: Indiana UP, 1988).

6. Mellor, *Romanticism and Feminism* 7.

7. Mellor, *Romanticism and Feminism* 7.

8. Ross 3.

9. William Blake, *Blake's Poetry and Designs,* ed. Mary Lynn Johnson and John E. Grant (New York: W. W. Norton, 1979) xxiv.

10. Mary Butts, *The Crystal Cabinet: My Childhood at Salterns* (Manchester, Eng.: Carcanet Press Limited, 1988) 237. All subsequent references to *The Crystal Cabinet* in this chapter will be cited parenthetically by page number in the text.

11. Helen C. White, *The Mysticism of William Blake* (Madison: U of Wisconsin Studies in Language and Literature, No. 23, 1927) 242.

12. Robert H. Byington and Glen E. Morgan, "Mary Butts," *Art and Literature* (1965): 171.

13. William Wordsworth, *The Prelude: A Parallel Text,* ed. J. C. Maxwell (London: Penguin, 1986) 51.

14. Percy Bysshe Shelley, *Shelley: Selected Poems, Essays, and Letters,* ed. Ellsworth Barnard (New York: Odyssey Press, 1944) 192.

15. Bryher, "Recognition" 162.

16. White 242.

17. See *The Crystal Cabinet* 294 n. 221.

18. Hazard Adams, "'The Crystal Cabinet' and 'The Golden Net,'" *Blake: A Collection of Critical Essays,* ed. Northrop Frye (Englewood Cliffs, NJ: Prentice Hall, 1966) 79.

19. Bryher, "Recognition" 162.

20. Evelyn Underhill, *Mysticism: A Study in the Nature and Development of Man's Spiritual Consciousness* (New York: World Publishing Company, 1955) 205–6.

21. William James, *Varieties of Religious Experience: A Study in Human Nature* (New York: Modern Library, 1929) 371–72.

22. James 418.

23. Richard N. Coe, *When the Grass Was Taller: Autobiography and the Experience of Childhood* (New Haven, CT: Yale UP, 1984) 115.

24. Jane Ellen Harrison, *Epilegomena to the Study of Greek Religion and Themis: A Study of Social Origins of Greek Religion* (New York: University Books, 1962) 68.

25. Underhill 73.

26. Toussaint was a Haitian leader for independence from France who was captured and died in prison in 1803. Wordsworth's sonnet entreats Toussaint to "take comfort. Thou has left behind / Powers that will work for thee; air, earth, and skies / . . . Thy friends are exultations, agonies, / And love, and man's unconquerable mind." From Stephen Gill, ed., *William Wordsworth* (Oxford: Oxford UP, 1984) 709.

27. Wordsworth 91.

28. Blake 208.

29. Adams 79.

30. Harold Bloom, *The Visionary Company: A Reading of English Romantic Poetry* (New York: Doubleday, 1961) 52.

31. Bloom 54.

32. Adams 82.

33. Qtd. in Blondel, *Mary Butts* 100.

34. Butts, *Traps for Unbelievers* in *Ashe of Rings and Other Writings* 330.

35. Byington and Morgan 171.

36. Byington and Morgan 178.

37. Byington and Morgan 170.

38. Qtd. in Blondel, *Mary Butts* 179.

39. Qtd. by Byington, in "The Writings and the World of Mary Butts," Tape 5, 1984.

TWO: A "WAR-FAIRY-TALE"

1. See Robert H. Byington's "Chronology" in *A Sacred Quest: The Life and Writings of Mary Butts,* ed. Christopher Wagstaff (Kingston, NY: McPherson & Company, 1995) 246.

2. Mary Butts, afterword, *Ashe of Rings and Other Wrintings* (Kingston, NY: McPherson & Company, 1998) 232. All subsequent references to this book in this chapter will be cited parenthetically in the text.

3. Sherry Ortner, "Is Female to Male as Nature Is to Culture?" *Woman, Culture, and Society,* ed. Michelle Zimbalist Rosaldo and Louise Lamphère (Stanford: Stanford UP, 1974) 86.

4. Louis Adeane, "Mary Butts," *World Review: New Series* 33 (November 1951): 26.

5. Robert H. Byington and Glen E. Morgan, "Mary Butts," *Art and Literature* (1965): 166.

6. "London after the War," *New York Times Book Review,* 9 August 1925: 7.

7. Bruno Bettelheim, *The Uses of Enchantment: The Meaning and Importance of Fairy Tales* (New York: Alfred A. Knopf, 1976) 5. Nina Sutton's biography, *Bettelheim: A Life and a Legacy* (NY: BasicBooks, 1996) has created a controversy surrounding Bettelheim's "violence" toward his patients and over the fact that he was not a trained analyst. This controversy, however, does not affect his assessment of fairy tales and their influence on children and adults.

8. Lillian Feder, *Ancient Myth in Modern Poetry* (Princeton: Princeton UP, 1971) 23.

9. In a diary entry in April 1921, Butts listed seven aims of her writing. Number one reads as follows: "I want to study and enjoy, and to enter if I can into the fairy world, the mythological world, and the world of the good ghost story." Qtd. in Nathalie Blondel, *Mary Butts: Scenes from the Life* (Kingston, NY: McPherson & Company, 1998) 100. This is one aim she strove for not only in her fiction, beginning with *Ashe of Rings,* but also in her short stories.

10. Qtd. in Blondel, *Mary Butts* 342–43.

11. Qtd. in Blondel, *Mary Butts* 326.

12. Qtd. in Blondel, *Mary Butts* 63.

13. James Joyce published *Dubliners* in 1914 and *Portrait of the Artist as a Young Man* in 1916. *Ulysses* was not published until 1922, although Joyce began initial work on the book in 1914. Butts, like Joyce, knew Sylvia Beach in Paris, and Harriet Shaw Weaver of *The Egoist* published four chapters of *Ulysses* with some excisions in 1919. By this time the novel had begun to appear in the *Little Review* in serial form in America in March 1918. Butts would easily have been familiar with Joyce's work when she began her work on *Ashe* in 1916.

14. Qtd. in Blondel, *Mary Butts* 50.

15. Qtd. in Blondel, *Mary Butts* 121.

16. Qtd. in Blondel, *Mary Butts* 147.

17. Qtd. in Blondel, *Mary Butts* 126, from a 1923 review in the *Irish Times* of her short story collection *Speed the Plough.*

18. Hugh I'A Fausset, "A 'War-Fairy-Tale,'" the *Manchester Guardian* 22 September 1933: 5.

19. John Ashbery, preface to Mary Butts's *From Altar to Chimney-piece: Selected Stories* (Kingston, NY: McPherson & Company, 1992) xii. Ashbery's assessment of Mary Butts's short fiction captures the writing technique of her fiction in general and serves as an accurate estimation and introduction to the technical aspect of her work. He writes, "The very features of her writing that taxed her earlier readers—her startling ellipses, especially in conversations; her drastic cutting in the cinematic sense; her technique of collaging bits of poetry and popular song lyrics . . . into the narratives—make her seem our contemporary. So do the freewheeling and disordered lives of her characters who can be wired in a very 1990s way. . . . One keeps getting the feeling that these stories were written yesterday."

20. Feder 63.

21. Byington and Morgan 177.

22. William Butler Yeats, *The Letters of W. B. Yeats,* ed. Allan Wade (New York: Octagon Books, 1980) 63. In a 1888 letter to Katharine Tynan, Yeats reveals at this point that his poetry is "almost a flight into fairyland from the real world, and a summons to that flight . . . it is not the poetry of insight and knowledge, but of longing and complaint—the cry of the heart against necessity. I hope some day to alter that and write poetry of insight and knowledge." Butts might not oppose "fairy tale" to "insight and knowledge" as Yeats does.

23. Linda Dégh, "Grimm's *Household Tales* and Its Place in the Household: The Social Relevance of a Controversial Classic," *Fairy Tales as Ways of Knowing: Essays on Märchen in Psychology, Society and Literature,* ed. Michael M. Metzger and Katharina Mommsen (Bern: Peter Lange, 1981) 40.

24. Maria Tatar, "Folkloristic Phantasies: Grimms' Fairy Tales and Freud's Family Romance," in *Fairy Tales as Ways of Knowing,* ed. Metzger and Mommsen 87.

25. Yeats 63.

26. Qtd. in Blondel, *Mary Butts* 100–101.

27. "Melita," *Dictionary of First Names* (New York: Facts on File Publishers, 1983), and "Melissa" (of which Melitta is a variant) *A Dictionary of First Names* (New York: Oxford UP, 1990).

28. See Gilbert Murray, *Four Stages of Greek Religion: Studies Based on a Course of Lectures Delivered in April 1912 at Columbia University* (New York: Columbia UP, 1912) 182. "*Sophrosynê,* however we try to translate it, temperance, gentleness, the spirit that in any trouble thinks and is patient, that saves and not destroys, is the right spirit."

29. Mary Butts, *The Crystal Cabinet: My Childhood at Salterns* (Manchester, Eng.: Carcanet Press Limited, 1988) 122.

30. "Van" is etymologically perhaps related to the obsolete word for a winnowing fan or basket. See *The Compact Edition of the Oxford English Dictionary* (Oxford: Oxford UP, 1971). The implication is that Van is like the basket or fan that separates the wheat from the chaff, the fraudulent from the authentic.

31. Fausset 5.

32. The 1933 edition of *Ashe of Rings,* published by Wishart & Co., London, reads as follows: "She would rehearse the turns of her screws on him at night; by day she would forget all about it" (79). Other quotations included in this text have slight variations in punctuation only.

33. It is interesting to note that by March of 1920 Mary Butts had immersed herself in studies of the occult and the magic of ritual in what she labeled the "4th Dimension." She and Cecil Maitland sealed their relationship through the ritual of sharing blood by cutting crosses on each other's wrists: "We sucked each other's cuts and kissed them, and lay back licking our own wrists." Qtd. in Blondel, *Mary Butts* 75.

34. Edward Fitch Hall, "Modern Witchcraft," *New York Herald Tribune* 8 August 1926: 8.

35. See Margaret Alice Murray, *The Witch-Cult in Western Europe,* foreword by Sir Steven Runciman (Oxford: Clarendon Press, 1967) 3. In his foreword to the 1967 reprint of her book, Steven Runciman explains that until the publication of Margaret Murray's study, the attitude toward witchcraft was "vague and unsystematic." Although her work has since had its skeptics and critics, it altered the prevailing

view of witches and promoted the theory that the "witch-cult was a survival of a pre-Christian religion in Western Europe, a fertility-cult which she called Dianic and which may have developed in Egypt" (4).

36. Qtd. in Margaret Alice Murray, Runciman foreword, 4. According to Thomas Cooper in his 1617 account, this yielding of the blood was to be "*sucked by Satan,* as a *sacrifice* vnto him, and testifying thereby the full *subiection* of their *liues* and *soules* to his devotion" (152).

37. Leon Surette, *The Birth of Modernism: Ezra Pound, T. S. Eliot, W. B. Yeats, and the Occult Movement* (Montreal: McGill-Queen's UP, 1993) ix.

38. Surette, *The Birth of Modernism* 6.

39. Dégh, "Grimm's" 41.

40. Margaret Alice Murray 154.

41. See Elaine Showalter, *The Female Malady: Women, Madness, and English Culture 1830–1980* (New York: Pantheon, 1985). In her chapter on male hysteria, Showalter explains that this malady paralleled the nervous disorders of women. Showalter records the evolution (in the 1910s) of shell shock in war-wounded men from the assumption of organic illness to "emotional disturbances produced by warfare itself." She continues by stating that it was a "compromise negotiated by the psyche between the instinct of self-preservation and the prohibitions against deception or flight. . . ." (170). It is interesting to note that Serge has avoided war altogether, but develops hysteria from his civilian fear.

42. Byington and Morgan 174.

43. It is interesting to note here that H. D., whom Butts knew and corresponded with, was also interested in the Hermetic tradition and in classical Greece and ancient Egypt. Nathalie Blondel notes in Butts's biography that H. D.'s biography by Barbara Guest, *Herself Defined: The Poet H. D. and her World* (Garden City, NJ: Doubleday, 1984) only mentions Mary Butts in passing and that "as early as 1963, Robert Duncan had raised the question of the unacknowledged influence of Mary Butts when discussing H. D.'s novel *Palimpsest*" (435), which was published in 1926, just a year after Mary Butts published *Ashe of Rings*. H. D.'s *Helen in Egypt* and *Hermetic Definition* may also reflect the influence of Mary Butts. It is most likely that they influenced each other. In *The Gender of Modernism* (Bloomington: Indiana UP, 1990), Bonnie Kime Scott notes that "unlike the epics of male modernists, H. D.'s poems center on the consciousness of female poet who finds a potent force for healing in the presence of female divinity in *Trilogy* and who writes herself out of patriarchal scripts through identification with the goddess in *Helen in Egypt*" (86). The interests of H. D. and Mary Butts may run in similar areas, but H. D. was far more of a feminist with a more experimental style in "respeaking myths of masculine classical culture from a woman's point of view" (86). As I argue in the introduction and throughout this book, Butts may indeed reinterpret myths from a female perspective, but she never fails to integrate the masculine view along with her own. In this way she deviates from other female modernists, whose emphasis was more rigorously and aggressively feminist. The reassessment was not so much of a struggle for Butts as it was a natural outgrowth of women's authentic place in relation to the past.

44. For further discussion of Basil Valentine's identity and writings, see John Read, *Prelude to Chemistry: An Outline of Alchemy Its Literature and Relationships* (New York: Macmillan, 1937) 183–87.

THREE: "DIS-EASE"

1. Robert H. Byington and Glen E. Morgan, "Mary Butts," *Art and Literature* (1965): 172.

2. Qtd. in Nathalie Blondel, *Mary Butts: Scenes from the Life* (Kingston, NY: McPherson & Company, 1998), 186. It is significant to note that in Byington's quotation, cited above, he cites the diary entry as "Eliot only writes of my quality, dislikes me and my work, I think." It seems Blondel would be the more accurate source—at least until the diaries are made available.

3. Jessie L. Weston, *From Ritual to Romance* (Garden City, NY: Doubleday Anchor Books, 1957) 149.

4. T. S. Eliot, "*Ulysses,* Order and Myth," *Selected Prose of T. S. Eliot,* ed. Frank Kermode (New York: Harcourt Brace Jovanovich/Farrar, Straus and Giroux, 1975) 177–78.

5. See Ruth Hoberman, *Gendering Classicism: The Ancient World in Twentieth Century Women's Historical Fiction* (New York: State U of New York P, 1997) 21–22.

6. Hoberman 22. Hoberman, in making the point here that Harrison argues for a return to the primitive one, when religion was not anthropomorphic and primitive peoples identified with the group, the totem, or tribe. Harrison explains in *Epilegomena to the Study of Greek Religion and Themis: A Study of Social Origins of Greek Religion.*(New York: University Books, 1962) that the first idea of totemism is the unity of the group; the second is "this human group is in a special relation to another group—this time of non-human objects" Harrison (120). Insofar as Mary Butts blends the idea of the group with the non-human through her longing to connect with her natural world, Butts is in alignment with Harrison. However, the fact that these things are part of what the group does as primitive people also supports my argument that Butts looks to the past to bring order through her use of myth. Her narratives are modern myths ordering while reminding readers not to forget origins that help build such myths.

7. Mary Butts, "Bloomsbury," *Modernism/Modernity* 5.2 (1998): 44.

8. Ruth Hoberman also argues that the female modernists she discusses (Naomi Mitchison, Mary Butts, Laura Riding, Mary Renault, Bryher, Phyllis Bentley) used myth to "challenge their culture's assumptions about gender" (22). I do not disagree with Hoberman on that point; however, my point is that Mary Butts can be set apart because she does use myth similarly to male modernists, and, although she may be challenging her culture's assumptions about gender, she does not do so by diminishing or arguing against a particular historical past. Instead, she wants women to find their own place and assert themselves as a viable part of that history.

9. Toril Moi, *Sexual/Textual Politics: Feminist Literary Theory* (New York: Methuen, 1985) 13.

10. Patrick Wright, *On Living in an Old Country: The National Past in Contemporary Britain* (London: Verso, 1985) 106.

11. Wright 106.

12. Mary Butts knew and admired E. M. Forster, and he admired her; in fact, there is correspondence between them in which he comments favorably on her work. However, Nathalie Blondel records in her biography of Butts that when E. M. Forster "was asked about her in 1949 he 'seemed to know little of her work'" (332).

13. Lillian Feder, *Ancient Myth in Modern Poetry* (Princeton: Princeton UP, 1971) 26.

14. Shelley Arlen, *The Cambridge Ritualists: An Annotated Bibliography of the Works by and about Jane Ellen Harrison, Gilbert Murray, Francis Cornford, and Arthur Bernard Cook* (Metuchen, NJ: Scarecrow Press, 1990) 1–2.

15. Martha C. Carpentier, "Jane Ellen Harrison and the Ritual Theory," *Journal of Ritual Studies* 81.1 (Winter 1994): 11.

16. Arlen 4–5.

17. Weston 121.

18. Jane Ellen Harrison, *Ancient Art and Ritual* (New York: Henry Holt and Company, 1913) v.

19. Harrison *Ancient Art* 35.

20. Robert Ackerman, *The Myth and Ritual School: J. G. Frazer and the Cambridge Ritualists* (New York: Garland, 1991). See Ackerman's book for a historical survey and clarification of the origins of and influences on the Cambridge Ritualists, the history of mythography, and modern literary criticism. Ackerman delineates influences on individual Cambridge Ritualists and the entire school of thought, which became important from the 1920s through the 1960s. Ackerman's study is especially useful in tracing the development of the myth-ritual theory and in identifying specific developments of thought concerning myth and ritual from the eighteenth century into the twentieth century. Carpentier's article draws much of its information from this source.

21. Carpentier 11–12.

22. Harrison, *Ancient Art* 29.

23. Leon Surette, "*The Waste Land* and Jessie Weston: A Reassessment," *Twentieth Century Literature* 34 (Summer 1988): 234–35. Surette sees Weston as writing religious history instead of anthropology, explores her association with the occult and with R. S. Mead, and contends that Weston's "study embraces the occult belief in a 'wisdom tradition' stretching back to antiquity, and further that recognition of Weston's occult thesis has consequences for our understanding of *The Waste Land*" (224).

24. Mary Butts, *The Crystal Cabinet: My Childhood at Salterns* (Manchester, Eng.: Carcanet Press Limited, 1988) 32–33.

25. Alicia Ostriker, *Stealing the Language: The Emergence of Women's Poetry in America* (Boston: Beacon Press, 1986) 32–33.

26. Ostriker, *Stealing the Language* 213.

27. Louis Adeane, "Mary Butts," *World Review: New Series* 33 (November 1951): 26.

28. Mary Butts, *The Taverner Novels: Armed with Madness, Death of Felicity Taverner* (Kingston, NY: McPherson & Company, 1992) 67. All subsequent references to *Armed with Madness* in this chapter will be cited parenthetically by page number in the text.

29. Marianne Moore, "A House Party," *Dial* 85 (September 1928): 260.

30. See Robin Blaser, "Here Lies the Woodpecker Who Was Zeus," in *A Sacred Quest: The Life and Writings of Mary Butts*, ed. Christopher Wagstaff (Kingston, NY: McPherson & Company, 1995), for a rather thorough evaluation of Nietzsche's

influence on Butts's novel and essay. Blaser examines the role of Nietzsche's presence in English literary thought and explores chronologically how Nietzsche would have affected Butts.

31. Jascha Kessler, "Recovering Mary Butts: Beauty and the Beast," *The Bookpress* 3.7 (October 1993): 14.

32. Feder 15.

33. Butts, *The Crystal Cabinet* 137.

34. Butts, *The Crystal Cabinet* 137.

35. Jane Ellen Harrison, *Prolegomena to the Study of Greek Religion* (Princeton: Princeton UP, 1991) 573.

36. Carpentier, "Jane Ellen Harrison" 23.

37. Northrop Frye, "Blake's Treatment of the Archetype," rpt. in *Blake's Poetry and Designs,* ed. Mary Lynn Johnson and John E. Grant (New York: W. W. Norton, 1979) 511.

38. Frye 511–12.

39. Weston 63.

40. Blaser, "Here Lies the Woodpecker" 192.

41. Robert McAlmon, *Being Geniuses Together 1920–1930* (San Francisco: North Point Press, 1984) 113.

42. J. E. Zimmerman, "Scylla," *Dictionary of Classical Mythology,* (New York: Bantam Books, 1971) 235–36.

43. Weston 75.

44. Weston 76.

45. Harrison, *Epilegomena and Themis* 68.

46. Blaser, "Here Lies the Woodpecker" 193.

47. Blaser, "Here Lies the Woodpecker" 193.

48. Robert E. Bell, "Picus," *Dictionary of Classical Myth*ology (Oxford, Eng: Clio Press Ltd., 1982) 283.

49. Harrison, *Epilegomena and Themis* 97.

50. David Adams Leeming, *The World of Myth* (New York: Oxford UP, 1990) 163.

51. C. G. Jung, *The Archetypes and the Collective Unconscious,* trans. R. F. C. Hull, *The Collected Works of C. G. Jung,* Bollingen Series XX (New York: Pantheon Books, 1959) 263.

52. Harrison, *Epilegomena and Themis* 110 and 113.

53. Harrison, *Epilegomena and Themis* 108–9.

54. Sir James George Frazer, *The New Golden Bough: A New Abridgement of the Classic Work,* ed. Theodor H. Gaster (New York: S. G. Phillips, 1972) 589–90.

55. Mary Butts, *Warning to Hikers* in *Ashe of Ring and Other Writings* (Kingston, NY: McPherson & Company, 1998) 290.

56. Harrison, *Epilegomena and Themis* 138.

57. Qtd. in Blondel, *Mary Butts* 207.

58. Qtd. in Blondel, *Mary Butts* 206.

FOUR: "VISIBLE PAN"

1. J. E. Zimmerman, "Pan," *Dictionary of Classical Mythology,* (New York: Bantam Books, 1971) 190.

2. Mary Butts, *Imaginary Letters* (Vancouver: Talonbooks, 1979). The introductory note tells us that a limited edition of 250 copies of *Imaginary Letters* appeared in 1928, but the text is dated "'Autumn, 1924,' at the Hotel Foyot in Paris, only a couple of years after Mary Butts left London and immersed herself in the frenzied Paris of the Twenties." It was greatly amended between 1926 and 1928. *Imaginary Letters* also appears in *Ashe of Rings and Other Writings* (Kingston, NY: McPherson & Company, 1998). All subsequent page references will be to this edition.

3. Mary Butts, *Imaginary Letters,* introductory note. All subsequent references to this novel in this chapter will be cited parenthetically in the text as *IL* followed by a page number.

4. Mary Hamer, "Mary Butts, Mothers, and War," *Women's Fiction and the Great War,* ed. Suzanne Rait and Trudi Tate (Oxford: Oxford UP, 1997) 232.

5. Butts, *Imaginary Letters,* afterword by Robin Blaser (Vancouver: Talonbooks, 1979) 64–65.

6. Patrick Wright, *On Living in an Old Country: The National Past in Contemporary Britain* (London: Verso, 1985) 114.

7. Bryher, "Recognition Not Farewell," *Life and Letters Today* 17.9 (Autumn 1937): 163.

8. Bryher, "Recognition" 163.

9. Louis Adeane, "Mary Butts," *World Review: New Series* 33 (November 1951): 24.

10. Robert H. Byington and Glen E. Morgan, "Mary Butts," *Art and Literature* (1965): 171.

11. Aleister Crowley ("The Great Beast") gives his opinion on why Butts chose weak or wounded men in his *The Confessions of Aleister Crowley* (New York: Hill and Wang, 1969) 880. When Mary Butts and Cecil Maitland went to visit Crowley and his occult group in Cefalu, Italy, Crowley became concerned about Maitland and felt Butts's influence played a major role in keeping him wretched. Crowley claims that with his attention, Maitland began to mend, but "the moment he showed the wish to become independent, the vanity of Mary Butts was wounded and her jealousy inflamed . . . she preferred to dull the anguish of the consciousness that she was a weakling, as she admitted, by keeping in abject dependence upon her a man on whom she could look down."

12. Frank Baker, *I Follow but Myself* (London: Peter Davies, 1968) 115.

13. Eve Kosofsky Sedgwick, *The Epistemology of the Closet* (Berkeley: U of California P, 1990) 251. As stated in the introduction, it is not the purpose of this study to delve into gay or queer theory; I leave that for the experts who will have much to explore in the work of Mary Butts. See also Judith Butler, *Bodies That Matter: On the Discursive Limits of "Sex* "(New York: Routledge, 1993); Eve Sedgwick's edited collection of essays, *Novel Gazing: Queer Readings in Fiction* (Durham: Duke UP, 1997); Annamarie Jagose, *Queer Theory: An Introduction* (New York: New York UP, 1996); and, perhaps from a different perspective, Michel Foucault's *The History of Sexuality: An Introduction,* vol. I. trans. Robert Hurley (New York: Random House, 1978) might prove helpful.

14. Butts, *Imaginary Letters,* afterword by Robin Blaser 75.

15. See Patricia Posluszny, *Thomas Nashe's Summer's Last Will and Testament* (New York: Peter Lang, 1989) 23. Nashe's allegory mourns the approaching death

of summer as it "discusses the transitory nature of life and points out in order of impermanence 'life's lustful joys'—wealth, beauty, strength, and wit." Butts's alteration of the line from Nashe not only plays on the notion of "queen" in discussing her character's homosexual lover but also makes a comment on the transitory nature of beauty, youthful lust, and youth itself.

16. Stephen Barber, "Lip-Reading: Woolf's Secret Encounters," in *Novel Gazing*, ed. Sedgwick, 405. It is, of course, important to note Virginia Woolf's relationships with gay men and to realize that Britain was still a homophobic and misogynistic society. The memory of Oscar Wilde's trial and imprisonment for homosexual practices (1895–97) was still in recent memory. Butts perhaps identified with these young men because she felt the same sort of (intellectual) isolation as a woman. Also, she choose to deal with that inequity by pursuing a lifestyle that was considered outrageous, especially for a woman.

17. Bryher, "Recognition" 163.

18. Mary Butts, *The Crystal Cabinet: My Childhood at Salterns* (Manchester, Eng.: Carcanet Press Limited, 1988) 122.

19. Butts, *The Crystal Cabinet* 123.

20. Butts, *The Crystal Cabinet* 115.

21. Butts, *The Crystal Cabinet* 198.

22. Qtd. in Robert H. Byington, "Interviews with Virgil Thomson, Eugene MacCown, Quentin Bell and Hugh Ross Williamson," in *A Sacred Quest: The Life and Writings of Mary Butts*, ed. Christopher Wagstaff (Kingston, NY: McPherson & Company, 1995) 43.

23. Byington, "Interviews" 46.

24. Byington, "Interviews" 46.

25. Robin Blaser, "Here Lies the Woodpecker Who Was Zeus," in *A Sacred Quest*, ed. Wagstaff 204–5. Anthony Butts was a painter whose early life parallels that of Val in the fairy tale version of their life, *Ashe of Rings*. Mary's love for Tony was unwavering, but his attachment to their mother alienated him from Mary, as did Mary's actions. Tony's comments on his sister's lifestyle and work were emphasized by the work of his close friend William Plomer. Douglas Goldring, however, in spite of his revelations of the details of Mary's life in *South Lodge*, respected her work and, agreeing with Ford Madox Ford's opinion, felt she possessed a "streak, at least, of genius." See Douglas Goldring, *South Lodge: Reminiscences of Violet Hunt, Ford Madox Ford and the English Review Circle* (London: Constable & Co., Ltd., 1943) 147.

26. Harcourt Wesson Bull, "Truth Is the Heart's Desire," in *A Sacred Quest*, ed. Wagstaff 56.

27. Qtd. in Nathalie Blondel, *Mary Butts: Scenes from the Life* (Kingston, NY: McPherson & Company, 1998) 306.

28. Jane Ellen Harrison, *Prolegomena to the Study of Greek Religion* (Princeton: Princeton UP, 1991) 96.

29. René Girard, *Violence and the Sacred*, trans. Patrick Gregory (Baltimore: Johns Hopkins UP, 1972) 8.

30. See Patrick Wright's assertion that Kralin is "to an extent formed after the image of John Rodker, the Jewish writer and leftist publisher who was also the father of her daughter" (Wright 123). Wright posits that Butts's Kralin is a retaliation

against Rodker, who had been accusing Butts of addiction and neglect of their daughter and who attacked her in his own *á clef* story, *Adolphe* (1920), and later in an anonymously published *Memoirs of Other Fronts* (1932). In a conversation with the author's daughter on 3 and 4 June 1996, in Dorset, England, Camilla Bagg made a similar claim about Kralin and Rodker; however, she stated that Rodker was just as much a neglectful father as Butts was a mother.

31. Mary Butts, *Warning to Hikers* in *Ashe of Rings and Other Writings* (Kingston, NY: McPherson & Company, 1998) 289.

32. Mary Butts, *The Taverner Novels: Armed with Madness, Death of Felicity Taverner* (Kingston: McPherson & Company, 1992) 171. All subsequent references to *Death of Felicity Taverner* in this chapter will be made parenthetically in the text.

33. Butts, *Warning to Hikers* 289–90.

34. Leon Surette, *The Birth of Modernism: Ezra Pound, T. S. Eliot, W. B. Yeats, and the Occult Movement* (Montreal: McGill-Queen's UP, 1993) 58.

35. J. G. Frazer, *The Golden Bough: A Study in Magic and Religion,* pt. 4. *The Scapegoat* (London: Macmillan and Co., Limited, 1913) 225.

36. Frazer, *Scapegoat* 408.

37. Adeane 26.

38. René Girard, *The Scapegoat,* trans. Yvonne Freccero (Baltimore: Johns Hopkins UP, 1986) 6.

39. Girard, *The Scapegoat* 12. See Girard's discussion of the scapegoat in the mid-fourteenth-century text of Guillaume de Machaut's *Judgment of the King of Navarre,* especially his discussion of historical persecution of the Jews and their function as scapegoats in societies frightened by the Black Death.

40. The anti-Semitism of Ezra Pound is, of course, well known and well documented. Leon Surette claims that "[o]ccultism . . . is frequently accompanied by some variety of political radicalism or subversion and . . . does not appear to have any particular ideological preferences. As with Nietzscheanism, the occult finds adherents across the whole political spectrum. . . . A case in point is the admiration that Allen Ginsberg, a left-wing Jewish poet, maintains for the right-wing and anti-Semitic Ezra Pound. Despite these differences, they share a sedition theory of history and culture, and a belief in the power of poetry to communicate revelations of ultimate reality" (*The Birth of Modernism* 45). In a society already disrupted by war and technology, Nick Kralin as seditious scapegoat fits neatly into this theory. The image of the Jew impinging upon established property and values offers a narrative movement toward ritual and communication, or revelation of "ultimate reality." It is also interesting to note the attention paid to Anthony Julius's *T. S. Eliot, Anti-Semitism and Literary Form* (Cambridge: Cambridge UP, 1996). Eliot's anti-Semitism, although not so flagrant as Pound's, has become a focal point of controversy in literary studies. Butts, along with her contemporaries, was not completely free of these prejudices in spite of, or perhaps because of, the fact that her first husband, John Rodker, was Jewish.

41. T. M., "A Memorable Novel," *Manchester Guardian* 9 December 1932: 7.

42. Dennis D. Hughes, *Human Sacrifice in Ancient Ritual* (London: Routledge, 1991) 152.

43. Frazer, *Scapegoat* 253.

44. Girard, *Violence and the Sacred* 258.

45. Barbara Wagstaff (under pen name of Leslie Rivers), "Alchemist of Reality: Recovering Mary Butts," *Poetry Flash* No. 133 (April 1984): 9.

46. Girard, *Violence and the Sacred* 258.

47. Cesáreo Banderos, *The Sacred Game: The Role of the Sacred in the Genesis of Modern Fiction* (University Park: Pennsylvania State UP, 1994) 19.

48. Harrison, *Prolegomena* 104.

49. Baker, *I Follow* 142.

50. Butts, *Warning to Hikers* 278.

51. Butts, *Warning to Hikers* 283.

52. Baker, *I Follow* 116.

53. Mary Butts, "Questionnaire," *Little Review* (May 1929): 21.

54. Butts, "Questionnaire" 22.

55. Butts, *Warning to Hikers* 269.

56. Qtd. in Glen E. Morgan, "Mary Butts," *Antaeus* 12 (Winter 1973): 144.

57. Jane Ellen Harrison, *Epilegomena to the Study of Greek Religion and Themis: A Study of Social Origins of Greek Religion* (New York: University Books, 1962) 564. Murray's memorial lecture included.

58. Butts, *Warning to Hikers* 295.

59. Butts, *Warning to Hikers* 294.

60. Butts, *Warning to Hikers* 294.

61. Butts, *Warning to Hikers* 294.

FIVE: "BRIGHTNESS FALLS"

1. Two modern collections of her stories have been published in Britain and America: *With and Without Buttons and Other Stories,* selected with an afterword by Nathalie Blondel (Manchester: Carcanet Press Limited, 1991), and *From Altar to Chimney-piece: Selected Stories,* preface by John Ashbery (Kingston, NY: McPherson & Co., 1992).

2. Christopher Wagstaff, preface in *A Sacred Quest: The Life and Writings of Mary Butts,* ed. Christopher Wagstaff (Kingston, NY: McPherson & Company, 1995) xiii.

3. Ashbery, preface, in *From Altar to Chimney-piece* ii and xi.

4. J. C. Squire, "The Modern Revival of the Short Story: Miss Mary Butts' Success," *Daily Telegraph* 8 March 1932: 16. Review of *Several Occasions.*

5. Rose Macaulay, "Stories Old and New," *Daily News* 12 April 1923: 7. Rev. of *Speed the Plough and Other Stories.*

6. Glenway Wescott, "The First Book of Mary Butts," in *A Sacred Quest,* ed. Wagstaff 12.

7. Rhys Davies, "A Note on Mary Butts," *Wales* 6.7 (1939): 207.

8. Qtd. in Nathalie Blondel, *Mary Butts: Scenes from the Life* (Kingston, NY: McPherson & Company, 1998) 99.

9. In their editors' notes, John Symonds and Kenneth Grant explain that "[t]he heart of Crowley is Magick, not magic, six letters instead of five, to affirm the identity of man (the pentagram) with God (the hexagram). Through Magick the human consciousness is made divine; hence Crowley the Magus is equivalent to a Logos,

an embodied Word, like Christ, Mohammed, Buddha." Crowley, *The Confessions of Aleister Crowley: An Autohagiography,* ed. John Symonds and Kenneth Grant (New York: Hill and Wang, 1969) 925. For definitions, see Aleister Crowley, *Magick in Theory and Practice* (Secaucus, NJ: Castle, 1991) xii.

10. Aleister Crowley, *Confessions* 878 and 922. Butts later denounced Crowley in an interview with the *Sunday Express* where she identified his Abbey of Thelema in Cefalu as filled with "profligacy and vice," presumably in response to his attack on her in his book *Diary of a Drug Fiend* (New York: E.P. Dutton, 1923). See Colin Wilson, *Aleister Crowley: The Nature of the Beast* (Wellingborough, Eng.: Antiquarian Press, 1987) 130. She quickly became disenchanted with Crowley after visiting his abbey. Butts had read widely in occult practices and magic before meeting Crowley. The brief encounter between them probably offered an equal exchange of information, and, in fact, Crowley most likely gained more knowledge from Butts than she did from him.

11. Robert H. Byington and Glen E. Morgan, "Mary Butts," *Art and Literature* (1965): 165.

12. See Robert McAlmon's letter to Norman Holmes Pearson in which he presents ideas for his "History of Encounters," unpublished typescript (Beinecke Library), that consists of "portraits" of various people he had known "through the years." McAlmon describes visiting Mary and Cecil at their apartment on the Rue Tombe Issoire and finding them engaged in a "black magic seance" involving a dead rat and magical rites. In his letter as well as in his "fictional" portrait, McAlmon paints a fairly nasty picture of Mary Butts as a drug-addicted, pretentious character willing to do or say anything to convince her victims to loan her money. Still, he concludes his description by insisting that "Amy's (Mary) one of the lasses who likes taking care of her man," an observation made by numerous people who knew Mary Butts.

13. See the introduction to the first edition of *Themis.* Jane Harrison, *Epilegomena to the Study of Greek Religion and Themis: A Study of Social Origins of Greek Religion* (New York: University Books, 1962) 545.

14. Mary Butts, "Ghosties and Ghoulies: The Uses of the Supernatural in English Fiction," *The Bookman* 83 (March 1933): 493. This collection of essays from *The Bookman* can also be found in *Ashe of Rings and Other Writings* (Kingston, NY: McPherson & Company, 1998) 351. It is interesting to note that an early, cryptic story titled "Magic" appeared in the *Little Review* in 1920. This was perhaps one of her initial forays into the topic, yet the story was never included in any collection. It does, however, explore an artist's ability to "present appearance in reality" and the knowledge gained from using magic supplies power to that individual. See Mary Butts, "Magic," *Little Review* 2.2 (July-August 1920): 3–6.

15. Virgil Thomson, *Virgil Thomson* (New York: Alfred A. Knopf, 1966) 87.

16. See Butts's series of articles "Ghosties and Ghoulies" in *The Bookman* 83 and 84 (1933) or the articles collected in *Ashe of Rings and Other Writings* (1998) for a discussion of authors Butts admired and whose work vibrates with these ideas in a way she approves. Some of them included Rider Haggard, John Buchan, May Sinclair, Lady Gregory, W. B. Yeats, Naomi Royde-Smith.

17. Frank Baker, *I Follow but Myself* (London: Peter Davies, 1968) 146.

18. Mary Butts, *Traps for Unbelievers* (Kingston, NY: McPherson & Company, 1998) 312.

19. Butts, *From Altar to Chimney-piece* 193. Unless otherwise indicated all subsequent references to short stories in this chapter will be cited parenthetically in the text.

20. "Withershins" and "Deasil," *The Compact Edition of the Oxford English Dictionary* (Oxford: Oxford UP, 1971).

21. Christine Downing, *The Goddess: Mythological Images of the Feminine* (New York: Crossroad Publishing Company, 1989) 2.

22. Downing 4.

23. Downing 4.

24. Butts, "Ghosties and Ghoulies" 387 and in *Ashe of Rings and Other Writings* 337.

25. Butts, "Ghosties and Ghoulies" 388 and in *Ashe of Rings and Other Writings* 337.

26. Butts, "Ghosties and Ghoulies" 387 and in *Ashe of Rings and Other Writings* 337.

27. Butts, "Ghosties and Ghoulies" 389 and in *Ashe of Rings and Other Writings* 343.

28. Jascha Kessler, "Recovering Mary Butts: Beauty and the Beast," *The Bookpress* 3.7 (October 1993): 13.

29. Butts, *Traps for Unbelievers* in *Ashe of Rings and Other Writings* 299.

30. Butts, *Traps for Unbelievers* 317.

31. Mircea Eliade, introduction, *The Sacred and the Profane: The Nature of Religion* (New York: Harcourt, Brace & World, Inc. 1959) 12, 13.

32. Eliade 12.

33. Qtd. in Blondel, *Mary Butts* 305.

34. Kessler, "Recovering" 13.

35. For discussions of what took place at Crowley's abbey, its bestial orgies, prostitution, treatment of children, and sexual practices see Crowley's own work and also John Symonds, *The Great Beast: The Life of Aleister Crowley* (London: Rider and Company, 1951); and Wilson. The name *Thelema* comes from Rabelais' *Gargantua and Pantagruel.* The only rule of the abbey of Thélème was "Fais ce que vouldras" ("Do as thou wilt").

36. In her diary in 1932, Butts claims that these objects were actually in Stein's home: "the mutilated altar-ornaments—I saw myself." Qtd. in Blondel, *Mary Butts* 305.

37. Butts, *Traps for Unbelievers* 330.

38. It is interesting to note that Aleister Crowley, in his *AL (Liber Legis):The Book of the Law,* (San Francisco: Level Pres, 1974), explains the development of aeons in the history of the world. His interpretation states that "[t]he first, that of Isis, is the aeon of the woman; hence, matriarchy, the worship of the Great Mother and so on. About 500 B.C. this aeon was succeeded by the aeon of Osiris, that is, the aeon of the man, the father, hence the paternal religions of suffering and death—Judaism, Buddhism, Christianity and Mohammedanism. This aeon came to an end in 1904 when Aleister Crowley received *The Book of the Law,* and the new aeon, that of Horus, the child, was born. In this aeon the emphasis is on the true self or will, not on anything external such as gods and priests." See the introduction to Crowley, *Confessions* 22. It is possible Mary Butts drew from this cosmology in her examination of the new civilization as children playing at games and trying to find their way by making up new, childlike rules and rituals to fit their society.

39. R. Ellis Roberts, "Short Stories," *New Statesman & Nation* 3.5 (12 March 1932): 340.

40. Evelyn Underhill, *Mysticism: A Study in the Nature and Development of Man's Spiritual Consciousness* (New York: World Publishing Company, 1955) 393.

41. Butts, *Traps, for Unbelievers* 323.

42. Robert McAlmon, *Being Geniuses Together 1920–1930* (San Francisco: North Point Press, 1984) 203.

43. Baker, *I Follow* 115.

44. Oliver Conant, "Countryside Modern," *New York Times Book Review* 26 July 1992: 23.

45. See Ashbery, preface xi.

CONCLUSION

1. Sandra M. Gilbert and Susan Gubar, *No Man's Land: The Place of the Woman Writer in the Twentieth Century*, vol. 2, *Sexchanges* (New Haven, CT: Yale UP, 1989) 5.

2. Gilbert and Gubar, *The Madwoman in the Attic: The Woman Writer and the Nineteenth-Century Literary Imagination* (New Haven, CT: Yale UP, 1984) 4. In their discussion Gilbert and Gubar cite Edward Said's "meditation" on the word *authority*, all examinations of the word indicating power or control.

3. Carl G. Jung, *The Archetypes and the Collective Unconscious,* trans. R. F. C. Hull. *The Collected Works of C. G. Jung*. Bollingen Series XX (New York: Pantheon Books, 1959) 160, para. 271.

4. Anne Baring and Jules Cashford, preface, *The Myth of the Goddess: Evolution of an Image* (London: Viking Arcana, 1991) xiv.

5. Mary Butts, "Vision of Asia," rev. of *The Vision of Asia: An Interpretation of Chinese Art and Culture,* by L. Cranmer-Byng. *The Bookman* 83 (Dec. 1932): 223–25.

6. Butts, "Vision of Asia" 224.

7. Barbara Wagstaff, telephone conversation with author, 24 May 1993.

8. Nathalie Blondel, *Mary Butts: Scenes from the Life* (Kingston, NY: McPherson & Company, 1998) 426.

9. Frank Baker, *I Follow but Myself* (London: Peter Davies, 1968) 135.

APPENDIX

1. Thomas McEvilley, preface, *The Classical Novels; The Macedonia/Scenes from the Life of Cleopatra,* by Mary Butts (Kingston, NY: McPherson & Company, 1994) ix.

2. Ruth Hoberman, *Gendering Classicism: The Ancient World in Twentieth-Century Women's Historical Fiction* (New York: State U of New York P, 1997) 43.

3. Hoberman 45.

4. Hoberman 52.

5. In her preface Butts acknowledges that she followed E. M. Forster's lead in showing the importance of the visit to Siwa. It plays carefully into the emphasis Butts places on spirituality in the life of humanity.

6. Butts, *The Classical Novels* 39. All subsequent references to either novel in the appendix will be cited parenthetically from this edition.

7. Hoberman 53.
8. Hoberman 54.
9. Hoberman 54.
10. Hoberman 46.
11. See Blondel, *Mary Butts* 380. Lindsay, *Last Days with Cleopatra* (London: Nicholson & Watson, 1935).
12. See Nathalie Blondel, *Mary Butts: Scenes from the Life* (Kingston, NY: McPherson & Company, 1998) 380–81 and 353–54.
13. Blondel, *Mary Butts* 381.
14. Qtd. in Blondel, *Mary Butts* 382.
15. Qtd. in Blondel, *Mary Butts* 335.
16. Blondel, *Mary Butts* 335. It is also interesting to note that this "shared sense of humiliation" in some ways accounts for Mary Butts's sensitivity to homosexual men. She shared with them a sense of the humiliation of being a woman in a patriarchal world and understood their struggle to survive in a world indifferent, and even hostile, to their needs.
17. In my interview with Camilla Bagg on 15 April 1998, she told me that among Mary Butts's papers is an unpublished novel, *Unborn Gods* that "seems to be merely an exercise in expressing what she thought about men and sex. . . . I think already she was beginning to feel that she had some sort of magic power with men, but what was she to do about it?" In writing about Cleopatra, Butts seems to know what to do about this magic power. Cleopatra uses her sexuality as a weapon of war and survival, just as Caesar and Mark Antony use swords and politics.
18. Hoberman 140.
19. Hoberman 142.
20. Julia Kristeva, *The Kristeva Reader,* ed. Toril Moi (New York: Columbia UP, 1986) 192.
21. Hoberman 142.
22. Qtd. in Blondel, *Mary Butts* 381.

Bibliography

Ackerman, Robert. *The Myth and Ritual School: J. G. Frazer and the Cambridge Ritualists.* New York: Garland, 1991.

Adams, Hazard. "'The Crystal Cabinet' and 'The Golden Net.'" *Blake: A Collection of Critical Essays.* Ed. Northrop Frye. Englewood Cliffs, NJ: Prentice Hall, 1966.

Adeane, Louis. "Mary Butts." *World Review: New Series* 33 (November 1951): 23–27.

Arlen, Shelley. *The Cambridge Ritualists: An Annotated Bibliography of the Works by and about Jane Ellen Harrison, Gilbert Murray, Francis Cornford, and Arthur Bernard Cook.* Metuchen, NJ: Scarecrow Press, 1990.

Ashbery, John. Preface. *From Altar to Chimney-piece: Selected Stories by Mary Butts.* Kingston: McPherson & Company, 1992.

Bagg, Camilla. Interview by author, Dorset, England, 1, 3, 4 June 1996.

Baker, Frank. *I Follow but Myself.* London: Peter Davies, 1968.

Banderos, Cesáreo. *The Sacred Game: The Role of the Sacred in the Genesis of Modern Fiction.* University Park: Pennsylvania State UP, 1994.

Barber, Stephen. "Lip Reading: Woolf's Secret Encounters." *Novel Gazing: Queer Readings in Fiction.* Ed. Eve Kosofsky Sedgwick. Durham, NC: Duke UP, 1997.

Baring, Anne and Jules Cashford. *The Myth of the Goddess: Evolution of an Image.* London: Viking Arcana, 1991.

Bell, Quentin. *Bloomsbury Recalled.* New York: Columbia UP, 1995.

Bell, Robert E. "Picus." *Dictionary of Classical Mythology.* Oxford, Eng: Clio Press, 1982.

Benstock, Shari. *Women of the Left Bank: Paris, 1900–1940.* Austin: U of Texas P, 1986.

Bettleheim, Bruno. *The Uses of Enchantment: The Meaning and Importance of Fairy Tales.* New York: Alfred A. Knopf, 1976.

Blake, William. *Blake's Poetry and Designs.* Ed. Mary Lynn Johnson and John E. Grant. New York: W. W. Norton, 1979.

Blaser, Robin. Afterword. *Imaginary Letters* by Mary Butts. Vancouver: Talonbooks, 1979.

———. "Here Lies the Woodpecker Who Was Zeus." In *A Sacred Quest: The Life and Writings of Mary Butts.* Ed. Christopher Wagstaff. Kingston, NY: McPherson & Company, 1995.

Blondel, Nathalie. Interview by author, Bristol, England, 3, 4 June 1996.

———. *Mary Butts: Scenes from the Life.* Kingston: McPherson & Company, 1998.

Bloom, Harold. *The Visionary Company: A Reading of English Romantic Poetry.* New York: Doubleday, 1961.

Blotner, Joseph. "Mythic Patterns in *To the Lighthouse.*" *Myth and Literature.* Ed. John B. Vickery. Lincoln: U of Nebraska P, 1966.

Bradbury, Malcolm, and James McFarlane, eds. *Modernism 1890–1930.* London: Penguin, 1991.

Bryher. "Recognition Not Farewell." *Life and Letters Today* 17.9 (Autumn 1937): 159–64.

Bryher papers. 12 June 23 (Beinecke Library).

Bull, Harcourt Wesson. "Truth Is the Heart's Desire." In *A Sacred Quest: The Life and Writings of Mary Butts.* Ed. Christopher Wagstaff. Kingston, NY: McPherson & Company, 1995.

Butler, Judith. *Bodies That Matter: On the Discursive Limits of "Sex".* New York: Routledge, 1993.

Byington, Robert H. "Interviews with Virgil Thomson, Eugene MacCown, Quentin Bell and Hugh Ross Williamson." In *A Sacred Quest: The Life and Writings of Mary Butts.* Ed. Christopher Wagstaff. Kingston, NY: McPherson & Company, 1995.

———. "The Writings and the World of Mary Butts." Tape 5. Proc. of a Conference at the University of California, Davis. 23–24 November 1984.

Byington, Robert H., and Glen E. Morgan. "Mary Butts." *Art and Literature* (1965): 163–79.

Carpentier, Martha C. "Jane Ellen Harrison and the Ritual Theory." *Journal of Ritual Studies* 81.1 (Winter 1994): 11–25.

Coe, Richard N. *When the Grass Was Taller: Autobiography and the Experience of Childhood.* New Haven, CT: Yale UP, 1984.

Conant, Oliver. "Countryside Modern." *New York Times Book Review* 26 July 1992: 23.

Crowley, Aleister. *AL (Liber Legis): The Book of the Law.* San Francisco: Level Press, 1974.

———. *The Confessions of Aleister Crowley: An Autohagiography.* Ed. John Symonds and Kenneth Grant. New York: Hill and Wang, 1969.

———. *Diary of a Drug Fiend.* New York: E. P. Dutton, 1923.

———. *Magick in Theory and Practice,* by the Master Therion (Aleister Crowley). Secaucus, NJ: Castle, 1991.

Daemmrich, Horst S., and Ingrid. *Themes and Motifs in Western Literature; A Handbook.* Tübingen: Francke Verlag, 1987.

Davies, Rhys. "A Note on Mary Butts." *Wales* 6.7 (1939): 207.

"Deasil." *The Compact Edition of the Oxford English Dictionary.* 1971 ed.

Dégh, Linda. "Grimm's *Household Tales* and Its Place in the Household: The Social Relevance of a Controversial Classic." *Fairy Tales as Ways of Knowing: Essays on Märchen in Psychology, Society and Literature.* Ed. Michael M. Metzger and Katharina Mommsen. Bern: Peter Lang, 1981.

DeKovan, Marianne. "The Politics of Modernist Form." *New Literary History* 23.3 (Summer 1992): 675–90.

———. *Rich and Strange: Gender, History, Modernism.* Princeton: Princeton UP, 1991.

Downing, Christine. *The Goddess: Mythological Images of the Feminine.* New York: Crossroad Publishing Company, 1989.

Dundes, Alan, ed. *Sacred Narrative: Readings in the Theory of Myth.* Berkeley: U of California P, 1984.

Eliade, Mircea. *The Sacred and the Profane: The Nature of Religion.* New York: Harcourt, Brace & World, 1959.

Eliot, T. S. "*Ulysses,* Order and Myth (1923)." *Selected Prose of T. S. Eliot.* Ed. Frank Kermode. New York: Harcourt Brace Jovanovich/Farrar, Straus and Giroux, 1975.

———. *The Waste Land, The Complete Poems and Plays 1909–1950.* New York: Harcourt, Brace & World, 1971.

Fausset, Hugh I'A. "'A 'War-Fairy-Tale.'" *Manchester Guardian* 22 September 1933: 5.

Feder, Lillian. *Ancient Myth in Modern Poetry.* Princeton: Princeton UP, 1971.

Felski, Rita. *The Gender of Modernity.* Cambridge, Mass.: Harvard UP, 1995.

Foucault, Michel. *The History of Sexuality: An Introduction.* Vol. I. Trans. Robert Hurley. New York: Random House, 1978.

Frazer, Sir James George. *The Golden Bough: A Study in Magic an Religion.* Pt. 4. *The Scapegoat.* London: Macmillan and Co., Limited, 1913.

———. *The New Golden Bough: A New Abridgement of the Classic Work.* Ed. Theodor H. Gaster. New York: S. G. Phillips, 1972.

Friedman, Susan Stanford, and Rachel Blau Duplessis, eds. *Signets: Reading H. D.* Madison: U of Wisconsin P, 1990.

Frye, Northrop. "Blake's Treatment of the Archetype." Rpt. in *Blake's Poetry and Designs.* Ed. Mary Lynn Johnson and John E. Grant. New York: W. W. Norton, 1979.

Gilbert, Sandra M., and Susan Gubar. *The Madwoman in the Attic: The Woman Writer and the Nineteenth Century Literary Imagination.* New Haven, CT: Yale UP, 1984.

———. *No Man's Land: The Place of the Woman Writer in the Twentieth Century.* Vol. 1. *The War of the Words.* New Haven, CT: Yale UP, 1988.

———. *No Man's Land: The Place of the Woman Writer in the Twentieth Century.* Vol. 2. *Sexchanges.* New Haven, CT: Yale UP, 1989.

Gill, Stephen, ed. *William Wordsworth.* Oxford: Oxford UP, 1984.

Girard, René. *The Scapegoat.* Trans. Yvonne Freccero. Baltimore, MD: Johns Hopkins UP, 1986.

———. *Violence and the Sacred.* Translated by Patrick Gregory. Baltimore, MD: Johns Hopkins UP, 1972.

Goldring, Douglas. *The Nineteen Twenties: A General Survey and Some Personal Memories.* London: Nicholson & Watson, 1945.

———. *South Lodge: Reminiscences of Violet Hunt, Ford Madox Ford and the English Review Circle.* London: Constable & Co., Ltd., 1943.

Hall, Edward Fitch. "Modern Witchcraft." *New York Herald Tribune* 8 August 1926: 8.

Hamer, Mary. "Mary Butts, Mothers, and War." *Women's Fiction and the Great War.* Ed. Suzanne Rait and Trudi Tate. Oxford: Oxford UP, 1997.

Hanscombe, Gillian, and Virginia L. Smyers. *Writing for Their Lives: The Modernist Women 1910–1940.* Boston: Northeastern UP, 1987.

Harrison, Jane Ellen. *Ancient Art and Ritual.* New York: Henry Holt and Company, 1913.

———. *Epilegomena to the Study of Greek Religion and Themis: A Study of Social Origins of Greek Religion.* New York: University Books, 1962.

———. *Prolegomena to the Study of Greek Religion.* Princeton: Princeton UP, 1991.

Hoberman, Ruth. *Gendering Classicism: The Ancient World in Twentieth-Century Women's Historical Fiction.* Albany: State U of New York P, 1997.

Homans, Margaret. *Bearing the Word: Language and Female Experience in Nineteenth-Century Women's Writing.* Chicago: Chicago UP, 1986.

Hughes, Dennis D. *Human Sacrifice in Ancient Ritual.* London: Routledge, 1991.

Jagose, Annamarie. *Queer Theory: An Introduction.* New York: New York UP, 1996.

James, William. *The Varieties of Religious Experience: A Study in Human Nature.* New York: Modern Library, 1929.

Julius, Anthony. *T.S. Eliot: Anti-Semitism and Literary Form.* Cambridge: Cambridge UP, 1996.

Jung, Carl. *The Archetypes and the Collective Unconscious.* Trans. R. F. C. Hull *The Collected Works of C. G. Jung.* Bollingen Series XX. New York: Pantheon Books, 1959.

Kessler, Jascha. "Recovering Mary Butts: Beauty and the Beast." *The Bookpress* 3.7 (October 1993): 1, 12–14.

Kristeva, Julia. *The Kristeva Reader.* Ed. Toril Moi. New York: Columbia UP, 1986.

Leeming, David Adams. *The World of Myth.* New York: Oxford UP, 1990.

"London after the War." *New York Times Book Review* 9 August 1925: 7.

M., T. "A Memorable Novel." *Manchester Guardian* 9 December 1932: 7.

Macaulay, Rose. "Stories Old and New." *Daily News* 12 April 1923: 7.

McAlmon, Robert. *Being Geniuses Together 1920–1930.* San Francisco: North Point Press, 1984.

———. "History of Encounters" and letter to Norman Holmes Pearson. Unpublished typescript. 8 Dec. 1952. Beinecke Library, New Haven, CT.

"Melissa." *A Dictionary of First Names.* New York: Oxford UP, 1990.

"Melita." *Dictionary of First Names.* New York: Facts on File Publishers, 1983.

Mellor, Anne K. *Romanticism & Gender.* New York: Routledge, 1993.

———, ed. *Romanticism and Feminism.* Bloomington: Indiana UP, 1988.

McPherson, Bruce. personal correspondence. 2 January 1998.

Moi, Toril. *Sexual/Textual Politics: Feminist Literary Theory.* New York: Methuen, 1985.

Moore, Marianne. "A House Party." *Dial* 85 (September 1928): 258–60.

Morgan, Glen E. "Mary Butts." *Antaeus* 12 (Winter 1973): 144–46.

Morris, Adelaide. "The Concept of Projection: H. D.'s Visionary Powers." *Signets: Reading H. D.* Ed. Susan Stanford Friedman and Rachel Blau Duplessis. Madison: U of Wisconsin P, 1990.

Morris, William. *The Collected Works of William Morris.* London: Routledge/Thoemmes, 1992.

Murray, Margaret Alice. *The Witch-Cult in Western Europe.* Foreword by Sir Steven Runciman. Oxford: Clarendon Press, 1967.

Murray, Gilbert. *Five Stages of Greek Religion.* New York: Columbia UP, 1930.

———. *Four Stages of Greek Religion: Studies Based on a Course of Lectures Delivered in April 1912 at Columbia University.* New York: Columbia UP, 1912.

Ortner, Sherry. "Is Female to Male as Nature Is to Culture?" *Woman, Culture, and Society.* Ed. Michelle Zimbalist Rosaldo and Louise Lamphère. Stanford: Stanford UP, 1974.

Ostriker, Alicia. *Stealing the Language: The Emergence of Women's Poetry in America.* Boston: Beacon Press, 1986.

———. "Thieves of Language: Women Poets and Revisionist Mythmaking." *Coming to Light: American Women Poets in the Twentieth Century.* Ed. Diane Wood Middlebrook and Marilyn Yalom. Ann Arbor: U of Michigan P, 1985.

Posluszny, Patricia. *Thomas Nashe's Summer's Last Will and Testament.* New York: Peter Lang, 1989.

Rado, Lisa, ed. *Modernism, Gender, and Culture: A Cultural Studies Approach.* New York: Garland, 1997.

———. ed. *ReReading Modernism: New Directions in Feminist Criticism.* New York: Garland, 1994.

Read, John. *Prelude to Chemistry: An Outline of Alchemy Its Literature and Relationships.* New York: Macmillan, 1937.

Roberts, R. Ellis. "Short Stories." *New Statesman & Nation* 3.5 (12 March 1932): 338–340.

Ross, Marlon B. *The Contours of Masculine Desire: Romanticism and the Rise of Women's Poetry.* New York: Oxford UP, 1989.

Scott, Bonnie Kime, ed. *The Gender of Modernism: A Critical Anthology.* Bloomington: Indiana UP, 1990.

Sedgwick, Eve Kosofsky. *The Epistemology of the Closet.* Berkeley: U of California P, 1990.

———, ed. *Novel Gazing: Queer Readings in Fiction.* Durham, NC: Duke UP, 1997.

Shelley, Percy Bysshe. *Shelley: Selected Poems, Essays, and Letters.* Ed. Ellsworth Barnard. New York: Odyssey Press, 1944.

Showalter, Elaine. *The Female Malady: Women, Madness, and English Culture, 1830 –1980.* New York: Pantheon, 1985.

Spurr, David. "Myths of Anthropology: Eliot, Joyce, Lévy-Bruhl." *PMLA* 109.2 (March 1994): 266–80.

Squire, J. C. "The Modern Revival of the Short Story: Miss Mary Butts' Success." *Daily Telegraph* 8 March 1932: 16.

Surette, Leon. *The Birth of Modernism: Ezra Pound, T. S. Eliot, W. B. Yeats, and the Occult.* Montreal: McGill-Queen's UP, 1993.

———. "*The Waste Land* and Jessie Weston: A Reassessment." *Twentieth Century Literature* 34 (Summer 1988): 223–44.

Sutton, Nina. *Bettelheim: A Life and a Legacy.* New York: BasicBooks, 1996.

Symonds, John. *The Great Beast: The Life of Aleister Crowley.* London: Rider and Company, 1951.

Tatar, Maria. "Folkloristic Phantasies: Grimms' Fairy Tales and Freud's Family Romance." In *Fairy Tales as Ways of Knowing: Essays on Märchen in Psychology, Society and Literature*. Ed. Michael M. Metzger and Katharina Mommsen. Bern: Peter Lange, 1981.

Thomson, Virgil. *Virgil Thomson*. New York: Alfred A. Knopf, 1966.

Underhill, Evelyn. *Mysticism: A Study in the Nature and Development of Man's Spiritual Consciousness*. New York: World Publishing Company, 1955.

Wagstaff, Barbara. Afterword. *The Crystal Cabinet: My Childhood at Salterns*. By Mary Butts. Manchester, Eng.: Carcanet Press Limited, 1988.

———. "Alchemist of Reality: Recovering Mary Butts." *Poetry Flash* No. 133 (April 1984): 4, 9.

———. Telephone conversation with the author, 24 May 1993.

———. "The Writings and the World of Mary Butts." Proc. of a Conference at the University of California, Davis. 23–24 November 1984.

Wagstaff, Christopher, ed. *A Sacred Quest: The Life and Writings of Mary Butts*. Kingston, NY: McPherson & Company, 1995.

Wescott, Glenway. "The First Book of Mary Butts." In *A Sacred Quest: The Life and Writings of Mary Butts*. Kingston, NY: McPherson & Company, 1995.

Weston, Jessie L. *From Ritual to Romance*. Garden City, NY: Doubleday Anchor Books, 1957.

Wheeler, Kathleen. *'Modernist' Women Writers and Narrative Art*. New York: New York UP, 1994.

White, Helen C. *The Mysticism of William Blake*. Madison: U of Wisconsin Studies in Language and Literature. No. 23, 1927.

Williamson, George. *A Reader's Guide to T. S. Eliot: A Poem by Poem Analysis*. 2nd ed. New York: Octagon Books, 1983.

Williamson, Hugh Ross. "Three Letters." *A Sacred Quest: The Life and Writings of Mary Butts*. Ed. Christopher Wagstaff. Kingston, NY: McPherson & Company, 1995.

———. "A Writer's Childhood: The Testament of Mary Butts." *John O'London's Weekly* (June 11, 1937): 388.

Wilson, Colin. *Aleister Crowley: The Nature of the Beast*. Wellingborough, Eng.: Antiquarian Press, 1987.

"Withershins." *The Compact Edition of the Oxford English Dictionary*. Oxford: Oxford UP, 1971 ed.

Wordsworth, William. *The Prelude: A Parallel Text*. Ed. J. C. Maxwell. London: Penguin, 1986.

Wright, Patrick. *On Living in an Old Country: The National Past in Contemporary Britain*. London: Verso, 1985.

Yeats, William Butler. *The Letters of W. B. Yeats*. Ed. Allan Wade. New York: Octagon Books, 1980.

Zimmerman, J. E. "Pan." *Dictionary of Classical Mythology*. New York: Bantam Books, 1971.

———. "Picus." *Dictionary of Classical Mythology*. New York: Bantam Books, 1971.

———. "Scylla." *Dictionary of Classical Mythology*. New York: Bantam Books, 1971.

A Chronological Listing of the Works of Mary Butts

(For a thorough bibliography of published writings by and about Mary Butts, see Nathalie Blondel's *Mary Butts: Scenes from the Life*. Kingston, NY: McPherson & Company, 1998.)

NOVELS

Ashe of Rings. London: Wishart & Co., 1933 (first published in Paris: Contact Editions Three Mountain Press, 1925). Reissued as *Ashe of Rings and Other Writings* (includes *Imaginary Letters, Warning to Hikers, Traps for Unbelievers,* and "Ghosties and Ghoulies"). Kingston, NY: McPherson & Company, 1998.

Imaginary Letters (with reproduction of the original line drawings by Jean Cocteau). Vancouver: Talonbooks, 1979 (first published in Paris: E. W. Titus, 1928).

The Taverner Novels: Armed with Madness. Kingston, NY: McPherson & Company, 1992 (first published in London: Wishart & Co. and New York: Albert and Charles Boni, 1928).

The Taverner Novels: Death of Felicity Taverner. Kingston, NY: McPherson & Company, 1992 (first published in London: Wishart & Co., 1932).

The Macedonian. Historical novel. London: Heinemann, Ltd., 1933 (first published in Kingswood, Eng.: The Windmill Press, 1933). Reissued as *The Classical Novels: The Macedonian/Scenes from the Life*. Kingston, NY: McPherson & Company, 1998.

Scenes from the Life of Cleopatra. Historical novel. New York: Ecco Press, 1974 (first published in London: William Heinemann, Ltd., 1935). Reissued with *The Macedonian* in 1998 as listed above.

SHORT STORIES

"Magic." *Little Review* 2.2 (July–August 1920): 3–6.

Speed the Plough and Other Stories. London: Chapman & Hall, 1923.
Several Occasions. London: Wishart & Co., 1932.
Last Stories. London: Brendin Publishing Co., 1938.
With and Without Buttons and Other Stories. Selected with an afterword by Nathalie Blondel. Manchester, Eng.: Carcanet Press, Ltd., 1991.
From Altar to Chimney-piece: Selected Stories. New York: McPherson & Company, 1992.

AUTOBIOGRAPHY

The Crystal Cabinet: My Childhood at Salterns. Expanded edition. Boston: Beacon Press, 1988. London: Carcanet Press, Ltd. 1988 (first published in London: Methuen & Co., Ltd., 1937).

PAMPHLETS

Traps for Unbelievers. London: Desmond Harmsworth, 1932.
Warning to Hikers. The Here and Now Pamphlets, no. 6. London: Wishart & Co., 1932.
(both reissued with *Ashe of Rings, and Other Writings,* cited above).

REVIEWS, ARTICLES, ESSAYS

"Questionnaire." *Little Review* (May 1929): 21–22.
"Vision of Asia." Rev. of *The Vision of Asia: An Interpretation of Chinese Art and Culture,* by L. Cranmer-Byng. *The Bookman* 83 (December 1932): 223–25.
"Ghosties and Ghoulies: The Uses of the Supernatural in English Fiction." *The Bookman* 83 (Jan. 1933): 386–89; (Feb. 1933): 433–35; (March 1933): 493–94; 84 (Apr. 1933): 12–14 (Reissued in *Ashe of Rings and Other Writings,* cited above).
"The Real Wordsworth," Rev. of *The Later Wordsworth,* by Edith C. Batho. *Time and Tide* 14.48 (2 Dec. 1933): 1446, 1448.
"Bloomsbury." Written in 1936 but not published until 1998 in *Modernism/Modernity* 5.2 (1998): 31–44.

POETRY

"Pythian Ode." *Transatlantic Review* 2.3 (1924): 235–39.
"Picus Martius." *Hound & Horn* 3.2 (January–May 1927): 230–33. Reprinted in *Soma* 3 (1932): 41–42.
"Thinking of Saints and of Petronius Arbiter." *Soma* 3 (1932): 43–45.
"Corfe." *Antaeus* 12 (winter 1973): 144–146. (first published in Louis Zukofsky's *An "Objectivists" Anthology.* LeBeausset, France: To Publishers, 1932).
"Two Ways of Not Seeing the World." *Antaeus* 12 (Winter 1973): 140.

(Mary Butts's poetry appeared in numerous little magazines in the 1920s and 1930s, in addition to those listed above, *The Egoist, Pagany, Larus,* and *Seed.* For a thorough listing of Butts's poems see Nathalie Blondel's *Mary Butts: Scenes from the Life,* cited above.)

Index